The Perpetual Migrant

Finding my way from the Abundance in Poverty to the Poverty of Abundance

JUZAR ALI

PAGE PUBLISHING, INC.
Conneaut Lake, PA

First originally published by Page Publishing 2019

ISBN 978-1-64584-019-0 (pbk)
ISBN 978-1-64584-020-6 (digital)

Printed in the United States of America

To my wife, Isfana, and my family with whom I share this journey.
To those whom I have not mentioned by name
but have nevertheless touched me.
To all of us who may have a story to tell.
And yes, we all have a story to tell, don't we?

PART I

Juku

CHAPTER 1

A Life on Elphinstone Street

As a child, my world was very small and sheltered, but even from an early age, I understood that the primary goal of my family was survival. I had a keen awareness that we were an immigrant family in a new nation, and our situation was always precarious. My world had very clear borders which ranged from my family's upstairs apartment to the walls of my father's "chemist and druggist" shop, just below, which opened onto Elphinstone Street. This location was no coincidence; it was the result of ambition, hard work, and a little bit of luck.

Elphinstone Street in those days was the place to be. Today, it is called Zaib-un-Nissa Street, and it still runs through the heart of Karachi's historic and commercial districts, but in the 1950s, it was one of the main thoroughfares in the capital of the new nation of Pakistan. It was a street of dreams, and it straddled two worlds that both seemed miraculous to me: the old world of the British Empire with all its colonial architecture, pomp, and circumstance and the new world of Pakistan with its bustling optimism, independence, and unfolding promise. Despite his very modest origins, my father, Hasan Ali, was a man of great ambition and vision. He knew there would be opportunities in this new country to form a new life. A better life. What's more, he understood the truth behind the adage of location, location, location long before it was even an adage, and he knew that he needed to be on Elphinstone Street. This was a time of change and independence. People were moving, planting new roots.

7

Now was an opportunity to reinvent oneself and reinvent the destiny of one's family. Elphinstone Street was the perfect place to build a dream—if one could find an opening there. My father saw that dream, and he risked everything to pursue it, even his own life.

In 1947, just two years before I was born, the Dominion of Pakistan was formed when an English barrister named Sir Cyril Radcliffe literally drew a line on a map of a nation he had never even visited before. It was an unenviable task he had been given, and sure enough, what followed was a wave of violence, genocide, and ethnic cleansing that led to the largest mass migration in human history. In other words, a living nightmare. It is a holocaust in the pages of history that very few people across the globe talk about.

As the British Empire ended its occupation of India, Hindus, and Muslims turned on each other with a startling ferocity, each fighting for territory and national pride. Neighbor against neighbor. Village against village. The ethnic and religious tensions that had simmered beneath the surface for the decades of British rule now erupted into riots and street battles, into mob killings and mass murders. Most of the slayings were achieved with knives, rocks, pipes, and pitchforks. Some people had access to even more deadly weapons, such as rifles and swords, and they wreaked havoc. Simple things such as fresh water became precious commodities as city and village wells were packed full of mangled human bodies.

One of the worst aspects of the violence was the intimacy of it and particularly the way it was intentionally waged against women and children. In both the Muslim and Hindu traditions, women were (and still are in many parts of the world) vessels of honor for their families. A woman's reputation is synonymous with the social standing of the family. Thus, one of the most effective methods of defiling an entire family was to violate the women: the mothers, the daughters, even the granddaughters. The more shame and pain inflicted upon the girl or woman, the better. Over one million people were massacred in the violence, but countless more bore—and still bearthe wounds, traumas, and stigmas of this systematic sexual violence.

As Britain quickly withdrew its government and military forces, the brand-new central governments of India and Pakistan had no time to develop the police and military capabilities required to respond to such a huge-scaled disaster. As the violence spun out of control, more than fifteen million people packed up what they could carry on their backs and began moving toward friendlier territory. This remains the single largest mass migration in human history, and it is steeped in misery. Muslims, Hindus, and Sikhs alike abandoned homes that their families had known for generations, even centuries. Muslims moved toward the brand-new nation of Pakistan. Hindus and Sikhs moved toward the new borders of India. My father was part of that migration out of India and into Pakistan. He endured the miles-long lines of refugees, the long days spent exposed to the brutal heat with little or no food and water, the roving bands of marauders who preyed upon the vulnerable lines of refugees. Most people were forced to board trains to cross the new borders. The trains were supposed to move safely between designated locations, but they quickly became enticing targets for bloodthirsty mobs and homegrown militias. Over and over, the packed trains were stopped and boarded by armed gangs with predictable results. There are many accounts of trains pulling out with more than five hundred people aboard, only to arrive at their destinations with train cars filled with nothing but blood.

Faced with the choice of being caught in the street violence or taking his chances on the train, my father boarded a train bound for Pakistan. It's a ride that should have taken no more than a few hours, but due to the conditions at the time, his journey took more than two days, with many long delays along the way. Every time the train stopped, he, like everyone, waited in terror. He didn't eat. He barely spoke to anyone. It was impossible to know in this time who was friend or foe, who might turn on you at any given moment. In my father's telling of the story, he kept his hand carefully placed on his chin, as if in a pose of contemplation. The only thing he was contemplating, however, was the ways in which Muslim men were often identified by mobs—by their beards and by their circumcised penises. If a suspected man couldn't be identified by one method, then he was often inspected by the other, in some cases quite brutally. My father did everything he could to become invisible and unobtrusive on that packed train in hopes of arriving at the other end of the journey alive and in one piece.

And thank God, he did.

Once he arrived in Pakistan with nothing but a suitcase in his hand, he made his way to Karachi. He had survived the journey, but now he had to figure out how to open a business. First, there was no safe way to transport a person's life savings across the border. There was no simple transferring money from bank to bank at this time. So people invented a method that is almost unthinkable in this day and age: an honor system based completely on word of mouth. People would very simply trade money. It required an incredible amount of trust (or desperation) and integrity to be effective. My father's life savings was stranded in India and needed to get to Pakistan. So he used family connections to identify Hindus who were migrating out of Pakistan to India. Then they traded their money. For obvious reasons, people usually traded in multiple smaller amounts rather than turning over their entire savings in one lump sum, so often it required numerous trading partners to acquire a significant portion of your own savings from back home.

Once he secured enough of his money, he had to find a location for a new business. My father had run a very small business in Indore, India, which he had left behind, and that lent him a small amount of credibility. Elphinstone Street real estate was a carefully guarded commodity, however. Every stretch of Elphinstone Street was run by a well-connected and wealthy businessman or landlord, and none of them appeared interested in renting to a Muslim immigrant fresh off the trains. My father opened a small shop elsewhere in the city, but still he pursued his Elphinstone Street ambitions relentlessly.

Finally, my father and his brother, Hashim Ali, came to know one of the landlords, a Hindu businessman that I grew up calling Mulji Chacha, or *Uncle Mulji*. Mulji Chacha was like the local godfather to the other small Hindu-owned businesses in the local areas and lanes and "galies." Nothing moved without his permission. There were small repair shop and local Hindu merchants who looked up to

Mulji Chacha's nod, even to communicate with the Muslim migrants. The side streets were called mochi gali, the street of the shoe repairmen. Apparently, it took a lot of cajoling to convince Mulji Chacha to believe my father and his brother were not troublemakers, but he must have seen something that he liked in the duo. He finally agreed to rent out a coveted shop space. Using the honor financial system, my father was able to scrape together enough goodwill money, or *paghri* as it was called, for the landlord. They settled on an amicable monthly rent, and my father set up his small pharmaceutical business, Venus Medico. This store would become the sun at the center of my universe for many, many years.

My father's experience running a chemist pharmacy shop served him very well as he established his position in this small world of 1950s Karachi. He was proud of his position in the long lineage of pharmacology, a skill that was born in his part of the world. The art of healing with medicines goes back almost as far as human history does, and it is one of the most respected of the ancient professions. There are Sumerian cuneiform clay tablets that are almost eight thousand years old and have prescriptions for medications written on them. There is a stone sign for a pharmacy with a tripod, a mortar, and a pestle in the Arcadian way in Ephesus, Turkey. This is the same Ephesus that was home to Mark Anthony and Cleopatra and to Mary Magdalene and where Paul read his famous letter to the Ephesians as recorded in the Christian Bible.

As far back as the sixth-century BC, Suśruta, who is considered the founding father of surgery, wrote one of the world's first great medical texts called the *Suśrutasanhitā*. This is the first known listing of medicinal substances, and it contains descriptions of 1,120 illnesses, 700 medicinal plants, 64 preparations from mineral sources, and 57 preparations based on animal sources. By the time my father came along, there were countless preparations from chemical sources as well, and his mind was a miraculous library of cures, treatments, and remedies.

After a time, the violence lessened and traveling became safer. When my father wasn't working, he was traveling back to India to visit his wife, my mother. These trips were very productive for him:

on one, he discovered a family friend who was willing to relocate to Pakistan and become my father's assistant, and on another, he managed to conceive me.

I was born in June of 1949, less than two years after the independent nations of India and Pakistan were born. I was born in Ahmedabad, India, but soon after I arrived, my father considered it safe enough to move my mother and me to Pakistan to live as a family. That's when my father rented the apartments just next door to the shop and upstairs. His dreams were coming to fruition. A modest but beautiful new life was blooming in front of his eyes. But like a flower growing from a crack in the sidewalk, it was never taken for granted. He knew there were much larger forces that could trample his dream at any moment, and he worked tirelessly to keep them at bay.

In addition to medicines, general remedies, and toiletries, my father's shop was also a dispensing pharmacy, which was uncommon and provided the business some great prestige. We had a qualified compounder on the staff who was legally authorized to mix and dispense medicinal compounds and tinctures to fill doctor's prescriptions. It was a place where doctors would stop by and discuss a specialty compound for a sore throat or a more complex prescription for an infectious disease, like tuberculosis.

I loved spending time in the shop. From my perch in the big front window, I could see merchants and well-heeled shoppers. I could watch the automobiles and those passing by the shops: the jewelers, the clothiers, the watchmakers, the arms dealers, and the other chemists. This street was so significant that horse-driven carriages, donkey carts, and camel wagons were not allowed. They were restricted to the side streets. I could hear the rumble of modern streetcars in the distance intermingling with tinkling bells as camel drivers brought their loads of supplies to the bakers, the confectioners, the shoemakers, the leather goods stores, and more. The cart drivers tied bells to the camels' knees so that people could hear the animals coming. Many years later, I would recognize that sound again when I first heard the jingle bells associated with American holidays or the ice-cream vendors in the neighborhood.

Directly across our shop was the cinema house, and I watched the lines of people waiting for tickets to the latest films. I could only imagine the things they watched on that silver screen. Those were the days when people dressed up to go to the movies, and it seemed very glamorous. Often, they showed American films, Westerns like *Shane* or comedies like *Roman Holiday*—glimpses of the wider world which I could not even dream of yet.

Although my world was small, it was not lonely. In our one-bedroom flat lived my mother, father, my two sisters, and me. In the flat just above us lived my father's assistant whom he had recruited in Ahmedabad, India. Just beneath us lived Kakajee Hashim Ali, my father's elder brother, along with his family. They had arrived in Pakistan with five children already and proceeded to have four more while living there beneath us. There was a constant buzz of activity as the families worked, played, prayed, and ate together. For the most part, the families stayed close and looked after one another, but there was a strange mix of camaraderie and competition between Kakajee and my father which I sensed even in my very early days. Sometimes, there was a delicate dance between family members as tensions simmered, and I would soon learn that the worst was yet to come.

One aspect of this new life that was very important to my parents was the appearance of success, and some of my earliest memories are of my mother carefully grooming me. My parents considered my appearance to be emblematic of the family standing, even as a small child, and my mother was determined that I project an air of success and style. I was scrubbed clean and my fingernails cut short and neat. My clothes were freshly washed and pressed. I was given a very modern haircut right out of the films that ran in the cinema house. It was clipped short around the ears and the back but left long on the top. Then with a dab of pomade, the hair was combed back from my face in a perfectly styled wave, almost like Elvis Presley's. My mother often went so far as to put a bobby pin in my hair to keep it in place. Then once I passed inspection, I could descend from the flat and spend the day lingering around the shop, playing with relatives and my father's business friends who often teased me about my carefully constructed look.

There was only one person more serious about my appearance than my mother, however, and that was *me*. If someone went to tousle my hair, I would duck my head and protect my hair by covering it with my small hands. If someone teased me, I would turn up my well-groomed nose at them. I can only imagine what I must have seemed like to my uncle, my aunt, my cousins, and the friends of my family as I, a four-year-old, protected my pompadour hairstyle with such a grim determination. Even I smile to think of it now.

When I wasn't lingering in my father's shop, I was often hanging about in my mother's kitchen, especially if she was making chapatti on a small primus stove. I would sit on a small stool as she mixed and kneaded the dough. Then she rolled the dough into balls the size of golf balls and wrapped each one in a cloth. Then one at a time, she would allow me to roll the freshly made chapatti and add sugar and that would be the best treat for me. The small apartment would fill with the delicious smells, and I waited eagerly for the first bread to come off the pan. When my mother would give me the bread, still warm and soft, it was the most delicious thing on earth.

My father came home in the evenings from the shop. We all listened carefully to Daddy's steps as he climbed up to the third floor and the way he would make his entrance. We paid close attention to how he responded to our greetings of *salaam*, for it would indicate how his day had been and how the evening would go. He had invented affectionate pet names for us all, so I knew that if he called me by my given name, Juzar, then things had gone badly. But if he called out to me as Juku, then it was all good, and it would be a fun night with a meal and stories and jokes.

This is how my days passed as my family worked very hard and prospered on Elphinstone Street. My small life was filled with family and friends. Occasionally, we all traveled back to India to visit my mother's family in Ahmedabad. We flew from Karachi on Indian Airlines, and it was a great treat to climb aboard that silver plane with its four gleaming engines, to sit in the cabin with the other well-dressed passengers, to feel the propellers churn the air as we zoomed down the runway and lifted into the sky, to see the whole city of Karachi becoming so small there against the Arabian Sea.

Then one night, as my fifth birthday approached, my father and his close friend, Saeed Chacha, gathered in our small flat, and I heard the adults talking. This was common, of course, but I could tell from the tones of their voices that they were having a serious discussion of some kind. Even that was not uncommon. What was uncommon was that I would be the subject of such a conversation. I did not know what they were talking about, but I knew it was about me. I could tell by the way my mother looked at me. I could also tell that she wasn't happy about whatever it was that the men were discussing. There was a sadness and loneliness in her eyes as if a decision was being made which she had no control over. I sensed through her that something was going to happen.

CHAPTER 2

A Thousand Miles Away

I remember the evening was hot and humid. The lights at the city railway station in Karachi were dim, and yet the hustle and bustle of the crowd at the railway station was exciting, so many people traveling to and from so many places I could not even imagine. The air filled with the distinct smell of the engine smoke, coal, and the sweat of the crowd. Going to places, like a railway station or an airport, for an evening outing was not unheard of, but still this was like a dream. I had been picked up and quickly put in the horse-driven carriage for the ride to the station with Daddy and Saeed Chacha, his close friend. We had luggage and a food tiffin box that Ma gave them.

Ma had been in tears as she stood near the door of the house when we left. I was five years old, and I could not understand what was happening, but I understood that I was at the center of all this excitement. I did not understand why she was not coming to the station with us for this outing. I remember the look on Ma's face as the horse-drawn carriage whisked Daddy, Saeed Chacha, and me away from her and to the station where we arrived at a platform where our train was waiting for us, and we clambered aboard and found seats together.

Soon after the night train left the station, I must have fallen asleep. The lights of Karachi faded in the distance behind us, and despite the excitement, exhaustion overtook me. I fell asleep to the rocking motion of the train. It wasn't long, however, before I was wakened by the clamoring of the train pulling into its first stop.

16

I soon learned that the railway station stops were the best part of the journey. The rail platforms were filled with people selling their wares: food, tea, clothes, luggage, local sweets, and gifts. The chant of chai garam meant "Hot tea, anybody?" It was a typical part of the soundtrack we grew up with in Pakistan, and as soon as we would pull into a station, the commotion would begin. Everyone would begin barking their wares, and people would pour on and off the train. I watched in wonder from my window. This was all new to me. My world was suddenly becoming much larger, but I felt safe in my perch in the train, next to my father.

It took three days and nights to cross one thousand miles of Pakistan and climb into the foothills of the Himalaya mountains, but finally we reached our destination: Murree. *Koh Murree*, as it was formally known, meant "hill station," and it was aptly named. At an altitude of seven thousand feet, Murree was founded by the British as a place where they could retreat for the summer months and escape the heat. As such, it looked very much like a European town with white picket fences lining the small country roads. Pretty stone walls surrounded churches, cemeteries, and convents. Many British citizens still lived there, and European-styled houses and lanes encircled a British club and brewery.

I walked with my father, holding his hand as we navigated the steep streets. Saeed Chacha walked with us, of course. Then as we came around a corner, I caught my first glimpse of the Presentation Convent School. I didn't realize it just yet, but this was my final stop on this journey. It was a severe-looking place, with stone buildings built high into the mountainsides, connected to one another by covered walkways and winding paths. Pitched roofs and church spires rose into the sky, and dark windows gazed down upon us as we walked onto the campus. There was an element of unwelcome sternness to it.

We were directed to the administrative building where my father introduced himself and me. Unbeknownst to me, all the arrangements had been made already. These were also before the days of paperwork or elaborate admittance processes. A small, frail but stern-looking Catholic nun came into the room, and once the introductions were complete, a large, burly man was summoned, and without any further ado, he picked me up, turned around, and began to take me away from my father. I still had no idea what was happening, but now it was frightening. This was no longer an adventure; this dreamlike trip was turning into a nightmare. I was being taken away by a nun and a strongman, and my father was just standing there, letting it happen.

I still remember my own shrill cries as I was whisked away, and I still see my father breaking down and sobbing. Saeed Chacha held his hands. Years later, he would be asked many times, "How could you do it, Hasan Bhai?"

His answer, as always: "Because it was best for him. He was to have the best of education."

My mother had little say in the matter and must have acquiesced with the belief and faith that my dad knew what he was doing. I was his only son, and this was the tough love he believed in. He came from a background where you had to make place for yourself. No one did it for you. For him, this was the start of a path he was creating for me no matter how difficult it seemed at first. I was entering a full-time boarding school run by a United Kingdom-based order of nuns, and I would be here for three years.

The Presentation Convent School was considered an elite institution that catered primarily to the British families who were still in Pakistan, foreign diplomats, army generals, and wealthy Pakistani families. My classmates were largely the sons of privilege, and even at five years old, it was easy to see that there weren't any other sons of small-time shopkeepers around the campus. I was immediately identified as an outlier, both by my classmates and by the adults who ran the institution.

Once the shock wore off and I realized that I would be on my own here, I settled into the daily routine as best I could. I was well-behaved, compliant, and studious. It seemed the only choice. Socially, I was quiet and kept to myself. After the warmth and close-knit nature of my family life at home, this place felt cold and isolated. I was terribly lonely, and it was the kind of loneliness that still resonates once in while even all these years later.

The weather didn't help. Long, bitter winters would grip the mountains and make everything miserable. The sky. The buildings. The boys. The refectory was the worst, with high vaulted ceiling and rows of long tables where the boys gathered for meals. Men with carts would move through the gloomy room and deposit a ladleful of porridge into the bowls on the table. The food was always horrible, and I quickly began to lose what little weight I had as a small five-year-old.

There were moments of levity though. Occasionally, one of the older, braver boys would play a prank that would send everyone into stitches. One prank that never got old was when someone would catch the corner of a nun's habit and yank it quickly off her head as she walked through these halls. The sight of those nearly bald heads would send us into stitches. The nuns looked almost like baby birds, with their dusting of feathery hair, their large eyes and waddles waggling angrily. I never pulled that prank myself, but the boys who did were like heroes to me for their gall and their ability to create laughter in this place.

During physical training, which is much like a physical education class, we were taught songs to sing as we exercised, and some of them were quite fun or funny as well, with their rhyming cadence. Some of the songs of those times were quite offensive too, a fact which I would recognize much later. For example, it was not uncommon for our instructors to lead us in a chorus of

> *Eenie meanie, minie, mo,*
> *Catch a n——er by the toe,*
> *If he hollers, let him go,*
> *Eenie meanie, minie, mo.*

Of course, many nursery rhymes have terribly racist origins, but it's still striking to me to think of a gymnasium of boys all having this kind of gibberish drilled into their minds and attitudes. But this was a time and a place with carefully constructed hierarchies of race, class, and social position. One of the most glaring examples of this hierarchy was bath time at the Presentation Convent School. Once a week, boys were taken to bathe according to their grade, so all the five-year-old, the six-year-old, the seven-year-old, and so on would be lined up and be marched to the tubs. Within our grades, however, we were carefully arranged. Later, it dawned on me that that arrangement was according to some status or color—white English boys were always at the front of the line, followed by the sons of more powerful Pakistani diplomats or politicians, and so on down the line until you arrived at the one little shopkeeper's son, *me*, standing at the very back. Did I really belong here? There were two large tubs, and two by two, the boys were put in the water to splash and bathe. Many boys found this to be an enjoyable part of the week as they played and laughed loudly, but for me, it was dreadful, standing at the end of that line and waiting my turn to climb into the same bathwater that every other boy had been in before me. By the time I was allowed into the tub, the water would be gray and cold. I bathed as quickly as possible so I could return to my room. I still remember the dark color of that bath tub water.

I was different in other ways too. All the boys waited anxiously for the mail to come every week, but I never received the same kinds of care packages that other boys got, full of goodies and socks, clothes, comic books, and other gifts from home. I could always look forward to letters from my family, but that was all. Meanwhile, the "tuck shop" was where the boys spent their "tuck" pocket money. Again, my parents never sent any, so that was something else that I could not enjoy like the others.

What my parents did do, however, was find a family for me. They couldn't afford to pepper me with pocket money or small luxuries, but they did arrange through friends to introduce me to the Esajee family who lived in Rawalpindi, a two-hour drive away. The Esajees ran a confectionary business, and they happened to have a store in Murree so they could easily visit me at school and take me for weekends. Usually, that meant I would hang about in the shop while they ran their business. This wasn't exactly exciting, but at least it wasn't school. Plus, it felt familiar after spending all my years hanging about in my own family's store. The Esajees were very kind to me. To this day, I owe them a lot. One of the brothers in the family reminded me of my dad with his strict no-nonsense demeanor. The only problem was the sweets. It was torture being around so many sugary delights and not being able to touch them. I would arrive from school half starved and spend the day surrounded by chocolates and sugar pastries, around peach jellies and gumdrops, around licorice ropes and candies. I had been raised by a strict and respectful father, so never did I steal a single gumball. Neither did I ask for any. And in the three years that I spent with this family, I can only recall three occasions where they broke down and offered me a taste from their inventory.

There was still a great deal of British influence in Pakistan at that time, so the Christmas holidays were still celebrated in many places throughout the nation. This was the one time of year that I got to travel home and see my family. The school closed for eight glorious weeks, and my father came to get me on the train. Soon, I would be back home, eating delicious food in my mother's kitchen, playing in the flat with my baby sisters, hanging around my father's shop, and basking in the company of family as we had our meals which were served on the *thaal*, a communal platter placed in the center of the low stool table. Oh, how I had missed these traditional Pakistani meals. It was a joy for me to be here and not in that school refectory, sitting at a long table and waiting for a ladleful of cold porridge.

Not only was my mother actively trying to fatten me up, much to my delight, but she also took a keen interest in my cleanliness. She never made a great display about it, but years later, she would confess to me that she was horrified by how dirty I was upon my arrivals home. She would spend hours cleaning my hair, my ears, my fingernails, my toes. Then well rested, well-fed, and well bathed, I would climb back on the train and return to school after the holiday break. My parents must have had some concerns upon seeing the condition that I always returned in, but what could they do from one thousand miles away? They were doing the best they could to secure a future for me. They had gotten me into one of the most prestigious schools in the country after all, but they did not have the political or financial clout to get me to the front of the bathing lines or to secure a "tuck" fund for me.

It must have been on my second Christmas holiday home when I finally asked them why they never sent care packages. "All the other boys get packages from their families."

Once again, my mother and father glanced at each other. And once again, it was only years later that I would learn the truth. They had been sending modest but loving care packages all along. Apparently, some of the older boys were stealing mine. Young boys like me were paired with an older boy to act as big brother and mentor in the boarding school. One of the duties of the big brother was to collect any mail or packages for the little brother. Apparently, my big brother was taking liberties with his position, and either no one noticed that he and his friends were stealing from me or no one cared to stop them.

Either way, when I returned to school for my third and final year, something curious happened. Each day of classes, there was a brief recess period where most of the boys would tumble out into the playground to organize soccer or cricket matches. I usually stayed to the edges of the playground with a book or talked with some of my more bookish classmates. Sometimes, we would create our own games with twigs, shrubs, and acorns which were all around. One day, however, a large, burly man—the same burly man who had so abruptly removed me from my father two long years ago when I had first arrived at the boarding school—walked out across the playground and came straight up to me. "Come with me," he said in Urdu.

Nervously, I followed him back into the building. What did this big man want with me? Had something happened? Was I in trouble? *What could I possibly be in trouble for?*

He led me on a strange path though, not toward the administration offices, but rather toward the kitchen behind the refectory. Finally, we arrived at our destination: the stove. "Sit here," he said, pointing to a stool beside the kitchen counter.

I perched upon the stool and watched as he plucked one egg from the icebox and then fetched a frying pan down from the cabinet. He lit the gas stove. He poured a dollop of oil. He fried the egg. I watched, mystified, still unsure why I had been called to witness this spectacle of a very large man cooking a very small egg. It smelled delicious though, making my stomach tense with hunger. At last, the secret was revealed to me: *this was my egg*. An egg just for me.

He slid the plate to me, along with a fork, and nodded. The egg was cooked perfectly—firm but tender in the whites, slightly browned upon the bottom, and just barely runny in the yellow center. This was the most beautiful item of food I had ever seen prepared at the school in all the time I had been here. I ate the egg like I was a wolf, like there would be no tomorrow.

When I was finished, the man placed the plate in the sink and walked me back to the playground. No one at recess asked me what the trouble was, and I didn't volunteer an explanation. I had no idea why that man had made me an egg, but I wasn't about to complain— or reveal my secret.

What's more, it didn't end there. From that point on, every day during recess, the big man would somberly walk onto the playground and fetch me, and every day I sat perched on the stool while he cooked me an egg. At first, I thought it must be some strange, wonderful kind of gift. Soon, I would learn that my father had called upon the school to discuss my weight loss among other things, and he had made arrangements for me to receive this "supplement" to my meal plan. What extra it cost him, I have no idea, but for me, this was huge. Like Pavlov's dog, each day, my mouth began to water as the big man prepared that egg for me, frying it perfectly. Each day, it was delicious, and it was from my parents that I would remember.

To this day, many, many years later, a fried egg is one of the small joys of my life. I still love the smell of them, the sound of them popping in the oil, the smooth texture of the white, and the exquisite taste of the warm yolk, particularly if it lapped up with a piece of buttered bread and jam.

Finally, my three-year primary schooling ended, and I was to return home for continued studies in Karachi. My three years at the Presentation Convent School were marked by the strict discipline which was enforced there and the sharp loneliness that I experienced. But they also instilled in me certain toughness even at that tender age. The experience was harrowing, and the memories are mixed, but one thing I never doubted in all that time was my parents love and the selfless intentions that made them do it. The emotional sacrifice my ma must have made, I cannot even fathom. The financial cost for my shopkeeper dad, I cannot gauge. What I do remember is that when I got back to Karachi and was told that I would not be returning to Murree the next year, I jumped with joy. I was back home and reunited with my sisters who were my best friends and playmates at that time.

CHAPTER 3

Mission Impossible

I was so glad to be back in Karachi that I didn't even mind if my father kept me close by and insisted I spend most of my time at the shop with him rather than run off and play. I was with my family once more, surrounded by my father, mother, sisters, aunt, uncle, cousins, and friends. I slipped easily back into the native languages of my family—Urdu and Gujarati. My father had strong opinions about many things, including languages. Being originally from Jabalpur and Indore in India, my father believed that Urdu was the language of the future and that any other language diluted the experience of Urdu.

Whatever language was being spoken, I was happy to let my mother groom me again and arrange my outfits. By ten years old, many of the other boys in our neighborhood had graduated to working as errand boys or else running in small packs on the streets, but my father had other plans for me. He didn't want me to be a typical shopkeeper's son, pressed into service with menial tasks. He certainly did not want me running in the streets where there was ample opportunity to get into trouble of one kind or another. He wanted me to have bigger opportunities. He wanted me to carry the family name and fortunes far beyond Elphinstone Street. From his vantage point, he saw exactly one route to such success: the Karachi Grammar School.

My father understood that to create world class opportunities for someone like me, an immigrant shopkeeper's son, it would require a world-class education, and the Karachi Grammar School was the one school in all of Karachi in 1957 that offered exactly that. Formed in 1847 by Reverend H. Brereton, the first chaplain of Karachi, the school began its life as the Karachi European and Indo-European School. It was modeled after the English school system and maintains, to this day, close ties to Cambridge University. By 1871, the school had adopted a motto from Horace: *Indocti Discant*, or "Let the unlearned learn." That was the clarion call that my father heeded.

By 1957, Pakistan had been independent for ten years, so the school was far more open to local students than ever before, but it was still an exclusive institution and a place of privilege. This was a school which educated princes and princesses from all over the Middle East and the Asian subcontinent, alongside the sons and daughters of the local elite. The school graduated—and continues to graduate—presidents, prime ministers, diplomats, writers, poets, producers, and even world-class athletes. Alumni include Benazir Bhutto, former prime minister of Pakistan and first elected female head of state of the Muslim world; Chaudhry Muhammad Ali, nuclear physicist and political defense analyst; Dail Jones, former party president of the New Zealand First party; Princess Sarvath al-Hassan of Jordan; Ghulam Mustafa Jatoi, former acting prime minister of Pakistan; Ambassador Thomas W. Simons Jr., former ambassador and Harvard scholar, and many, many more.

The school was close enough to walk to, and my father looked upon those walls with the greatest respect and no small sense of cunning. How was he, a small-time shopkeeper, going to get his son enrolled alongside international royalty and local elite? This was more than a simple matter of tuition cost or access; the school was famously competitive, requiring a difficult entrance exam and interviews. What's more, there would be only one opportunity to enter the school, right at the beginning of term for the students in my age-group. There would not be another chance for me to apply until high school, and by then, it would almost certainly be too late and much more competitive.

My father knew this would be a delicate mission, requiring a perfect alignment of introductions, interviews, test scores, and timing. How was he going to pull off this mission impossible?

*****

Venus Medico was a popular gathering place. In those days, a pharmacist was often the most trusted health-care professional that the average person could easily visit. My father was not just the guy who sold medicines; he was almost like the family doctor. He could diagnose and treat myriad minor ailments, such as sore throats, indigestion, respiratory infections, gastrointestinal distress, muscle aches, or swollen joints.

He was fast becoming a respected health-care professional, but he had also invested in a miraculous piece of machinery that ensured his popularity: *a refrigerator*. It was an old Kelvinator with the wide body, rounded corners, and chrome handle. It was a huge, lumbering appliance, and it seemed to fill up half the shop, but it was the only working refrigerator for blocks in any direction, so it became a kind of destination unto itself. The refrigerator allowed my father to offer more than just the typical array of throat paints, carminative mixtures, and tinctures; with the Kelvinator, he could also offer his customers specialized medicines, such as insulin, which needed to remain chilled. The true genius of the Kelvinator, however, was that my father could provide a glass of ice-cold water when people drifted in out of the scorching Karachi heat. I remember nearby shopkeepers and their staff bringing in water in bottles and asking that these be stored in the Kelvinator for cooling. Often, my dad's chemist shop sounded more like a barbershop as people sat about sipping tea or a cool beverage, relaxing, and talking about their problems and their lives. Wide-ranging discussions would ensue about their bunions or sore backs, their jobs or their children, their taxes or politics or upcoming elections. People came in with newspapers, sat down for a while, "solved" the world's problems, and moved on.

To make matters even more interesting, the building had been built in an age before widespread electricity, let alone household fans or air conditioners, and therefore designed with maximum ventilation in mind. My father's chemist shop opened from the back into the neighboring stamp collector's shop to achieve a cross-breeze. Cross-ventilation was the design feature of the day. This also achieved a hilarious cross-pollination of ideas. Someone might walk into the neighboring shop looking for a rare collectible stamp from Italy only to find they are participating in the discussion going on in our shop, debating the merits of requiring a special license for taxi drivers, and then finally make their way home with a nice therapeutic shampoo for dandruff.

This was also how my father worked on many of his pet projects and missions. When he wanted more walk-in business, he would discuss it openly with the many people passing through his shop and the adjoining ones as well, mixing the different advice and ideas like pharmaceutical ingredients. "You should advertise in the newspaper," one man suggested. "So people know what you have here."

"You should have a sale," another man offered. "That will lure them into your shop."

My father would listen and debate the merits of each idea until he arrived at prescription of his own, often combining elements from many ideas. In this case, he decided that his shop needed more interesting window displays to advertise and entice.

That became my job. I was the head window display officer, and I took my position very seriously. Using pamphlets and advertisement materials brought by the pharmaceutical representatives, I would adorn these window displays. At times, I would walk down the street, if allowed, to see what others were doing. We had no monies to upgrade this in any truly professional manner; hence, we used what we had. When a new product or marketing gimmick was presented to him by his suppliers, my father would say, "Juku! Do something with this window!"

The other aspect of my job was simply keeping the window area clean. One downside to a street front store and cross-ventilation was dust, dust, and more dust. It got everywhere. My father's staff usually stood behind the counter with a duster nearby, maintaining this constant vigilance. The showcase windows were no different; they required cleaning and constant upkeep.

When my father set his sights upon the Karachi Grammar School, he turned, once more, to his open source brain trust for their opinions, ideas, and assistance.

Right away, he was met with skepticism. "Karachi Grammar?" one customer said. "You'll never get your little Juku in there."

Others agreed. "It's too tough," they said. "Only the rich go to that school," they said. "You should think of another school," they said.

I listened to all this commentary from my position in the window display area where I was meticulously arranging displays of new over-the-counter medicines and new-and-improved products. I swept the grime away as quickly as it blew in from the street and made decorative flourishes out of ticker tape and ribbons. From my perch in the window, I observed that no matter how many people tried to persuade him to abandon his quixotic quest, my father remained determined.

The debate raged on for weeks even as the deadline for admission began to loom on the calendar. "You just don't have the connections," one man said to my father. "You don't have the clout, man."

"Can you even afford that?" asked Mulji Chacha, our landlord.

Then one day, just as my father was going on about how he was going to get his son a world-class education if it killed him, in walked one of his regular customers, Mr. Haidermota, who was educated and had a professional job in Karachi. He was considered a scholar. He often wore a Western-styled suit when he came by the shop to pick up his lozenges or have a sore throat examined. On this day, he walked into the shop and couldn't help noticing the conversation that was going on all around him. "Karachi Grammar School?" he asked.

"Yes," my father replied.

"Why, I know someone who works there," Mr. Haidermota said.

For just one moment, the shop became so quiet you could have heard a pin drop.

*****

The first step was the test. With a personal introduction, Mr. Haidermota was able to help arrange for me to take the admissions exam which would evaluate my skills in math and English. The test was famously rigorous and known for weeding out all but the most knowledgeable of students, even at early ages. My father had paid dearly to send me to a distinguished primary school all the way across the country; now we would find out if all the investment and sacrifice were worth it. The monthly tuition fees for this school would be a quarter of our monthly family income in those times, but that did not deter my dad's determination.

On the day of the exam, the three of us—my father, me, and Mr. Haidermota—walked to the school. I walked between the men, holding their hands. I felt nervous but thrilled as we approached the impressive stone building. It was flanked by a wide playground on one side and a cemented drive on the other and designed to present a full view of the massive structure with its arched doorways, its ornate, castle-like windows, its layered roof and trellised greenery growing over the beautiful entryway. It looked more like a palace to me than a school. I knew I was fortunate to be able to walk into this building, but I also couldn't help feeling intimidated by the place and fearful of how we would be received. I couldn't shake the feeling of that cold, dirty bathwater left over for a shopkeeper's son.

Once inside, Mr. Haidermota made his introductions and the adults all talked while I peered around. It was the beginning of a school day, and the classes—standards as they were called—were about to begin. It seemed that students were everywhere, moving through the halls and courtyards. I could tell right away that this was a better place than the Presentation Convent School. It had more light and open spaces. Students seemed happy and boisterous as they moved toward their classes. Even the adults seemed kind here, but there was a strict decorum that was every palpable. The man talking with my father was firm but respectful, and he offered me a smile as we said hello.

Finally, it was time for me to take the famous admissions test. I was escorted to a small office while my father and Mr. Haidermota waited outside. Later, I would learn that both men were anxious and spent the whole time pacing the floor. At the time, all I knew was that I had a quiet room, a chair at a wooden table, and a test booklet which was laid in front of me. If I had been nervous before, I quickly put those thoughts away and went to work. I had very little control over what my father and the other adults decided for my future, but this was one thing I could do for myself and for my family. As I peered over the test, I recognized everything. All my weeks and months of lonely studying and reading were now paying off. I carefully completed the grammar section. I recognized much of the English and methodically moved through the constructions, the vocabulary, and the conjugations. I wrote my short essay. Then I arrived at my favorite section: the mathematics. Even as a child, I loved the orderliness of numbers and the way they worked together in complex yet sturdy relationships.

When I finished the test, we said our goodbyes and left the school. They would notify us in a few days' time to let my father know how I had done. The next few days around the chemist shop were full of nonstop chatter as people stopped by for a cold drink from the Kelvinator and, among other topics, asked how I had done. My father would just shrug. "It's in God's hands now," he said.

Finally, word arrived: I had passed the test. Everyone at the shop was ecstatic. There was pride all around, but these were the same people, of course, who, just weeks ago, were saying that it couldn't be done. The celebration was short-lived, however, when my father realized that the next challenge was his: the interview. The admissions test was the first hurdle. Next, he would have to sit for a one-on-one interview with the headmaster for his interview. This was already going to be a high-pressure situation for my father, but to make matters worse, the interview was going to be held in English.

"In English!" my father exclaimed. "The whole interview!"

The only English my father knew at this point was the little he had taught himself from reading the pharmaceutical pamphlets and products instructions that came with his inventory shipments. The whole shop burst into excited chatter.

"Do not worry," Mr. Haidermota said calmly when he arrived at the shop and heard the news. "I will help you."

"How? Can you take the interview for me?"

"I will coach you," Mr. Haidermota replied.

Mr. Haidermota spent the next week working with my father. By day, my father worked tirelessly in his shop, and by night, he practiced English phrases and understanding. During all these tense preparations, my mom was a reassuring presence, filling the house with her calm energy, her good food, and her kind prayers. "Thank you, Ruby," my father would say after one of her countless small kindnesses. That was his affectionate nickname for her—Ruby. There was something so strong and unspoken between the two of them that I always admired. My father was the outspoken public face of the family, and my mother was the quiet, strong foundation. She always did what she could to support her family in her own way, especially in these times of heightened stress.

When the day of the interview arrived, Mr. Haidermota brought over a Western-style suit for my father to wear, and he helped my father tie a tie for the first time in his life. Then the three of us set off for the school once again. I knew my father was nervous, but he kept his composure behind a firm visage.

Now it was my turn to wait outside while my father went with the headmaster into the corner office with the big wooden table. It was early in the morning, just as students were arriving for school, and as Mr. Haidermota and I sat waiting, I couldn't help noticing how many students arrived by automobile. I could see out the door and across the yard to where they were being dropped off. This was striking to me. Almost no one we knew had a car at this time, but here was a parade of vehicles rolling to a stop in front of the school to deposit these students from all over the city.

Minutes passed slowly, but finally, my father and the headmaster emerged from the corner office. At first it was difficult to tell how the interview had gone based upon the men's faces as they shook hands and said goodbye. But when my father turned toward Mr. Haidermota and me, there was no mistaking the smile that wrinkled the very corners of his mouth and eyes. He had done it. He had achieved the impossible. He had gotten his little Juku into Karachi Grammar School. The two grown men were so excited that they embraced right there in the hallway. "He's in!" my father said. It was time to go back and celebrate with the family and send Maulvi Sahib to the sweetmeat shop for some Gulab Jamun. Let us recite the Salwaat. Mission impossible had been accomplished.

CHAPTER 4

The Little Mouse

For the first time, I found myself enjoying school very much. I had always loved to read and to learn, but up until now, school had been a lonely and difficult experience. Everything was different at Karachi Grammar School, right from the beginning. Instead of being separated into strict social castes, we were separated into "houses." Houses are an old English tradition where students are grouped at random, and the members of each house bond over their unique traditions and look after one another, both socially and academically. The older members took the younger members, like me, under their wings and introduced us to everything the school had to offer. There were sports and clubs. There were debate teams and extracurricular activities. There were school festivals and grand occasions, such as Boxing Day, dances, sporting events, and awards ceremonies. It was clear to most everyone that I lived in a different social stratum outside the walls of the school—I arrived on foot, not in a chauffeured car, and no one had ever heard of my family before—but we all wore the same school uniform inside these walls, and that's all that seemed to matter.

The courses were challenging, of course, but wonderful. I was placed in the lower B section, which were the most basic of classes. I sat with twenty other students in a room. The wooden desks were built to seat two students side by side, and we went through our schedule this way. The teachers were strict and dedicated to their subjects. Some of them lived right on campus, and they would sweep into the room to deliver their lessons on history, science, English, Latin, and more. My favorite subject, as always, was mathematics, but I quickly fell in love with geography too. I loved the maps of distant places and the names of far-off cities. I could imagine the mountain ranges of Europe, the plains of Africa, the jungles of Brazil, the skyscrapers of New York. Many of the students and teachers were here from such a variety of nations that it became easy for me to imagine traveling to their home countries, to imagine seeing the beauty of their cities and towns. In my mind, I was already a world traveler.

When one subject was finished, the teacher would pack up and move on to the next classroom and the next instructor would sweep into our room and begin a new subject. We would stand up as they walked in. As always, I was a quiet student, small in build, skinny but determined as ever to compete and succeed. I might not have the same background as my peers, might not have the social clout they had inherited through their parents, but I could work as hard as they did, or harder. It wasn't long before one of the older boys in my house gave me my first nickname, Choe, which is Urdu for "little mouse." "Juzar Choe," he would say, "all work and no play make for a dull mouse." Then he would cajole me away from my books to play cricket in the large quad.

Each afternoon when school let out, I would stream off the campus with all my classmates, and my father or one of the men from his shop would meet me outside the school to walk me home. "Goodbye, Juzar Choe!" my new friends would call as they climbed into family cars.

Back at the chemist shop, I kept up my duties as chief window display officer. What's more, I had earned a promotion and was also a backup cashier. Each day, I reported back to my father how school had gone. I could tell my father was proud, not because of the way he talked to me but by overhearing the way he talked to other people. To me, my father was always strict, loving, and no-nonsense. He set expectations high for himself, his family, and close friends and, therefore, did not make a fuss when those expectations were met.

With other people, however, he would gush about his son at Karachi Grammar School. He would retell stories that I shared with him. He would share the good marks I received on papers or tests. At moments, he sounded so thrilled that you might have thought *he* was the one attending school. Some of the moments that seemed to make him proudest were when the doctors would stop by the shop. In those days, physicians not only wrote prescriptions for medicines, but they also often wrote down the exact ratios and ingredients they wanted their medicines to be made from and for a dispensing prescription in grains and grams. There might have been larger chemist shops in town, more upscale locations or greater inventories, but my father had two secret weapons that no one else in the city could claim: Khan Sahib and Maulvi Sahib. People came from across the city to acquire their expertise as compounders.

To me, Khan Sahib was practically an uncle. I spent nearly every day with him in the shop, and often Maulvi Sahib would be the one to gather me from school. Khan Sahib and Maulvi Sahib were well-known throughout the city for their skill and expertise in mixing prescription medicines. Maulvi Sahib was also the regular salesperson. Physicians and general practitioners would come from all over to have them make their medicine, and they would refer their patients to Venus Medico because we always custom-made prescriptions exactly as the doctor's asked. Khan Sahib was a large man, like a bear, and he had to squeeze up the small ladder to get into the small, raised compounding booth at the back of the shop. He invented a basket system on a rope so he would not have to go up and down the ladder all day. He would lower a prescription to me, and I would race it outside to a waiting car where my father would be chatting with the doctor. Throughout all of Asia, there has always been a tremendous respect for healers and teachers. Doctors were often both, and so it was not uncommon to hear people greet them with the term of utmost respect—*ustad* or *master*.

To me, doctors were almost like gods. If one walked into the shop, everyone dropped what they were doing to attend him. If one pulled up outside in his car, then someone instantly ran to the curb to see how we could serve. No one asked for payment when a doctor picked up his order. "We will take care of it later," my father would say, and sure enough, they each had their ways of settling their bills discreetly.

Doctors might have been gods, but there was one way in which my father now stood toe to toe with them: their kids all went to the same school together. "How is little Juzar?" a doctor might ask.

"He won the Most Improved award this year," my father would reply.

To the untrained eye, my father probably seemed nonchalant as he talked about his kid with these passing physicians, but to those of us who knew him well, it was clear to see how it filled him with pride.

Then one day, I came home with something foreign. A birthday party invitation. This was not just any invitation however, for I had been to parties before. This invitation was custom ordered on a fine cream paper. This invitation was handwritten in a beautiful calligraphy with expert flourishes and perfect black ink. This invitation came from a mansion in Garden East. It had been delivered to me at school. Invitations just like it had been delivered to everyone in my class, in fact. I had never heard of such a thing—imagine inviting an entire class of students to your home. Where would they all fit? How would you feed them? My imagination ran wild when I thought of what this birthday party might be like.

"Garden East?" my father said as held the invitation carefully. The family was sitting together for *thaal*, gathered around our low table. "That's miles away."

"We could take the tram," I offered.

"The tram does not run to this part of Garden East. They do not *want* a tram clattering through their neighborhood there."

I looked to my mother, hoping that she might have some suggestion. I could see her thinking quietly, but nothing appeared to come to mind. I knew that a hired car or a carriage was out of the question. Too expensive. If there was no streetcar, then I didn't know what the other options might be. Surely there must be some way to get to the party though.

Finally, my father announced, "It is impossible," and he set the invitation down.

That was the end of the discussion.

Sure enough, the date of the party came and went, and I could only imagine it from the stories that my classmates told when they arrived back at school. The big, beautiful cake. The games on the lawn. The music and prizes. It seemed like everyone in the whole class had been there.

Except for me.

So be it, I thought as I went about my studies, and soon the memory faded as life at school continued. But then, a few weeks later, it happened again: another invitation arrived upon my desk.

This one was from a different student, but it was in a similar cream envelope, written in a similar beautiful calligraphy in a similar gorgeous ink. I rushed home after school with the invitation, but unfortunately, it was almost the exact same scene playing out before my eyes. My father turned the invitation over gently in his hands and looked at the address of the house where the party would be held. PECHS was a high-end residential area at that time.

I had no idea where that was in relation to Elphinstone Street. My entire world was built upon a small sliver of Karachi that extended only as far as I could walk from this block where my home was. Places like Garden East and PECHS might as well have been as far away as those Brazilian jungles that I dreamt of in geography class or Beverly Hills. I listened to stories about visiting societies, which were wealthy enclaves much like the gated communities of today, the same way I listed to stories about visiting London, Paris, or New York.

"Impossible," my father said once more, and once again, I missed the party.

Despite my general lack of transportation and party appearances, I was developing some wonderful friendships at school. I fell in with a small pack of boys from my class, and we became something like the Magnificent Seven from the silver screen. Only we were the Magnificent Nine. There was Burjis, the natural leader of our group. He was clever in school and good at sports He had a great charisma and was very popular in our grade. Ejaz was the brains of our operation. He was very smart and had a keen memory. He seemed to know something about everything. Shahid was our comedian. He was short and strong, like a wrestler, and he was a master of cheeky tricks. Anwar was the solid boy of the group. He came from a rich family and always had the newest comic books. Mohammad Ali was our nerd, and then there was Shafi. Shafi was the erudite consummate gentleman who's fantastically beautiful handwriting was the envy of the school. His intellectual and analytical skills at that age could only be matched by Tommy, a mathematics genius, who also made a hobby of memorizing the dictionary!

Bernard was the silent one but a solid guy, a dark-skinned local Christian boy, but he came from a relatively poor family as far as I could gather. His father seemed a strict, hardworking, principled person, and the family lived in a poverty-stricken area of Karachi. They reminded me of my own family in many ways, and the two of us had a common bond based simply on our family's socioeconomic status amid the opulence we saw around us. He was the only other student that I knew of, besides myself, who did not arrive to school by car. Rather, he rode to school each day on the handlebars of his father's bicycle. He literally biked out of the slums to attend school beside princes and princesses. Unlike me, however, Bernard was a muscular boy and a very good boxer. He had the most street sense among us.

Finally, of course, there was me. The little mouse. I was small and quiet, but I was an enthusiastic member of our gang. From my father, I had learned the value of strong friendships, and from the beginning, I felt a great sense of loyalty to my gang. We all shared a wonderful sense of ambition and adventure. Together, we offered one another a wide range of perspectives, experiences, and world views. We could also field an impromptu cricket team at the drop of a hat and accept a challenge from the boys of another house.

It was only a matter of time, however, for the inevitable to happen: another birthday invitation. This time it came from one of my own good friends, Burjis, but it was that similar fine paper, that similar calligraphy, that similar upscale address on the invitation. My heart sank when I saw it land upon my desk. "Juzar Choe!" Burjis laughed. "That's the saddest look for a boy who just got invited to a party."

"I won't be able to go," I admitted to him.

"Why not? Do you have a dentist appointment that day?"

"No," I replied. "I don't have a car. I have no way to get there." I just shrugged not knowing what excuse to give them

"Pshhhh," Burjis said. It was a funny sound he made when he was being incredulous. "I'll send a car for you."

"You'll what?" I asked, not sure if I had heard him correctly.

"I'll ask my father to send a car for you. Cancel your dentist appointment," he joked.

On the day of the party, my mother spent extra time fixing my hair and adjusting my clothes. It had taken some careful persuasion to convince my father to let me climb into an unknown car and go to the party, but she had been successful, and now she wanted to make sure I looked good when I arrived.

My father waited by the curb with me until the black car rolled to a stop and the chauffeur came around to let me in. He and my father exchanged polite words as I slid onto the wide smooth back seat and planted myself next to the half-open window. I smiled at my father as I pulled away, and then I was gliding through the city in the back of a very nice automobile. We went down roads I had never seen and drove past shops, parks, and mosques I knew nothing about. We wound our way through neighborhoods I had only heard of, and finally, we arrived upon the long, curved slope of Burjis's driveway.

His home was beautiful, a large bungalow set upon a huge green lawn and concrete driveway. Many other cars had already arrived for the party, and the driveway was crowded. The chauffeur escorted me through the house toward the sounds of music and laughter. We passed a living room full of beautiful furniture and a dazzling white carpet. We passed a study full of books and leather chairs and a mahogany desk. We passed beneath a crystal chandelier which sent rainbow prisms of light dancing across the walls. Finally, we arrived at the party which had taken over the back of the house and spilled out across the patio and into the big backyard where I could see a game of cricket being played. Adults mingled, and kids ran every-where. "Juzar Choe!" someone shouted, and I turned to find Burjis and the rest of our gang hovering around a table which was laid out with the most amazing food. Sweetmeats and fried bread. Cakes and biscuits as we called them there. Roast lamb meat and sandwiches cut into triangles. "What are you doing here?" Burjis asked with a big smile. "I thought you had a dentist appointment!"

I was so happy to be at the party and see my friends.

CHAPTER 5

Eggs and Butter

Exactly as my father had hoped, the Karachi Grammar School was changing my life in many wonderful ways. I was making great strides with my studies, and I was voted Most Improved Student in my first year, which led to me being promoted to the advanced classes. I was still a quiet, shy boy, but I was discovering clubs and activities, such as the debate team and elocution contests, where I could thrive, and I was forming enduring friendships with my classmates.

It wasn't just me being transformed, however. The school held several annual events that were known throughout the city as being social occasions of the highest caliber, and that's where my father and mother, an immigrant shopkeeper and his wife, would hobnob with Karachi's elite families and political class. Much like me, my parents were quiet and reserved at such events, careful not to draw attention to themselves. I imagine that they probably felt out of place at events like this, but I could tell that they enjoyed the experience very much.

There was one event that loomed larger than any other on the school calendar each year, called Boxing Day. This was the event that students prepared for year-round, an event so big that it warranted its own school holiday. It was so popular, in fact, that even prime ministers and presidents of Pakistan were known to attend as chief guests.

Not to be confused with the English holiday, our Boxing Day event centered around the sport of boxing. A full-sized ring was erected in the school courtyard, surrounded by rows of seating, and the best athletes from within the school would compete in each division. Students trained and competed to be able to enter the ring on this occasion, and even I tried for a while to hone some boxing skills. What I lacked in size, I thought I might make up for in quickness, but alas, it quickly became clear that the talents of Juzar Choe lay elsewhere. One punch and I would be out for the day.

On the night of the event, music filled the school halls as the school band serenaded the crowd. Politicians, sports figures, celebrities, and socialites appeared among our faculty and families, and everyone was dressed formally, elegantly, and beautifully. The school headmaster turned into master of ceremonies, a senior faculty member was the ringside announcer, and a celebrity panel of judges graded each fight.

By now, my father had invested in a suit of his own and was quite adept at tying a necktie. It was truly an occasion, however, to see my mother dressed in a beautiful silk sari of rose red or magenta or gold. In those days, a sari was still considered the most formal of attire, and my mother looked completely transformed from the woman that I knew around the house or in the market or at the shop. It was magic to see my mother like this, passing beneath the hanging lanterns and saying hello to the socialites of Karachi. She had an uncanny ability to converse in English even though she did not have much grasp of the nuances of the language. It was like a superpower—her ability to read people's faces and body language, without understanding their actual words, and then reply perfectly in mono syllables.

The boxing matches would ensue throughout the evening, the awards would be announced, and then, finally, when the ceremonies were drawing to a close, we would anxiously wait for the principal of the school to announce what we would all be waiting for: "This occasion has been such a success that I hereby officially declare tomorrow to be a holiday!"

A great cheer would erupt in the courtyard, for that mean that the school would be closed the next day, which was a very rare treat for us.

*****

Despite the new suits and saris and despite the new social circles that my family now occasioned, our fortunes still rose and fell daily, depending on how the shop was doing. I was becoming keenly aware of these two unique worlds that I lived in: the world of Karachi Grammar School with its prestigious events, elite company, and lavish birthday parties and the world of my neighborhood with its local characters, overcrowded apartments, and work around the shop. At school, there was a wonderful sense of strength, prestige, and continuity, as if nothing could interfere with the time-honored traditions of the place. At home, on the other hand, life felt far more precarious, and it was always led by events at the shop. Family life and shop life were interconnected to such a degree that it was sometimes hard to tell where one ended and the other began. If things did not go well at the shop, then that was reflected in the home. If sales were slow, an unexpected loss occurred or there was a problem with suppliers, then the mood of the whole family took a nosedive. The worst was when some city official arrived, seeking to enforce some obscure and possibly fictitious rule, just to extract a bribe from the shop. Those occasions sent my father into fits of frustration and anger, and they were becoming more and more common. Many people, including may father, were beginning to complain quite bitterly about the government which appeared to be riddled with corruption and turning a blind eye to its citizens as these vulturelike officials preyed upon us.

If things were going well, however, then life was good. My father could be a strict manager, but he also treated his team like family, and it wasn't uncommon to arrive back at the apartment and find the whole staff of the shop gathered around the table for *thaal* or just relaxing in the living room. My sisters and I didn't mind this at all. These were the happy times even if it meant the dinner had to be divided up even further than usual. After all, we spent as much time with these guys as we spent with our own parents. Sometimes, my sisters, Rashida and Akila, and I would get together and plan a variety show for everyone. We made a stage out of one end of the living room. We installed curtains made from bed sheets strung over a clothesline. Then we would perform popular songs from the radio, reenact book or movie plots that we knew of, or even perform some interpretation of current events: a royal wedding, an intriguing murder trial, or a rousing win by the national cricket team over the Australians. Whatever it was, it was bound to be riddled with "Ali humor," our unique and ridiculous interactions and interpretations.

It was especially fun if my father was feeling relaxed and lending his energy to the show too. The whole room would be full of laughter and applause, and in the end, I would award the official prizes for Best Actress, Best Comedy Skit, and Best Singing Voice, and so on to my little sisters. Their prizes were coins, hairpins, chocolates, or some other small treats or treasures. I loved my sisters dearly, and we had a wonderful close relationship full of fun and jokes. If we were especially lucky, my father would call out, "Ruby, make some sweet dish!" That meant that he had good news. My mother would make a traditional egg custard which was something like a crème brûlée or the egg *maesub*, a fantastic sweet dish made with eggs, butter, and milk. The good news could be almost anything—we might have had a good sales day, landed a new supply account client, or my father might have secured a new product for his inventory. It was usually something quite small by today's standards, but big news for a struggling family.

It was also common for the family of adults to share domestic duties like childcare. My sisters, cousins, and I always enjoyed special occasions such as the *Laylat-ul-Qadr*, the Night of Decree and Power, the Night of Worship and Destiny. For the adults, it was one of the most sacred events of the year, a celebration of the night when the first verses of the Holy Koran were revealed to Prophet Muhammad (SAW-PBUH). To observe this night is the equivalent to one thousand months of prayer according to Muslim belief. This was a night of blessings and mercy from Allah Subhanaho, and even more importantly, this was the night that angels brought the annual decree down from heaven. Ma would lay out the prayers clothes, washed and ironed, upon a chair with the *bukhr* underneath to give its characteristic beautiful essence. Even the preparation for the night was exciting to us at that time.

For the children, there was another kind of excitement in the evening: *fun*. We were gathered into slumber parties, left with babysitters, and handed packets of the good stuff. The good stuff included candies, fruits, nuts, and other goodies which we would get to eat through the evening. Our cousins from downstairs would sometimes come up to join us, depending on how well our fathers were getting along. Most of the time, it was just us and the kids of our family friends though. The Miabouy family with my childhood friends, Rukhsana and Mamu, were our most common companions. Finally, my mother, father, auntie, uncle, and all the adults would head off to the mosque for the 11:00 PM prayers, leaving the horde of children with Maulvi Sahib, my father's shop assistant and compounder. It was party time for us kids. I still remember he, being a devout Muslim himself, would be on the prayer mat during this evening while we as kids would create our own entertainment.

We, too, were instructed to say our prayers, which we did for a short while, and then the night would dissolve into games and fooling around. It was exciting to be up so late, to have all the children together, and to outnumber the adult by so many. Maulvi Sahib tried to keep at least a slight sense of solemnity for the occasion, but we giggled and told jokes. We sang songs, teased one another, and played chase and shot tops around the room until Maulvi Sahib spoke sternly to us. Then we quieted down for a few moments, waited until things had settled down, and started all over again. We did not fear his temper the way we did our own fathers', and it was liberating. I can remember many times hearing my cousins being loud and rowdy in their apartment just beneath us, with lots of running around and yelling. Ten people lived in that one-bedroom apartment with about three hundred square feet. Then suddenly, it would turn quiet as footsteps came in from outside and began to ascend the staircase. Everyone listened to determine if it was my father or their father coming home. If it was their father, my Kakajee, there would not be another sound from the apartment below. It was pin-drop silent for the rest of the night once he arrived home. My father and his brother were both like that: they ruled their homes absolutely and strictly. My Kakajee had a temperament that was sourer than my father's though.

He could be much harsher in his discipline, and his bad moods could last for months. To make matters worse, Kakajee had taken a new job as a traveling salesman, so as my father was slowly becoming a successful business owner, his clout in the community was also growing, which had the unfortunate effect of making Kakajee, his older brother, extremely sensitive to anything he perceived as a social slight. For example, if the two brothers went to a party together and the host greeted my father first, Kakajee could descend into an icy anger and there could be bad blood for months. Even in a culture which cherished its traditions and social customs, Kakajee was known to take it way too far.

The tension between the brothers was bad enough, and it often scared me as a young boy, but even worse was the tension that arose between the families. When the brothers were at war over some small violation, the families followed suit. An icy tension would suddenly spring up between me and my numerous cousins who lived just beneath us. During those times, anything might be perceived as an act of aggression. For example, water. Fresh water was stored in a cistern on the roof of the apartment building, and it flowed straight down through a pipe to reach the apartments. Thus, if we were using the water on the third floor, it affected the flow of water to the second and first floors. Something as simple as washing dishes could be construed as an intentional act of sabotage, and the family tensions would spiral to new lows. The worst for me as a young boy was to be walking on my way to school, to market or to Venus Medico, and to be passing through the already filthy alley and then suddenly have garbage rain down upon my head. Someone was throwing it from the window above. I never saw who threw the garbage while I was walking, but to this day I don't think it was a coincidence that every time it happened to me, our families happened to be at war. I am sure both families were to share the blame.

But tonight at least, under the protective watch of Maulvi Sahib, my sisters and I were able to play freely and without fear while the adults were out at mosque, greeting their destinies. The end of Ramadhan heralded Eid and Eid brought Eid. An envelope with a little money that we would each receive from our elders and our "uncles" as "fun money" for us to spend as we wished. It was a competition between siblings for who got the most and it depended on who got the most and it depended on who was the favorite of that "uncle."

*****

My father was known to help people out with their medical problems even if they didn't have the resources to pay. Sometimes, people would pay him back years later for a treatment or remedy. Other times, they might barter with him for some other goods or services. This is exactly how we found ourselves with several hours of free services at a photography studio. My mother like the idea and decided to make a family occasion out of it. It was a beautiful October evening, and our aunt Mami Fatima was visiting from India. We had a fun time getting dressed up and piling into the family car that had arrived with my aunt. A family drive was a special treat indeed. We had our photos taken at the studio, but it was what happened afterward that made the night so unforgettable. It was getting late, near midnight, and as we were driving home, we had to pass near the military barracks and armory. Normally, this would have been routine, just a darkened facility behind fences and off the main road. Only tonight, the military base was a hive of activity. Something was clearly happening. Men were running everywhere, and vehicles were pouring out through the gates: troop carriers, armored vehicles, and even tanks. At first, it seemed thrilling, but very quickly I picked up on the fear that the adults were feeling as they watched that sight. We drove quickly home and shuttered ourselves indoors even as the military convoys roared through city streets, fanned out across Karachi, and began setting up checkpoints at intersections.

This was before phones were common in houses, and we did not have one. There was no internet or television. The radio was playing its normal broadcasting. We had no way to discover what was happening outside our windows, but we knew that it was something serious. We barely slept that night, and in the morning, we finally learned what was going on. The first newspaper to arrive was the

English language paper, so I read the news to the family: the civilian government had been overthrown in the night. General Iskandar Mirza led the army to topple Prime Minister Feroz Khan Noon and the Constituent Assembly of Pakistan. We were now under military rule.

At first, there was a great deal of confusion. What exactly did this mean? People woke up to find their government was gone, but they went about their daily activities anyway, waiting to see what would happen. General Mirza announced a slew of directives. He installed General Ayub Khan as the chief martial law administrator. He announced a host of anti-corruption measures to scrub the public sector of all the bribery, embezzlement, kickbacks, extortion, and cronyism. What's more, he ordered that businesses all over Pakistan stop hoarding and open their full inventories to customers with strict price controls. Many businesses had been strategically hoarding basic supplies, such as butter, eggs, or even cooking oils, to drive up prices. As a result, those staples had become like luxury goods, only tasted on special occasions. Similarly, inventories of imported items like china, glassware, linens, or kitchenware were manipulated as well. As soon as people heard about the military order, they rushed into the streets to form long lines at the grocery or other shops. My mother quickly sent me out as well, and I jumped into line at the grocery. I jostled to keep my position, clutching the few rupees in my pocket. When it was finally my turn, I purchased a box of butter and two dozen eggs. I was ecstatic. I could practically taste the eggs as I walked quickly home.

In the days after the coup, the city was on cloud nine. The military seemed like angels sent to deliver us from the thousand small miseries and indignities that plagued our lives. Business was regulated. Government services became efficient. Soldiers were everywhere on the streets, and people walked up and thanked them.

It was only thirteen days later when Ayub Khan, chief marshal law administrator, deposed General Mirza and appointed himself president of Pakistan. Soon after that, the soldiers faded from the street corners, and eventually, the new military-supported government began its own descent into corruption and turmoil. But for now, we had eggs and butter. We were living the good life.

CHAPTER 6

A House Divided

People settled into the new normal quite quickly after the initial excitement of the coup faded. Life went on for me quite as before, both at school and at home. Usually, those two worlds of mine remained far apart from each other. I could spend my mornings alongside some of the most privileged kids in the nation and then return home in the afternoon to the hustle of work and family in the shop and our small, crowded flats. I could spend weekends visiting my new friends in their suburban mansions and enjoying sleepovers where the living room was converted into a movie theater with a reel to reel projector, and then the chauffeured car would drop me back off on Elphinstone Street where I would walk down the dirty little alley behind the shop.

Our alley (*galli*) was truly nasty, and unfortunately, we all had to pass through it every day to reach our apartment. Just half a block off Elphinstone Street, I had to jump through filth and feces to reach the door of our building. One section of the alley was the neighborhood garbage dump, and another section of the alley was crowded with encroachments. Thus, everyone in the area emptied their rubbish bins from their windows into the alley where squatters erected makeshift tents made from boxes and lived amid the filth. To make it even worse, the public urinals overflowed into the alleys, making them more unpleasant. Often my sisters and I would hold our noses as we leaped over rivulets of sewage that trickled past our building door, and yet when we would reach our home on the third floor, it was heavenly clean with the west-facing windows open for ventilation in the shotgun flat. It was nirvana compared to the conditions below and behind us.

My friends from school knew where I lived, but they did not come to my home. I didn't know what they thought of my location. After all, we were right there on Elphinstone Street, one of the best locations in the city if we faced the front. But our actual apartment was like something out of a slum. I almost felt like an impostor. Occasionally, one of my friends would stop by Venus Medico with his father or driver to say hello or, possibly, even to make a purchase. Sometimes they would just pull up to the curb to shout a greeting and then move along. I remember how awkward I felt about that at first, waiting upon my friends and their families. Despite our growing friendships, I wasn't sure what they would think about this other world that I lived in or how this might affect our friendship. My father, too, seemed slightly unsure of how to respond to my friends. He was polite and welcoming to them, but he never encouraged me to invite them over to the apartment or to any family events. It seemed like he too wanted to keep the worlds quite separate. There was something coming, however, that was forcing me to think of this more and more: my own birthday.

By now, I had been to many birthday parties for my school friends, and they were great. At that age and time, birthday parties were the grand occasions of our friendships, the social outlets of our often-regimented lives. It was clear to me how my friends gained respect and social currency by hosting one of these affairs when it was their turn, and I knew that it was now my turn. I wanted desperately to host a good birthday party, but I was also nervous about inviting my friends to walk through the filthy alley to reach my family's small apartment.

My father also hesitated when I asked him about it. It wasn't so much that my father was ashamed of his situation, for he would often remind me to be proud of our family heritage, our core values, and our hard-won successes no matter how small. "Mian, apni awkaat mat bhoolna," he often said in Urdu. *Boy, don't forget who you are.* He stressed this often, especially as I shuttled back and forth from my new life at school.

On the other hand, he was also keenly aware of his own image and reputation, which he considered incredibly valuable business assets. It did not need to be common knowledge, for example, that he stepped over a puddle of piss and garbage to enter his own home from an alleyway overrun by squatters. That wasn't exactly the image of success and professionalism that he hoped to project to the doctors and clientele of the shop. He never hesitated to invite his own friends though, and on occasion, he would even coax some of the relatively influential ones in the local police or governmental circles, albeit at a lower level, to use their influence to improve the surroundings.

Now he had to consider my friends, however. He had grown more comfortable with my gang from Karachi Grammar and their families over the past months, and after some discussion, he agreed to let me host a small event. There would be no pony rides, and I certainly wasn't about to invite my entire class to the apartment, but I was going to host a real birthday party. I was going to invite my school friends to my home, combining these two worlds that I lived in. It was thrilling and nerve-racking at the same time.

My mother helped me plan the food and the games. Ma was a great cook, and she would always be there with tasty food, depending upon the occasion, be it Eid or a gathering of friends or just on the spur of the moment if needed. My sisters helped me decorate with balloons and streamers, and on the day of the party, my friends were wonderful. Despite all my worries, they didn't care about the alley or the small apartment. We played together as we always did, looking at comic books, talking about cricket, and playing board games like snakes and ladders, ludo, or Chinese checkers. The most popular activity, however, was something I had never even thought of as an entertainment: playing on the balcony. I had done it for years, of course, mostly by myself. I would often sit and watch people pass beneath. One of my favorite ways to pass the time was to sit on the balcony and pretend I was in the press box at an international cricket match. I was the English language commentator for the radio, of course, and I would deliver the exciting play-by-play. It was amazing how many thrilling comeback victories Pakistan managed to achieve under my careful watch.

In all that time, it never occurred to me that my balcony perch could be exciting for guests, particularly the guests who came from sprawling homes with wide lawns and garden walls. But my friends had never experienced anything like it, this ability to hang over Elphinstone Street, one of the busiest thoroughfares in the city, and watch all the people, carts, cars, and commotion. We could shout down to passersby and have funny exchanges. We could compete to see who threw a jelly bean the farthest across the street. My friends had a blast. We would play all sorts of make-believe games based just on the number plates of the cars passing down the street.

Finally, my mother presented a small-but-delicious birthday cake, and then I opened my gifts. I received a top that year, and we all took turns wrapping the string carefully around the device and then shooting it through the air until it landed and spun off wildly across the floor. By the time everyone left to go home, I was beaming with satisfaction. My party had been small, but it had been a success. It felt good to be able to offer something in return after all the invitations to parties, sleepovers, dinners, and rides in cars that had been extended to me by now.

The only problem with the birthday party was that my Kakajee, Kaki, and cousins were stewing in the apartment beneath us. Kakajee and my father were in the middle of a bad feud, and the families were not talking. This made things very awkward as I walked past their crowded apartment when I escorted guests to and from my party. My cousins pretended to ignore us, but from the corner of my eye, I could see the sharp looks that came my way as we passed by their open door, and they were like daggers.

A few weeks later, some exciting news swept through Karachi. The president of the United States, Dwight Eisenhower, was coming to Pakistan. This would be the first state visit by any Western leader since the nation was formed, and it was clear that Karachi would roll out the red carpet for the US leader and World War II hero. In much the way that I felt thrilled to host a good birthday party, the whole nation of Pakistan now seemed thrilled for the opportunity to display our unique hospitality and host the American delegation. More than just an official visit, this was a chance for Pakistan to shine in an international spotlight and demonstrate a fabulous state welcome.

Even at school, we talked about the visit while city officials began to plan the events. A grand parade was organized which would escort President Eisenhower directly from the airport to the presidential palace. Of course, there was only one road through the center of downtown that would be suitable for such an occasion, one road that was wide enough, perfectly located, and offered a handsome view of both Karachi's historic downtown architecture and the commercial activity that continued to thrive there: Elphinstone Street.

The US president was going to pass right by my father's shop. He would pass right past our home. More importantly, he would pass just beneath my balcony.

I immediately began preparations of my own.

On the day of the parade, my friends came over once more, and we all made decorations for the balcony. We painted Pakistani and American flags onto poster boards. We painted signs that said "Welcome, President Eisenhower" in Urdu and in English. We made streamers out of paper and tied balloons to the balcony rails.

Meanwhile, the streets filled with people. Faces appeared in all the windows up and down Elphinstone Street and crowds gathered in every doorway and on each balcony along the route. It was heaven for a gang of schoolboys who could shout back and forth with the excited crowds, who could play catch with members of another balcony, hoping not to lose their ball into the sea of humanity below, and who could work on group cheers and chants.

When the parade came into view, it was spectacular. The city leaders rode at the head of the procession in a shining black convertible. Behind him came marching bands and military processions, traditional dance troupes, and mounted guards dressed regally in their ornate attire and carrying their ceremonial swords which gleamed in the sunlight. We all felt very proud of our nation. The US president rode with President Ayub Khan of Pakistan in a state carriage drawn by six beautiful horses. As they drew near, we chanted and yelled until both presidents finally looked up and spotted us on the balcony. They both smiled and waved at our wild cheering.

The next day at school, we made quite a spectacle of ourselves again, this time retelling the story of the president's wave and how we had earned it. Nearly everyone had been to the parade, of course, but not many people had had a vantage point such as ours. Before the end of the day, everyone knew all about our balcony adventure. It was a wonderful feeling for me. Not only had we seen a spectacular parade, but I had also been able to offer something valuable to my friends. My classmates might live in the finest houses in Karachi and they might travel to school by chauffeured car, but they did not have a balcony over Elphinstone Street. That was something only I could offer. The best seat in the house!

Unfortunately, the joy I felt at school was short-lived as I still had to return home each night to the tensions that were flaring between my father and Kakajee. The families were practically at war right now, and it was terrible to be a kid caught in the crossfire of these adult rages, especially since we lived together in such cramped quarters. The most recent grievance up was caused when I was coming home from school a few days ago and ran across my Kakajee in the stairway. He glared at me, and I mumbled a greeting as I scurried past him out of fear.

Sure enough, my "lack of respect" turned into the latest flash point, and my name was bandied about whenever the warring factions began their heated conversations. By now, the war had spilled over into the community, and people had begun to take sides, depending on who they were closer friends with. My father had his group of friends who commiserated with him and supported his position, and my uncle had his group as well. What's more, Kakajee's oldest daughter, my cousin, had married, and now her husband lived in that tiny apartment with the whole family too. What should have been a time of joy and welcome was used a weapon of exclusion even when my cousin became pregnant and began to show. Everywhere I turned, there seemed to be more and more complications. And what was it all about? If there was such a thing as death by a thousand paper cuts, then this was war of a thousand insults. The competitive streak that ran in our family helped them to achieve great things, but it also created strife where none was necessary.

Each night when I said my prayers, I carefully included my family, hoping for reconciliation soon. I wanted to be the peacemaker. Up until now, there had always been something that brought the brothers back together—a religious night of atonement, a family friend who could negotiate the crisis, some turn of events that required a united front, and so on. This time, however, the division seemed so wide that I wondered what could possibly bridge this gap?

My questions were soon answered, and it was not what I had hoped for.

Late one night, we heard a commotion begin to stir downstairs, loud enough to stir us from our sleep. Normally, at this hour, all was quiet, but we could hear the scrambling of feet and the urgent voices. The unmistakable sound of Kakajee yelling reached our ears, and within minutes, there was a banging on our apartment door. My father raced to answer the door, and one of my cousins stood there ashen faced and with fear in his eyes.

"Fatima Bahen is not well," he said, referring to his elder sister in the seventh month of her pregnancy. "It's the baby."

And just like that, months of feuding disappeared. All the insults and garbage thrown at one another, water hoarding, and warring factions vanished. This was an emergency, and now nothing mattered but the family. My father dressed in a flash and was out the door. My mother did the same, and we trailed after her. Fatima Bahen was in pain, her belly cramping. My father quickly called upon a nearby friend of his with a car and arranged to take Fatima Bahen to the hospital where he knew the doctors. Fatima disappeared into the car along with her husband, my father, and Kakajee, and they vanished into the night. There was nothing for the rest of us to do but wait, and we did it together. My mother helped with the youngest of the cousins. The older cousins played together quietly and waited.

We passed the hours until finally my father returned home. "Fatima will be fine," he said. "So will the baby. They were able to stop the bleeding, and everything looks fine. She will stay in hospital for a few days to be sure."

Kaki sobbed with relief. Without saying much, it was clear she was grateful. I hated the fact that my cousin was in the hospital and that Fatima Bahen had almost lost her baby, but I was so glad to see a thaw in the relationship of the two families. Fatima Bahen would be all right, and the family war was over. For now, at least.

CHAPTER 7

The Jolly Cricket Club

By the time I reached twelve years old, things were going quite well for me and my family. I was thriving in my studies, I had a small coterie of school friends, I had a great group of neighborhood friends as well, and I was taking on a larger role at my father's shop. Venus Medico was thriving, and by now, we had even installed a telephone handset in the house. Of course, we did this by running an extra-long phone line out the shop window, through the alley, and up into the apartment through the third-floor window. My mother had to ring a buzzer to make a call, which got one of the shop assistants to lift the phone receiver. Then she could provide directions, and the shop assistant would place the call for her from the main telephone next to the cash register. Once placed, she could continue the call from her handset in the living room.

This also meant I could speak on the phone with my friends, which was a nice luxury and very convenient for a boy amid a heated campaign. I just happened to be running for the top office of our neighborhood cricket club, and it seemed very presidential indeed to be able to place a telephone call to my good friend Eba and ask for his support. Eba was one of my few neighborhood friends who had a phone in his house too. I knew to keep my calls discreet, short, and to the point, of course. I was tying up the shop phone, and every call cost money.

On the other hand, this was cricket. By now, cricket was more than just a passing hobby, more than just a way to spend time at recess, more than just something to chat about with customers at my father's shop. Cricket had bloomed into one of the great passions of my life. The national cricket heroes like Fazal Mahmood, Hanif Muhammad (the Little Master), or Saeed Ahmed were like gods to me, and the very sight of a cricket bat would send my young heart racing. I dreamed of playing for Pakistan one day and having that *moment* like when Fazal Mahmood bowled Pakistan to a stunning twenty-four wins over England at the oval, with six wickets in each innings. I spent hours practicing my bowling technique: in the park, in the alley, in the living room. Wherever I was, I could hear my imaginary crowd roaring for me and in all the imaginary games I played with myself in the small apartment, and of course, I always managed to lift Pakistan to a beautiful victory.

These were the wild and free days of Pakistani cricket too, and nearly anyone could form a club and play inter-league matches. There were city clubs like the Karachi Blues and their rivals, the Karachi Whites. Clubs were formed at schools, among branches of the military, and even in the workplace. One of the best squads in all of Karachi was hosted by Pakistan International Airlines. At my own school, cricket was dominated by the older boys from each of the houses, so I did what any aspiring national superstar with more heart than physical stature would do: I helped form a neighborhood club of my own.

The Jolly Cricket Club was born on the Polo Ground, a large public playground where neighborhood teams and groups of kids would gather to play. On a clear Sunday morning, the Polo Ground verged on chaos and we were in full gear. *Why the team was named Jolly Cricket Club, I do not recollect. We were, after all, a very competitive bunch on and off the field and I soon realized that egos and tantrums don't take long to develop or entrench, no matter what age.* The pitch itself only requires twenty-two yards, of course, so the wide Polo Ground could accommodate many separate matches simultaneously. The problem was that everyone's outfields overlapped. As the matches heated up, cricket balls and outfielders flew in every direction, racing through one another's competitions. It was organized chaos, but somehow, the matches managed to coexist in a wonderful way.

My neighborhood friends and I had been coming here since we were little, and now we had taken our commitment to the next level. To the amusement of many, we took everything about our club very seriously, including the election of officers. So far, I had been campaigning among my closest friends—Eba, Abde, Hunaid, Aziz, and Idris. Zulfiqar and Zoaib had recently joined us too, and they brought in a whole new perspective on cricket. They were smart kids on the block, at times nerdy, and they had their own passions for cricket to share with the group. This weekend, I would give my most important speech to date to the entire club. Several other candidates would also give speeches, and then we would hold the election. Up until now, I held the position of secretary and had done an outstanding job of keeping all the official club records. I had statistics from every match. Without even looking, I could tell you who scored the most runs on our team, who dropped the most catches, or who was in the running for each of our annual awards. Now it was time for me to make a run for the top elected position: *captain of the Jolly Cricket Club.*

Just then, I heard my father's voice yelling up through the alley from the shop. "Juzar!" he yelled.

"Yes," I replied, putting my head out the window.

"Come, help."

"Of course," I replied.

My father had hired a new errand boy named Wali Mohammed, who was just a couple years older than me. Wali needed help delivering a large shipment of medical supplies to one of the banks across town to their pharmacy for their employees, so I would assist him. By this time, my father had worked magic to secure an import license for his business. No one knew exactly how he did it, for those licenses were incredibly difficult to acquire, but somehow, after years of working his midlevel connections and cajoling government officials, he had managed it. Immediately, it began to pay dividends. My father could order rare and hard-to-find treatments, vitamins, cosmetics, and other items directly from the producers in other nations. Soon, the word was out, and my father was not only selling these treasures in his own shop but was also supplying them in bulk to other shops around the city. He found himself with exclusive contracts to supply businesses with their health-care supplies. In those days, a large business, like a bank, provided their own infirmary for employees. They would stock medicines, vitamins, first aid supplies, and more. They might even have their own pharmacist or doctor on location.

Thus, Wali and I climbed aboard a city bus to deliver our packages of supplies to a bank pharmacy several miles away. It was a treat for me to go on these errands, one of the few times that I could travel around the city without close adult supervision. My father kept strict tabs on my comings and goings, even to the Polo Grounds and back. His watchful eye seemed ever present. These crosstown deliveries were brief adventures where it was just Wali and me out in the streets. We were close enough in age to enjoy each other's company, and we both were drawn to the many distractions on our way home. Often, we would take the scenic route back to the shop so that we could explore the street vendor stalls and buy a sweet. We would pause for the street magicians and the animal tamers—the men with bears on leashes or snakes in baskets or monkeys that played tiny organs. One time, Wali and I bought a pack of firecrackers, and we set them along the train tracks so that we could startle passengers on board the trams with our small explosions. We got a great kick out of that.

Of course, one of the problems with having well-connected father is that his friends are everywhere. By the time we returned to the shop, he had already heard about our firecracker mischief. Someone had seen us and reported the incident to him. He hung up the phone just as we walked in the door. He was livid. He sent Wali to do some other errands, and he sent me to stand in front of the shop in the withering heat of the full sun as a punishment. This was one of his favorite punishments. I stood there for nearly three hours until the heat of the sun and my father's anger blended into the same thing, both making me sweat soaked and woozy. Finally, one of my father's good friends, Mohammed Husain Chacha, stopped by the shop and convinced him to let me come back inside where I could see the staff watching me from the corners of their eyes and trying not to laugh.

On this trip, however, I knew that I couldn't afford to anger my father. It was too close to the cricket club elections, so Wali and I went straight to the bank and back, enjoying the sights along the way, but not stopping for any amusements, sweets, or pranks.

*****

My father closed the shop every day for lunch. School let out around one o'clock in the afternoon, and I would hang about the shop until lunchtime, and then we would climb the stairs to join the rest of the family for the meal. After lunch, he liked to take a nap, but not before he had his feet massaged. He would lie out the sleeping mat facedown and instruct me to stand on his feet and read to him. He had purchased subscriptions to English language magazines like *Reader's Digest* for me, and he insisted that I read aloud to him as I shifted my weight back and forth, working his feet into the mat. I remember reading the *Reader's Digest* version of "The Fall of the Third Reich." Inevitably, he fell asleep before I had finished reading the second paragraph, but he would wake up if I stopped, so I churned through one article after another while he dozed.

It seemed an absurd practice at the time, with no relevance to the life we were going through, but my father carried many mysteries about him, and we children knew better than to pry. Sometime later, I would overhear my mother ask him, "Why do you make Juzar read to you if you fall off to sleep?"

"It does not matter whether I hear it," he answered. "It matters that he can read and read English, and he must."

Here was a man who hardly knew English, subscribing to these magazines so that I would be proficient in English.

When he woke from his naps, he would return to the shop. Sometimes, I would join him, and other times, I would remain and study. This week, as the cricket club elections loomed, I went down to the shop with him to keep myself distracted.

Sure enough, Tahir Bhai was carrying on about the movie that he had seen last weekend, *Ben-Hur*. Tahir Bhai was a diehard movie enthusiast, and while I was out playing cricket, he spent every

Sunday afternoon ensconced in the Capitol Cinema across the street from the shop. Movies were becoming very popular at the time, and visits to the cinema were considered very trendy, especially if they were playing the latest releases from Hollywood. Tahir Bhai was our resident hipster in that regard. The Sunday matinee was almost a religion for him, and he would block his time for this. Only something catastrophic or totally unavoidable would alter his plans. He would pout his way out of any shop duties or other obligations if he had to, even with my father. That matinee was his time. He gained such satisfaction from getting a ticket and watching movie with a couple of *paans* in his mouth. I had been to the theater myself on a couple occasions and witnessed him beaming and smiling away in his own peace.

All the following week, he would provide his analysis of the film. He would carry on with every customer or friend, offering his assessment of the acting, the costuming, the story line, and the details. Oh, he loved the details. He especially relished finding small mistakes or inconsistencies. *How come Charlton Heston has so much blood on his face in one moment, and then suddenly he is clean again? When did he bathe? When did that actor change his shirt?*

Often, it was more fun to listen to Tahir Bhai carry on about the movie than it was to see it, especially if Maulvi Saheb got into the conversation and began teasing him. Those two were like the odd couple—complete opposites. Tahir Bhai was skinny and short, a diminutive figure with a personality bordering on obsessive compulsive, while Maulvi Saheb was tall, deeply religious but more genial. There was a lot of respect between them, yet a lot of fire, and they loved to tease each other about their quirks and idiosyncrasies. Lucky for the rest of us, these were many and hilarious.

While we were all in the shop, listening to the two banter, a customer walked in whom we recognized. This was one of the newer customers who had begun arriving after my father secured his import license. Along with the brisk business came these other people that my father was forced to deal with: government officials. Despite the martial law, it was hard not to notice that things were slowly slipping back to the way they had been before the coup. The military leaders which had been hailed as heroes were slowly becoming the very thing that they had replaced. The access to the power and the money were changing them. Government was slowly becoming riddled with corruption once again, and even these low-ranking government officials felt free to wield their little power over shopkeepers like my father. This customer had become notorious in our shop. He came for an expensive face cream that we imported. He would place special orders for specialty items like this, and then tell us to put it on his tab, which he never paid.

Sure enough, he gathered up his face cream, hung around long enough to feel properly appreciated, and then left without paying. I could see my father's face darken as he watched the man make his merry way down Elphinstone Street.

Meanwhile, from the other direction, I saw my neighborhood friends Eba, Abde, Akhter, Hunaid, and Idris coming down the street. *What terrible timing*, I thought. My father was surely in a sour mood after that government official had stiffed him again.

My friends would often pass by as I worked at the shop. They would watch from the corners of their eyes to determine if it was safe to come in or if they should just keep on going. Inevitably, the only reason they were there was to lure me away from the shop. They always wanted to play cricket, go to the movies, or just hang out along the streets or parks. Today was a Friday, so they were thinking of cricket. The Jolly Cricket Club held practice at the Polo Ground on Friday afternoons, and I went as often as I could. As discreetly as possible, I responded with the corners of my own eyes, alerting them that my father was not in a mood for visitors. Of course, he was difficult to read in the best of times. Occasionally, he would demonstrate flat out disapproval when my friends wandered by, but often he would show nothing but a flat affectation that kept everyone on eggshells. On very rare occasions, I would meet his glance and find him smiling, and then with a gleam of approval in his eye, he would wave at me, implying "You may go. It is okay."

For whatever reason, to my surprise, this just happened to be one of those days. My friends passed by and kept going down the sidewalk, and as I looked cautiously from them to my father, I found him smiling. He had seen them walking. He also knew about cricket practice the elections on Sunday. He flashed me that wave of his hand, and I practically jumped for joy. I loved it when he did that. I ran out the front door and yelled to my friends who were a block away already. They turned around and cheered when they saw me running toward them. I could practically feel the cricket ball in my hand already and hear the roar of my imaginary crowd.

Late that night, I was back at home, and we were all asleep on our mats when someone began yelling up to our apartment from the street. At first, I just rolled over and drifted back to sleep, but the yelling persisted, and suddenly my father was up and going to the balcony to see what the matter was that had prompted this call. Apparently, the wife of a friend had come down with something that seemed rather serious. My father quickly dressed and left with his friend. I waited up for as long as I could, eager to know what was happening, but eventually fell asleep again. I only awoke when my father came back into the apartment to find his keys to the shop. It must have been past three o'clock in the morning by now, and he was going to open the pharmacy. I was already dressed, so I ran downstairs with him to help. "What is it?" I asked.

"Wahid's wife is sick," he replied.

"Is it bad?"

"Yes," he replied. "We took her to the hospital."

"Then why are you opening the shop?"

"Because she needs medicine." He waved a clutch of small papers with prescriptions written on them. They must have been from one of his doctor friends. My father woke up Tahir Bhai, who lived above us, and began to carefully fill in the prescriptions.

"What does she have?" I asked, feeling emboldened by the late hour and the intimacy of the situation. Normally, my father did not like to be peppered with questions, especially as he worked. He glanced up at me as if he were deciding whether to answer me. Then he said, "TB."

Tuberculosis. Even as a boy, I knew about this disease. For centuries, it had been one of the most relentless killers of people around the world. It was contagious, deadly, and indiscriminate although it was known to plague the poor quarters of most cities. It had been immortalized in world literature as many artists, writers, and historians had succumbed to the disease themselves. Herodotus describes it in ancient Greece, and it is impossible to listen to Chopin without sensing the melancholy and rage that the virtuoso composer must have felt as he slowly wasted away.

In the 1950s, however, new medicines had been invented which, for the first time, offered hope for survival. My father had access to this medicine, isoniazid and PAS. As I watched him mix the prescriptions, I felt overwhelmed by the enormity of the struggle, and I was filled with admiration for my father, working in the middle of the night to save the life of this woman. I knew it was only one part of the larger effort to save her, but my father's contribution would be significant.

When he finished with the compound, he told me to go back to bed.

"I want to come with you."

"No," he said. "I may be gone for a while. On Sunday, Wahid' wife was still in the hospital, but she was doing much better. Her condition had stabilized and then improved slightly. It was still soon to tell, but it looked like she would survive."

That news filled me with joy as I headed to the Polo Ground early in the morning to stake out a pitch for the Jolly Cricket Club. I met Eba, and we claimed a nice patch of flat ground and converted into pitch by hammering in our wickets. Then we practiced bowling and batting with each other. After a while, the rest of the team came along for the midday matchup with a rival club of ours. We got beaten handily on the pitch, but the day was not over yet. We still had our elections. One by one, the players who were running for captain, vice-captain, secretary, and treasurer stood up and gave fiery speeches about their dedication to cricket, their unwavering loyalty to the Jolly Cricket Club, and their remarkable talents that would make them the absolute *best* captain, vice-captain, secretary, or treasurer. When it was my turn to speak, I turned in a passionate oration of my own. I might have been diminutive in physical stature, but I had a real fire for this club. I also had two years of experience in debate clubs and elocution contests. I countered every argument that had come before me. I rattled off impressive statistics. I wove in poetry and quotes from none other than Mohammed Ali Jinnah, father of Pakistan, and Winston Churchill, the British Bulldog. In a bit of daring, I compared myself to Hanif Muhammad, the Little Master. I raised my voice and gesticulated for emphasis although I was careful to never lose my cool. In short, it was one of the best, most passionate, powerful speeches of my life. I could almost feel myself being transformed into club office bearer even as I spoke. "A vote for Juzar Ali is a vote for the future!" I told them. "It is a vote for the many victories that we will share as brothers on the field of cricket!"

A round of applause greeted me as I finished, breathless. I was on top of the world. True to his word, Eba stood up and said some words in support of me. I felt very proud. Then the team voted for Eba to be captain.

"What?" I demanded. "You weren't even running for captain."

Eba just shrugged his shoulders. "That was a great speech you gave," he said.

"How did it go?" my father asked when I returned to the shop that afternoon.

"I am the secretary again."

"Who won the captain race?"

"Eba."

My father grunted. Even I had to admit that Eba had always been the natural choice for captain. He was the most skilled of us all, and he had a mind for strategy on the field.

"How was your speech?" my father asked.

"It was moving."

"Let's hear it," Maulvi Saheb said.

"What?"

"Give us your speech!"

"Yes!" Tahir Bhai said.

Before I could begin, however, a customer walked through the door. It was the government official again. "Hello," he said as a formality.

Everyone nodded to him.

He had come for some cosmetics for his wife—the expensive ones, of course. He was taking her to a formal dinner that he described to us as very important. My father waited on the man himself this time. He helped the official find everything he needed, and then he did the unthinkable: he asked the official to pay for the items.

"Put it on my tab," the man said, as always.

"No," my father said. Apparently, he had had enough of the man and his tab. "Your bill has grown too high," he said. "You must pay for these items now."

The man looked stunned. "Do you know who I am?" he asked.

"Of course, I do," my father said, giving him a respectful nod. But my father clearly wasn't going to budge from his position.

"You can't be serious."

"I am just a shopkeeper," my father replied. "But I must have payment for my goods."

The government official looked around at me and all the shop staff. Then he flew into a rage.

He yelled that he had never been treated so disrespectfully in his life. That we would feel the brunt of his wrath. That we were lucky to even have a business. That he knew one hundred people who would run this pharmacy better than we did. That we didn't know who we were messing with. That we would regret this day.

Then finally, he stormed out of the shop. This was the power and struggle of one of the P's, I was to learn later: *Panga, Pawaa, Paisa.*

A moment of stunned silence hung in the air. Maulvi Saheb and Tahir Bhai looked at each other. Wali wrung his hands around the broom handle in the back of the shop. I looked to my father, and he met my gaze.

"Well?" he asked. "How about it?"

"How about what?" I inquired.

"That speech," he replied. "Let's hear it."

The woes that this disgruntled government official would bring to us would have to wait for another day.

CHAPTER 8

Surprise

I could tell something was wrong with my mother. It was subtle, and I pretended not to notice, but I could hear it in the way she cleaned the kitchen—with a little extra brusqueness to her movements and a little extra clatter when she put things away. I could tell by the way she sighed occasionally throughout the day or by the way she slipped into stony silences. I could see it in the way she avoided looking at my father when he came into the apartment. Something was going on.

Of course, it was perfectly common for our parents to keep information from the children; we were still informed of family affairs on a need-to-know basis. Most often, we were simply told what to do and when to do it. So for days, I waited for it, whatever was bothering my mother. Sooner or later, it would reveal its face. After a week, a hint arrived: a new sleeping mat. It just appeared in the family stack of sleeping mats, as if it had always been there. *But who was going to be sleeping on it?*

Next, I noticed that someone—either my mother or father—had carefully cleaned out the one closet to make some extra room. *Room for what?* I was dying to know.

Finally, it was revealed. As we gathered around our low table for *thaal*, my father announced very nonchalantly, "Your sister is coming to live with us."

"Who?" Rashida and Akila asked at the same time. My two little sisters had both sensed the disturbance in the careful balance of the apartment too, but now they both looked at our father with inquiring eyes. "Our sister?"

"Shirin Bahen," I said, and my father nodded. Shirin Bahen was his daughter from a previous marriage. He and my mother had both been widowed before they knew each other. My father had had one child in his previous marriage. My mother had had none.

We had known about this half sister of ours for years, and I had even met her once while we were on a trip to India to visit family. She lived with her aunt in Ahmedabad, and my father took me with him when he went to visit her. I remembered a dark-eyed girl, quiet and older than me by about eight years. But why was she coming here? How long was she staying? What would she bring with her? We had so many questions for our parents, but one look at our mother's face told us not to pursue the excited questions we had. Not now, at least.

Later, we would learn that Shirin Bahen's grandmother had died, and so my father decided to have her come live with us. But for now, all we knew was that some huge change was coming to our little world, and it was both exciting and uncomfortable.

Shirin Bahen arrived while I was at school. I came home one afternoon, and she was sitting on the chair in the apartment. "Hello," I said, staring at her. She was even bigger than I thought she would be, and prettier.

"Hello," she replied, sitting calmly and spreading her long skirt over her knee. She was a teenager by now, which startled me a little. I knew her age before she arrived, but it's one thing to know that a seventeen-year-old girl is coming to your home, and it's another thing to see a seventeen-year-old girl sitting in your mother's chair. The only thing I knew about teenage girls was what I learned at school: they are *mysteries*.

"That's my mother's chair," I said.

"I know. She told me to sit here."

My mother bustled about the apartment, preparing the afternoon meal and putting Shirin Bahen's things away in the closet, taking every inch of that newly available room. My mother extended the traditional hospitality one would expect for a visiting family member, but there was a stiffness to her formality, and it was clear to all of us children that Mother was not happy about having this teenage girl suddenly living with us. Not only was Shirin Bahen practically a stranger to us, but she was also a legacy from other life that my father had had years ago in another country with another woman. It was hard to even imagine for me. I peered at Shirin Bahen and wondered, *Did she have her mother's eyes? Her mother's nose or hair? Was that her mother's confidence that she seemed to wrap herself in?* I didn't know if that could be an inherited trait, but she seemed to have it from somewhere. Clearly, she felt as awkward in this situation as anyone, and she could sense my mother's frustration too, but she seemed to have a calm and assured demeanor anyway. I admired that.

Father came up for lunch and gave Shirin Bahen a warm smile. He had already greeted her when she first arrived, so there was no need for any further scene. He settled in as if it were any normal workday and dug into his lunch. We all followed his lead, and then after lunch, everyone went about their business like there was nothing unusual at all going on—except there was a whole new person in the room.

It was during this time that I had become involved with several debate clubs and speech teams, and often I would compete in elocution contests that were hosted by a school, college, or our *jamaat*, which was a type of local community religious-based association. The debates and speeches were most often delivered in English, which made them doubly tricky. Not only did I have to be eloquent, clever, well versed in fact and flawless in my logic, but I also had to do it all in a second language.

My father was thrilled by the contests though. He thought they were demonstrations of strong character, moral fiber, excellent upbringing, and uncommon abilities. He was also passionate about a strong command of English. He considered it a priceless advantage in the world, one that he himself did not have, but he would make sure his kids possessed. Not only had he been born into the British Empire and all its strict hierarchies of class and language, but he also recognized what an international language of commerce, politics, medicine, and travel it was.

In the evenings, my father would come home tired but, soon after dinner, would sit on the *talaie*, or sleeping pad, legs stretched out in front of him. He would then ask Rashida and Akila to stand on his legs and massage them while he had me get started. This was preparation for the debate, contest, or public speaking event I was to participate in. I would put up a makeshift podium, usually Ma's Singer sewing machine stand, and then start my rehearsal. He would time it and pay careful attention to every aspect of my delivery. He did not offer many corrections, though; I had to wonder how much of the English he understood at all, especially the *big* English words I would use to impress the audience. But he listened with rapt attention, and his support and pride were unmistakable. We would practice and practice, day after day, until I would become disgusted with it, but not him. He never tired of the practice.

He rarely attended the actual events, but that was common. Public debate and speaking contests were often held during the time when the shop would be open for business and or during the day at youth assemblies, either at school or at the community centers. They were organized in a way reminiscent of a sports event, with multiple competitors and crowds of supporters for each sliver-tongued gladiator. My close-knit group of friends would be there to create that enclave of loud support, clapping and cheering as I stepped to and from the podium. They would break into rapturous applause at appropriate moments in my speeches. They were my secret weapon, inspiring me with confidence and making me seem charismatic and persuasive. There was another speaker in my age-group that I often competed with, and he, too, had a group of friends that supported him. Often the events seemed more like team sports than individual contests as the two crowds tried to outdo each other. It was great fun, and I won many of the competitions. I loved the look on my father's face when I would bring home a trophy, and he would beam with pride and place it on the shelf with the others. He was never effusive in his praise, of course, but later, at the shop, I could hear him bragging about me to his friends, and every once in a while, his friends would get excited and ask for a dramatic reenactment, which I provided, filling in details about the roars of my crowd. Those were great moments as my father presided over these sessions in his shop. Here was a man who didn't finish high school and barely spoke English orchestrating these elaborate speeches and orations. You could just see this family legacy forming in his own excited imagination.

He wasn't just living through his kids, however. In addition to running his successful business, my father had begun to help organize a neighborhood activist association. While General Ayub Khan was ruling through martial law, he declared that he would install a system that was more orderly than before, so he went to the United States to have a look at their democracy. Upon his return, he implemented the electoral college system of representation in Pakistan. It would be years before national elections were held, but political parties still existed, and Ayub Khan gave them certain authority and responsibility. It was a kind of "democracy to suit the dictator." Importantly, however, instead of appealing directly to the citizens for popular votes and support, politicians now would work to secure the support of the local electoral representative of the neighborhood. Thus, whoever the electoral representative was, he wielded a lot of clout in local communities. He was the voice that would represent local interests, and he was the wheeler and dealer that would secure benefits for the community in return for his vote. Incidentally, it seems it mirrored the indirect franchise that the delegates and caucuses in United States represent.

My father became part of a rebel party of "progressives" who wanted to influence the local dealmaking in the matter of local activism and ultimately take over as the electoral representative from the neighborhood. He would often host impromptu strategy meetings at the house. "Ruby," he would say, "prepare a meal for ten people. We are having a meeting!"

Often, his meetings would overlap with my own get-togethers, and the dinner parties would turn into freewheeling affairs of neighborhood community activists engaged in animated conversation. Often, I would be recruited to take notes, write letters, and help prepare speeches for the older men. My relationship with his friends was unique. I was their secretary, their child, and their protégé. To me, being close to my father's friends was a matter of honor, which I cherished because it meant I was giving something back to my father.

Behind the scenes, there was still family tension though. Once the house had quieted down and it was just the family again, the strain between my mother and Shirin Bahen was still there and growing worse. My mother did not appreciate he disruption to her family dynamic or much of anything about this adolescent girl who had been dropped in our home by fortune and my father. Little things, like the way Shirin Bahen stacked dishes before they were completely dry or the way she left the sleeping mats, became more upsetting than they normally would have. My mother had begun to complain openly about the girl too, which put the rest of the children in the awkward position of having to choose sides. Of course, we reflexively chose our mother's side, and that only exacerbated things.

But then something interesting happened: final exams. As the academic term was ending, students across the city began to hunker in preparation for their course examinations, and it impacted everything from the crowds at movie theaters to weekend cricket matches at the Polo Grounds. It was the season of studying. Shirin Bahen and I were no different from the rest, and we both focused our attentions on our studies with even more rigor than usual. What's more, we both had our academic weak spots. Currently, I was struggling with arts, and Shirin Bahen was hard-pressed to score well in English and literature. Naturally, we sought help and found tutors who could assist each of us. The problem was that the tutors each lived in a different neighborhood. What had begun as the season of studying had now become the season of walking. Shirin Bahen and I walked great distances together to our tutor's residences. We met in the early afternoon, when school was out, and we walked several miles through the blazing heat to reach her English tutor. Then we would walk to my arts tutor. These long travels initially started with a distant companionship, but as we spent hours crisscrossing the city together, I really got to know Shirin Bahen. We talked as we walked, and before long, I had a much better appreciation for my sister and everything that she had been through. I understood her position with my mother much better than I had before although, I must say, I remained quiet in that understanding.

Suddenly, I was the person who could mediate some tensions at home. I could explain to my mother what Shirin Bahen's perspective was, and vice versa. It didn't always help or solve every problem, but it made things much better after that. Shirin Bahen and I had a common goal, which was to do well on our exams, and that created a new dynamic in the house which would turn out to be a positive force. It also helped each of us to have a motivational partner when it came to trudge across the city for tutoring and study sessions.

Of course, things never stay the same for long, especially in Karachi. Not long after our exams, something new crept into the house. This time, it was my father who betrayed the telltale signs: the sighs and the stony silences, the preoccupation and seriousness, even at dinner. My mother kept the house quieter than usual and was strict with us about not disturbing our father.

Immediately my curiosity took over. What could it be this time? What was causing my father so much stress?

It didn't take me as long to find out what was going on this time because it was related to the shop. Naturally, it quickly became the stuff of shop talk, especially something this serious. Apparently, the drug inspector had charged my father with violating the law because he imported and stocked a medicine that was manufactured illegally. My father did not know about the illegal aspect of the product; all his paperwork was kept meticulously and revealed perfectly legal import documents and receipts for the medicine. Normally, this might have been a situation that was quite easy to fix with relatively minor penalties and a clarification of the process. In this case, however, it seemed that someone inside the government was eager to prosecute the case and make a severe example out of my father and his shop. We never knew for certain who was behind the political push to punish my father, but immediately we all thought of that government bureaucrat and his expensive face creams—the one who had threatened us.

Whoever was responsible, this was legal action that threatened to shut down the shop completely, crush the family beneath financial penalties, and possibly even imprison my father. For a family of modest means who were struggling so hard to get ahead, this threat loomed over our heads like thundercloud. This could take away everything.

Once it became clear just how serious the situation was, everything changed. The assemblies at the *thaal* turned from freewheeling political rallies to emergency business meetings. The discussion often hinged on whether we could afford a high-priced attorney with excellent credentials and connections in the government or whether we could afford *not* to hire a high-priced attorney with excellent credentials and connections in the government and risk losing everything. My father enlisted all his friends, associates, and colleagues to find out any information they could and to defend him publicly. Even though it was a sprawling metropolis, Karachi was still a small town in many ways, and sure enough, my father's troubles made it into the newspaper. They were small articles, buried in the city business section, but still, they were my father's private business affairs being aired out in front of the whole city, and he hated finding anything related to his case in there. Every evening for as long as I could remember, newspaper boys would scarf up their armfuls of the *Leader and Evening Star* and race down the street, shouting the headlines and selling their papers as fast as they could. We always looked forward to getting the paper every morning and evening. This was the source of nearly all our news, our politics, our entertainment and gossip. The evening papers even carried salacious pictures (salacious by 1960 Pakistani standards, mind you) of Western movie stars like Jayne Mansfield, Sophia Loren, or Marilyn Monroe. Schoolboys like me and my friends were constantly squirreling away such treasures and pinning them to our bedroom walls when our parents weren't looking. The newspapers kept tabs on the whole city, publishing everything from student test results to the latest cricket scores, even as they inspired the Hollywood-themed fantasy lives of an entire generation of Karachi schoolboys.

Now, however, we had something far less appealing to scan for each morning and evening at the shop: my father's legal troubles. My father decided he had no choice but to hire the expensive attorney even if it bankrupted him. The alternative was even worse than bankruptcy. He vowed he would keep us in school unless there was no other alternative. Our weeks and months dragged on like this, always waiting for some legal action to occur, for some deadline to arrive, for some decision to be made, for some official to provide the next piece of information, for some court date to arrive, and then for some article to appear in the newspaper. There were so many court dates, which led to so many articles. My father's case slowly wound its way through the legal system, and we all did whatever we could to keep the shop running smoothly, to keep the family fed on a smaller budget, and to cut out any kinds of extra expenses. By now, I was old enough to work behind the counter at the shop and assist customers, not just run errands and do odd jobs. I took pride in my ability to assist in my father's time of need, and it gave him some peace of mind to know that his son was able to handle the job. I had been watching my father diagnose people's ailments and assist them for so many years that it seemed natural for me to step in and help as best I could.

During the month of Ramadan, the shop closed at Maghreb, as always. My father would come home, and then we would wait for the Azaan and then namaz and then iftar. My mother would have cooked some goodies, and we would all chat and discuss the day's events. I loved it when he would suggest, "Juku, let's go for a walk."

Despite all the troubles, this was the most delightful quality time. I would spend hours with him, just walking at his side, chatting. We often discussed things like school, medicines, politics, or current events. We never discussed the legal case on these walks. And often, we discussed nothing at all. We would walk along in a contented silence, just enjoying each other's company as we cruised for miles through the streets of Karachi or sometimes walk to Frere Hall, a nearby park of gardens and fountains. I loved these walks with my father, and to make them even sweeter, if things had taken a good turn with the case and he was in a good mood, we would occasionally stop for a late-show movie on our way home. My father made these small treats feel like treasures. They were for me some of the best times I had with my father. Being a man of few words and strict discipline, he did not believe in conveying his warm sentiments too much. These long walks provided an unspoken closeness though that I cherished, and occasionally he even surprised me with a smile of approval.

CHAPTER 9

The Pendulum

The court case dragged on for months, and my father was forced to spend much time and money on his defense. Some weeks, he practically lived in the court buildings as he went to file briefings or wait for hearings and appointments with different officials. Often, he would be gone from sunrise to sunset, leaving me in charge of the shop while he was away. After the initial thrill of the responsibility wore off, I found myself struggling to occupy the time of the pharmacy team. Over the years, I had spent countless hours in the shop myself, serving the directives of my father. It had never occurred to me what a fine art it was to keep everyone busy and productive. The days had natural ebbs and flows of customer traffic, and during the quiet times, my father seemed to have an endless list of tasks: cleaning, stocking, researching, delivering merchandise, distributing fliers, and more. When the tasks had been accomplished, my father drove interesting conversations and engaged his friends and customers. In other words, even when he didn't look busy, he was networking and tending to his professional, political, and social relationships which were all closely interwoven and had a magical tendency to revolve around the Kelvinator refrigerator.

Now without my father to drive the activities, to-do lists, and conversations around the shop, I found myself trying to fill his footsteps and keep everyone busy and engaged. Granted, my father's team had been working together for years, so they didn't need much encouragement to do their jobs well and keep everything running smoothly. Still, I wanted to do a good job for my father and prove myself to the rest of the team. I found myself adapting games and tricks from home and school to use in the shop. For example, during slow afternoons, I brought a version of our famous family quiz shows. I would play show host and ask my "contestants" tricky questions about the different products and services offered in the shop. *Contestant number one, in what country is our best-selling skin cream produced? Contestant number two, what would you recommend to a customer who walked in complaining of a sore tooth? Contestant number three, what are the ingredients of an effective laxative?*

Maulvi Sahib, Tahir Bhai, Wali Mohammad, and the other shop helpers would try to answer the questions accurately and rack up points. Everyone responded enthusiastically to the game, and we would have funny little awards ceremonies, complete with teasing and bragging sessions.

Another thing I brought from school was my official "newspaper," *Gupistan* (*Stan* meaning "nation" in Urdu and *Gup* meaning "clever lies"). For years, I had been writing playful news articles about school friends, entertainment figures, and current events. My school friends, especially Burjis and his parents, were my fans and patrons for this publication and always got a kick out of this when I would share an edition with them. The customer friends who would come to Venus Medico, too, got a laugh out of this. My articles were very tongue-in-cheek and riddled with inside jokes and humorous asides. They might be compared to modern articles from *The Onion*. Unlike the Pakistani newspapers, I was not afraid to lampoon the president and his cronies in addition to my more lighthearted pieces. It was hard not to notice how the longer the military ruled the nation, the fewer articles appeared in the newspapers that were related to domestic issues. As "President" Ayub Khan continued his dictatorial reign, the news tended to focus more and more on foreign affairs, international crises, and Pakistan's standing in world events. Anything to avert attention from what was happening in local government or politics. Instead, the papers would dedicate entire sections to Queen Elizabeth of England since she announced that she would be visiting Pakistan for the first time as part of a regional tour of ex-commonwealths.

The US presidential elections garnered a lot of coverage as well. Currently, Pakistan was a key partner with the West in several treaty organizations, such as the Southeast Asian Treaty Organization (SEATO) and the Central Treaty Organization (CENTO). Cold War tensions were growing all over the world, and these treaty organizations were built to counter the Soviet Union and the expansion of communism in both Asia and the Middle East. As long as Pakistan proved to be a faithful partner in these organizations, the West appeared willing to overlook the constitutional violations of Pakistan's leadership. In fact, one of John F. Kennedy's first decisions as president of the US was to schedule high-level meetings with Pakistan to shore up the allied position in Southeast Asia. He would send his vice president, Lyndon B. Johnson, to meet with the Pakistani government, so naturally, the Karachi newspapers were filled with news about Pakistan's great importance in the Cold War efforts and President Ayub Khan's pivotal role in international relations and his significant influence with the US and Western leaders.

I, on the other hand, ran articles such as "US Leaders to Pay Final Respects to Dead Pakistani Constitution," "Pakistani Government Regrets Move to Islamabad: Food in Karachi Much Better," or "Corrupt Politician Has Pet Monkey on Government Payroll." I used the articles as a prop to do what my father did so skillfully—engage his customers and his staff and keep a constant thread of interesting conversation running throughout the day. And it seemed to work. Customers would ask for the latest installment of the "news," and the staff enjoyed either discussing my ideas or teasing me about them. At times my stories were related to making fun of local politicians or even tongue-in-cheek items such as "Pakistani Man Bites Dog." Occasionally, people warned me to keep my opinions to myself, but largely people found them amusing, and I exercised some discretion in deciding who I would share my satirical pieces with.

When my father would return to the shop from his various outings, there was no telling what mood he might be in. He was always a complicated man, sensitive yet very private and difficult to read. Now the constant stress and turmoil took a toll on him. His emotional pendulum was swinging in wide arcs. Sometimes, he would arrive back after some small victory, and he would be in a great mood. Other times, he would arrive back after some setback, and he was distraught. I quickly mastered the art of deciphering his moods at a glance. Often, I could tell his emotional state before he even walked through the door based upon the way he carried his shoulders, the set of his face, or the briskness of his step.

No matter how bad things got, he was usually able to find refuge in his shop. He loved helping his customers, and he could throw himself into his work. He continued to diagnose minor ailments for people, help people find the rare items they were looking for, or open the shop in the middle of the night for emergency situations. Even through his own ordeal, my father continued to be the kind of guy who would drop everything to help a friend or acquaintance in a difficult spot. In fact, in some ways, he seemed even more dedicated to his friends, family, customers, and neighbors. It was as if the legal troubles reminded him of just how precarious working people's situations were and how much they depended upon one another in times of need. When larger forces aligned against a person—whether they be illness, medical emergency, business or legal problems—people had to stick together to survive. There were no deep pools of resources for the working class—neither family nor public money to dip into. There were no high-ranking connections to lean upon, just the complex web of friendships and working relationships that people like my father made for themselves. Their lives were vulnerable and precarious, and those social and familial connections were the thin ropes of their safety net.

My father was known as a man who energetically built those types of connections for himself and the people around him. He was a consummate networker and a hustler in the best sense of the word. Now in his time of need, he was calling in favors and turning to as many people as he possibly could to find help against this troubling government suit against him. At the same time, however, he was also still hustling for his friends. I remember late one night, a friend of my father's appeared in the street below our window and began shouting up to my father. "Come quickly!"

"Do you need something from the shop?" my father asked from the balcony.

"No, not the shop. Huseini Bhai is in trouble."

"What kind of trouble?" my father asked.

"He has been arrested."

"What? I'll be right down."

We all watched my father dress quickly and race out the door. My mother did not come back to bed after that; she didn't like it when my father disappeared on his middle-of-the-night missions. Inevitably, he was off to cajole, bribe, tap his network of connections, and call in favors. She was always afraid that he would wind up getting himself into trouble even as he worked to get his friends *out* of trouble. We kids eventually fell back asleep, but even when we awoke, there was no father. My mother was cooking in the kitchen, wearing the stony expression on her face that she wore when she was tired and worried. The shop was open as the kids all left for school, but still no Father.

Finally, by the time I returned home from classes, my father was back at home, preparing for lunch. We were all dying to know where he had been all night. It turns out he had been unable to free his friend from jail without the judge's order which could only be secured in the morning, but they had gotten on very good terms with the prison guards who allowed my father to stay and keep his friend company. My father had stayed up all night in the jail cell playing cards with his friend. Now he was exhausted, but happy and hungry. He had done well for his friend who was also now at home with his family.

As his own legal situation continued to preoccupy my father, I found that not only was he trusting me to run the shop for him while he was away, but he was also trusting me to look after my own education goals. He still wanted to receive reports and updates, but he was far less involved than ever before. I found it liberating. I loved my father dearly, but it could feel stifling to be beneath his intense gaze all the time. Now, at last, I had some autonomy, and it felt good to be out from beneath the scrutiny of his attention. Of course, I continued to take my studies very seriously. I knew that my father had worked relentlessly to put me in this position with a chance to have a bright future, and I was determined to make something of it.

Returning home from school one day, I could tell something was wrong. My father was not at the shop, and everyone seemed slightly on edge. "Your father is in a bad mood," Maulvi Sahib told me. I knew from the expression on his face that he would not tell me any more details even if he knew them. His first loyalty was always to my father, and it was improper to gossip about his personal situation, even with his son. There was a fine line between shop talk and personal business, and Maulvi Sahib was very good at navigating that line.

Later, we would learn that his friend had refused to lend some assistance in some matter. If there was anything my father took more seriously than winning his legal case, it was the loyalty of his friendships, so this was a doubly bitter blow to him. Anyone who was close to my father knew that his ego was closely tied to his emotions, and they both were quite sensitive. Unlike his brother, he wasn't a man of outbursts and fiery rages. His anger was contained and cold most times. It wasn't uncommon for my father to closet himself, not only get quiet and distant, but he would also physically isolate himself as well. He would disappear for hours, or even days. Sometimes, would stay in the top floor apartment of our building where he had access to an extra room.

My mother bore the brunt of these episodes even though she rarely if ever was involved in the initial offense, and she was usually the one who finally smoothed things over. She had a lot of patience and tact when it came to these situations. Her most effective strategy was to simply wait it out and let the tide settle before she formed a delegation made up of family members or close friends (or some combination of the two). These delegations would visit my father to pay homage and to offer food, consolations, and sympathies. They would reaffirm my father's role as leader of the family and of his small empire. Finally, he would agree to return home.

Sure enough, this latest offense turned into a full-blown crisis and required a delegation to be sent to the top floor of the apartment building on day three. I led the expedition, up the rickety stairs to the dingy door where my father was sequestered with his anger and hurt feelings. We brought him dinner, which he accepted when he finally opened the door. He allowed us inside, which was a good sign that he was open to negotiation. Eventually, the conversation swung around to how much he was missed at home and in the shop. "Everyone is asking for you," I told him.

Finally, he agreed to come back downstairs.

The family was overjoyed to see him come through the door, and later, my mother would offer me a small smile of gratitude for a job well-done. Now would begin the enjoyable part of this cycle as the pendulum swung in the opposite direction. When my father returned from his exiles, he would overcompensate for his absence with energetic play, fun family outings, and other small surprises. Eventually, this emotional pendulum would come back to center and things would return to normal, but for now, the days were filled with fun. My father was thrilled to hear about my schoolwork. He teased and played with Rashida and Akila.

The next night after dinner, he surprised us all by hiring a *ghora gari*, or horse-driven buggy, for a ride to Clifton in the moonlight. Rashida and Akila squealed with delight when he announced the news, and we all gathered up pillows, blankets, and treats to take with us. It was a fun ride and a beautiful night, clomping along through the city. When we reached our destination, we all strolled along, and then we all took our pillows and treats to make a picnic along the Jahangir Kothari Parade. The parade was a huge and elaborate stone promenade with high walkways, sweeping stone staircases, beautiful architecture and a gorgeous open-air dome set high atop columns. It was donated by a Parsi merchant and philanthropist as a gift to the city, and it was one of our favorite places in Karachi. We had a beautiful evening, and everyone was in a good mood.

The playful spirit did not end there, however. Somehow, my father convinced everyone to compete in a game to see who could change out of their street clothes and into their night clothes the fastest. As soon as the buggy arrived back at our alley in Elphinstone Street, we all leapt out of the carriage and raced to the back door. Up the stairs we ran, discarding clothing at every landing. My mother was the only one not participating in this silly contest, and she gathered up our clothes as she brought up the rear of the party. Finally, we were all tucked into our bedrolls, still giggling and glowing from the fun of the evening. Rashida and Akila did give me the run for my money as we competed in this game

As kids, amid the turmoil and stresses of day-to-day marginally financial security, we lived for moments like these. They were so sweet and special to us all, and we welcomed the swing of the pendulum to this fun side whenever we could see it happen or make it happen and treasured every moment of it. Through these periods, my mother was the quiet soul. How she, at times, managed to give me some extra money to buy something I wanted was beyond me. But she did. I wanted to buy skates and go skating in Frere Hall Gardens with Eba. She made it happen.

Later, we were the proud owners of a TV at home. TV had just been introduced in Pakistan. It was a big step touting progress and modernity by the government. Initially, it was only available in public parks like Jahangir Park near our home, and I was allowed to go once in a while to see some shows on it. Of course, a lot of programs were geared toward government propaganda. Later shows like *Dr. Kildare* were the local hits, and the interest it piqued in medicine for me around my family environment of Venus Medico was but natural for me.

CHAPTER 10

Parade Season

By now, the official capital of Pakistan had moved seven hundred miles north to Rawalpindi, but Karachi was still the cultural capital of the nation as well as the international transportation hub of Southeast Asia. Nearly anyone from the West who was flying into this part of the world landed in Karachi for stopover. Likewise, nearly anyone traveling out of southern Asia to the West was bound to spend some time in the city. So naturally, when the Queen of England scheduled a visit to Pakistan, she would land in Karachi. President Ayub Khan planned to meet her at the airport and treat her to another of Pakistan's warm welcomes—a parade down Elphinstone Street.

What's more, Queen Elizabeth's parade was going to be even more spectacular than the one for Eisenhower. This would be the first royal visit since Pakistan became independent from the British Empire. The Queen would be landing in India first before making her way to Karachi, so there was an even greater sense of competitiveness than usual. Pakistan needed to demonstrate its ability to outdo our neighbor to the west, so the parade was going to be even larger and more magnificent than any others. Elphinstone Street was going to be transformed into an international showcase of Pakistani heritage, strength, and warmth to welcome the English monarch and her husband, Prince Philip, Duke of Edinburgh.

Everyone in the city was looking forward to the spectacle. "Juzar Choe!" Burjis said when he saw me at school. "You must invite me to your party."

"What party?"

"I know you're having a party for the Queen."

"Bah," I said, shrugging as if it were no big deal. "It's just a queen."

I joked with him for a moment, but of course, he was invited to my party. He was my closest friend at school by now, and he often had me over for dinners with his family, sleepovers, and even just to do homework together. His family were very warm and caring with their welcome for me and very generous with their private transportation, shuttling me back and forth from their home to my own.

Burjis was still very popular at school, and it wasn't long before everyone knew about my front-row balcony seat to the Queen's parade. Suddenly, everyone wanted an invitation to a Juzar Choe party. I had the hottest ticket in town.

Of course, I still lived in a very small apartment with a very stern father, so the final invitation list was largely unchanged from the birthday list of years ago. These were still my closest pals and the boys that my father knew best.

Again, we decorated the balcony with flags and signs. Again, we practiced chants and played with the crowd. And again, when the parade finally arrived, we piled onto the balcony to enjoy the spectacle. This year, of course, we were joined by the newest member of the household, my sister, Shirin Bahen, and a few of her friends from school too. Our little party was growing bigger. As usual, we made an occasion out of it with homemade treats and drinks for everyone.

By now, Karachi was no longer a sleepy seaport town; it was a thriving metropolis of over one million people and every single one of them appeared to be out on the parade route this day. Also, this time, we were friendly with my cousins, crowded onto the balcony just beneath us too, which was great fun.

The parade itself was fantastic. Once more, the city leaders rode at the head of the procession, followed by the marching bands and military processions, the traditional dance troupes, and mounted guards dressed in their ornate attire. There were more modern displays as well, including shining new fire engines, military vehicles, and flatbed trucks converted into floats and covered with flowers and girls in white dresses. We hollered loudly at the girls until they waved back at us. In fact, we made an art out of getting people to notice us with our group cheers. We were warming up for the main act, of course.

And here she came. The thirty-four-year-old Queen wore a dress made of shining gold and a stylish hat to match. She rode in a long white Cadillac convertible, sitting up on the back deck alongside President Khan. We went crazy, along with the rest of the crowd. The Queen looked gracious as she smiled and waved to the cheering throngs. But we wanted her to wave to *us*. We let go with one of our group cheers, but she did not seem to hear us through the crowd. We tried one more time, just as her motorcade was right in front of us. *One, two, three.* And we shouted at the top of our lungs, "Hip hip hooray!"

They were silly chants, but they did the trick. Queen Elizabeth looked around for her cheering section, and she found us up on the balcony. She gave a wide smile and a wave to what must have seemed to her a ridiculous gaggle of schoolboys with their homemade signs and flags, and we went wild.

Just three months later, the new US Vice President, Lyndon B. Johnson, landed in Pakistan for meetings with the government. He, too, landed in Karachi, was met by President Ayub Khan, and treated to a lavish parade down Elphinstone Street. We were becoming professional celebrators! Once more, Karachi pulled out all the stops for the visiting dignitary: the marching bands and military processions, the organized crowds of schoolchildren waving American flags, the waves of confetti floating on the air, and the majestic displays of heritage such as the horse brigades, the swordsmen, and traditional dancers.

We made American flag posters to hang all over the small balcony. We enjoyed the crowd and the spectacle out on the street, and we were thrilled when the parade finally began to roll past, with its military vehicles and shining fire trucks. We danced with the bands and waved wildly to the passing convertibles which transported politicians, generals, and celebrities, such as Fazal Mahmood, the captain of the Pakistani national cricket team.

President Johnson rode in a long black convertible, and he waved to the thick crowds of cheering people. Unlike other dignitaries who had passed along Elphinstone Street, Johnson liked to jump out of his car and mingle with the crowds. No one knew what to do with him as he repeatedly stopped his motorcade and came smiling into the throngs of people. To me, he seemed like a huge man who wore a huge hat and waved a huge hand. He was famous, even here, for his Texas cowboy hat. His smile seemed generous though, and this trip would lead to one of the most charming episodes in US-Pakistani relations. As Johnson rode along the parade route, he spotted a group of camel carts parked on a side street. Apparently, the vice president from Texas was terribly curious about the beasts and wanted to see them up close, so he stopped his motorcade once more and jumped out. He spoke briefly with the drivers and pet the animals. The press was all around him, of course, and he smiled for the clicking cameras and shook hands as he prepared to depart. "Y'all come see us in Washington sometime," he said. It was something he often said.

Someone translated his words to the camel drivers, and to Johnson's surprise, one of the drivers, a poor man named Bashir Ahmad, immediately took him up on his offer. The press ran with this personal interest side story, and soon Johnson was being asked follow-up questions about whether he was really going to host Bashir Ahmad in Washington, DC.

Johnson could easily have brushed the issue aside and forgotten about his exchange with the camel cart driver, but he rose to the challenge with great spirit. Not only did he arrange for Ahmad to travel to the United States as part of the People to People program, but Vice President Johnson also personally met him upon his arrival in New York and then hosted him at his Texas ranch. Ahmad was treated like a visiting dignitary in Washington, DC, and when it became clear that the poor camel driver was lost amid the place settings of formal dining rooms, Johnson arranged to have more casual group meals of finger foods, such as fried chicken, stuffed celery, deviled eggs, or corn on the cob. In other words, the US vice president went incredibly out of his way to host this poor camel driver, to make him feel at home, and to protect him from embarrassing exchanges with dinner companions or the press.

Ultimately, the trip became a successful public relations event for Johnson, but that did not lessen his thoughtfulness. His final act of kindness was to send Ahmad through Saudi Arabia on his way home so that he could visit Makkah. Makkah is the birthplace of Muhammad and is considered the holiest city in all of Islam. When Muslims kneel to pray, they face Makkah, and every year millions of pilgrims travel to visit the city, especially during hajj. As a very poor cart driver, Ahmad never thought he would be able to fulfill this most sacred duty, but Vice President Johnson gave him this special opportunity. It was reported that Ahmad cried when he received word of the special gift.

Long after the parade was over, we eagerly followed the news of Bashir Ahmad's travels in the daily newspapers. Back in my father's shop, we scanned the morning and evening papers, looking for the latest story or tidbit. We were impressed by Johnson's acts of friendship and generosity. We were thrilled with Ahmad's great adventure. And if truth be known, we were all a little jealous of the poor camel cart driver. It was like winning the lottery, and we all daydreamed out loud about what we would do if Vice President Johnson plucked us out of the crowd and suddenly we were whisked off to America.

Of course, there was still the depressing news to hunt for too—anything to do with my father's case. His expensive lawyer had won a concession from the government plaintiffs, however, and the case was going to be heard directly by a high court. We all waited with great anticipation for that day to come. It was nerve-racking, but whatever was decided there would be the outcome. By now, the case had already dragged on for so long that it almost seemed impossible that it would ever end. I knew for certain that my father wouldn't stop fighting until either he won the case or died trying. It had become the thing that drove him from morning to night. With a high court hearing pending, my father was back into the full swing of his case once again, meeting with lawyers and tracking down international records regarding the pharmaceutical company that we were accused of collaborating with.

In the meantime, I was trying to make good use of all my extra time in the pharmacy. I read everything I could get my hands on, whether it was the inserts from the medicine packages, trade journals that my father had around the shop, or even medical ingredients labels that might reveal some secrets of chemistry and healing. I had begun practicing my own prescriptions as well. I would invent a patient with a malady, and then I would write a diagnosis and construct a prescription. Afterward, I would get feedback from Maulvi Sahib, our expert compounder, and he would offer me advice and explain the fine points of the medicines and their numerous combinations. After a while, I began practicing with the actual ingredients, mixing my own prescriptions and compounds.

Family life was very busy at this time, but occasionally, I would still be able to attend my friends' parties. Whether it was Anwar's or Burjis's party, it was great fun, as always, and it felt good to be out with my friends again after so much work and stress which seemed to have taken over my life lately. Kandy and other girls would be there too, and we all enjoyed the food, the music, and the yard games.

Finally, the court date arrived, and my father packed his documentation together in a case, put on his nicest shirt, and went back down to the city courthouse. Today was the big day when he would finally have his official hearing. As per usual, I stayed behind and watched the shop as he disappeared down the street with his entourage of friends, colleagues, and supporters. We tried to have a normal day around the shop, but everyone was on pins and needles waiting for his return—hopefully. There was still the possibility that he would be convicted in that courtroom and taken to jail.

Nearly all my father's customers knew about the court date too, so we were peppered all day with questions as people came through the door. "Any news?"

"Not yet."

Then ten minutes later, a neighbor would walk through the door. "Any news?"

"Not yet."

Conversations swirled all day, and even my mother seemed flustered, which was highly unusual. She was an amazing woman who could keep her composure through nearly anything, yet here she was calling down to the shop to ask me to fetch a cup of flour for her because she forgot it at the market this morning. Then she needed help with a squeaking door which was driving her mad. Then she called down just to ask if there was any news.

"Not yet," I replied as gently as I could.

Finally, Maulvi Sahib looked up through the window and shouted, "Seth Saheb is coming!"

Here came my father, walking down the street with his lawyer and his entourage. One look at them told us everything we needed to know: they had won the case. They all wore broad smiles and walked with jaunty confidence in the strides. They laughed and talked loudly as they came down the sidewalk, and we all poured out the door of the shop to greet them on the sidewalk.

"We won," my father said. I could see that he was thrilled, yet he kept his composure. "Let us say a Salwaat."

The rest of us, however, burst into excited chatter. This was excellent news. I ran around to the alley and shouted up to the third-floor window. "Ma! Ma! They're back!"

She appeared in the back balcony almost immediately, as if she had been hovering nearby. "What happened?" she asked.

"Daddy won," I said, doing my best to imitate his composure. "He won the case."

Just then, my father came around the corner too. He was beaming when he looked up and saw his wife. "Ruby," he said, "it's time to make some sweet dish."

It turns out he had been completely acquitted, and it was all over. There was a lively celebration at the house that evening, and the next morning, we were all up early to read the newspaper. After all the months of reading about this case, we were hoping to see the good news there at long last. Sure enough, there it was, a small article about the case and the court verdict. My father was very pleased to read that article. He felt that his reputation, honor, and pride had been dragged through the mud, and at last they were publicly restored. To him, it was not just a wrong case; it was a threat to the respect he had established in the community and in the circle around him. Tahir Bhai made many Xerox copies of the news item so there would be plenty to pass around. We used to tease Tahir Bhai about his compulsive Xerox copying which he used to squirrel away all kinds of files, receipts, medical documentation, and more, but today we just cheered when he passed the copies around.

CHAPTER 11

The Monabao Connection

For some time, my father, Mr. Fix It, had been helping family and friends navigate the complicated legal systems as they migrated back and forth across the border between Pakistan and India. That often-hostile border not only split two new rival nations, but it also split tens of thousands of families and friends. For centuries, family lineages had been spread all over the region, but within a generation, these new borders had appeared, along with this deep animosity between sovereign nations. Now there was very little freedom of movement for most people, especially in times when political tensions were amped up between the nations. My father, of course, was not one to be deterred. He learned this new system like the back of his hand and kept up with every new law or policy, every turn in foreign relations that might affect the movement across borders. He also had several friends in government whom he could rely on to keep him informed or to expedite paperwork, visas, and other legal hurdles.

One of the people my father helped come to Pakistan was a young man named Tahir Bhai Dairywala. He, a family friend, was a handsome young man. He came to Pakistan to try his prospects at making a life for himself. Karachi presented its challenges, certainly, but it was still a place where a person with some ambition, energy, and connections might make a life for himself. In addition to being a family friend and relation, Tahir Bhai was a smart young man, very street-smart, and my father took an interest in his success. He provided a reference that helped Tahir Bhai find work as a technical engineer.

My father couldn't help observing that a young man out to make a life for himself would surely need a wife. Tahir Bhai agreed. Yes, he would absolutely need a wife. What a coincidence that my father happened to have an eighteen-year-old daughter who had just graduated from school!

Shirin Bahen and Tahir Bhai Dairywala met at a family meal, and they hit it off almost immediately. This was how many marriages happened at this time: families would identify what they thought of as ideal matches and place the couple together in these arranged situations. If the couple hit it off, then the union would be endorsed all around and the couple would be engaged to be married. If either of the partners had serious objections, then the union could be called off. Minor objections carried no weight. So in a way, these marriages were well orchestrated, if not totally arranged. Certainly, some families placed more pressure than others on their children to find the arrangement suitable, but my mother and father were not cut of that cloth. It wasn't long before my family happily announced Shirin Bahen's engagement to the rest of the extended family and friends.

My father was very happy about the engagement, but one thing troubled him. As he reflected upon his eldest daughter, his soon-to-be son-in-law, his extended family, and the important occasion that a family wedding was, he couldn't help feeling that the event should be held in India, not in Pakistan. India is where Shirin Bahen was born and spent most of her life. India is where most of her family lived. India is where my mother's and father's family roots lay, not to mention Tahir Bhai and his whole family. None of the Indian relations would be able to travel to Pakistan for a wedding, especially with the difficulty of getting a visa from the other side of the border.

On the other hand, a Pakistani wedding party certainly couldn't travel en masse to India either. Or could it?

"That's insane," his friends said as we talked about the wedding at the shop. "It's nearly impossible to get *one* person across the border. How will you move a whole wedding party?"

Everyone agreed. It was completely unheard of at this time—large parties of people crossing the border for social occasions. There were all kinds of official and unofficial obstacles standing between them and India. To any normal person, that minefield of passport offices, visas, customs, military checkpoints, local police departments, and more would appear an impenetrable wall of obstacles blocking that border crossing. But of course, my father was no normal person. Once more, he looked upon a challenge and decided that he would take it head-on. He conferred with the bride-to-be and her fiancé, and they arrived at a decision: "The wedding shall take place in India."

First, the Pakistani wedding party had to be finalized. It included our family, of course, and as soon as it became known that Hasan Bhai was planning this, there were many enthusiastic participants. Of course, my Kakajee Hashim and his family, the Jupiterwala clan, and a confederation of other cousins and close family friends were included, well over forty people in total. Next, my father went about securing visas and passports for the entire party. This was the work of a magician, pulling strings and recruiting help from his network of friends and connections until he had traveling papers for more than forty people in his possession. I can only imagine what his friends in the passport office must have said to him when he walked in with this outlandish request, but somehow, he prevailed.

Once all the official documents were secured, the travel arrangements themselves had to be organized. My mother's extended family and friends in India agreed to host the Pakistani travelers. Despite all the tension between Shirin Bahen and my mother over the years, Ma came through when the family needed her. Not only was her family in India going to host the wedding party and many of the wedding events, but my mother also helped Shirin Bahen choose her wedding clothes, plan her parties, design her jewelry and henna.

In the meantime, train tickets were secured. And more train tickets. And again, more train tickets. There was no direct travel from a Pakistani city to an Indian city, so there would be multiple stops and trains involved. The families were buzzing with excitement as all the plans slowly but surely came together. In our house, it's all we talked about for weeks—what we were going to wear, who we were going to see, how many parties there would be, and what kinds of food we would enjoy. We had never been part of such an event, a traveling wedding party. And to make it even more exciting, our sister was the guest of honor.

Finally, the countdown ended, and the day of departure arrived. All forty-plus members of the wedding party gathered at the Karachi City Railway station and prepared to board the train to the Khokhrapar. This was the tiny town on the Pakistani side of the border crossing. The train platform had the air of a carnival as we all gathered there with our suitcases and travel trunks, with our traveling clothes, baskets of food, and our excited shouts of greeting. Such a motley crew! There were elderly relatives and baby cousins. There were middle-aged bachelors and young families trying to keep track of their broods. Coolies, who identified themselves by wearing bright red turbans on their heads, swarmed over our party and found plenty of work helping everyone with their luggage in exchange for a few rupees.

I was glad to see my cousins from both my father's side of the family and my mother's. My mother's people were the Jupiterwalas. They were wonderful people and a great support for our family. They had been in Karachi for many years and had established a small but successful chain of supply companies. They lived in a commercial district of the city, some ways from Elphinstone Street. Their house was something like a home in the French Quarter of New Orleans, with a door onto the street and a nice courtyard in the back. Of course, their home wasn't nearly as ornate as many French Quarter establishments these days, and there was no Bourbon Street! As kids, we loved visiting them. It was a treat to escape the cramped quarters of our own flat and play cricket in the courtyard. It was almost like going for vacation, and they often invited us to stay the night and spend weekends. Their family was our comfort zone, and we were there for them when they needed us. And now we are going on this great adventure together.

Everyone was a little nervous about this crazy trip across the border, but there was a certain safety in numbers that allowed us to lose ourselves in the hustle and bustle of it and feel thrilled about it all together. It was as if the wedding celebrations had already begun. We all piled into the cars and jostled for positions in the seats, stuffing baggage and food into overhead racks and running through the aisles. I could see many of the other train passengers eye our group warily.

The train ride took days. It was over twenty-four hours just to get to Khokhrapar, the exit point on the Pakistani side of the border. The adults passed the time by talking politics, telling stories, playing cards, and sharing jars of tea or sweets from their baskets. The smaller children passed time by playing chase in the aisles or elaborate games of snakes and ladders on the floor of the train as it rocked and creaked from station to station. As always, the best part of the train ride was rolling into a new station where the local vendors would be waiting—the confectioners and sellers of sweet, the tinkers and newspaper boys, the food stalls and women selling beautiful dyed fabrics. There were entertainers, policemen, porters, and passengers from all over Pakistan jostling for position along the train platforms and throughout the stations. I was old enough now to step off the train and enjoy the experience of wandering through the vendors, smelling their cooking, watching their magic tricks, buying a bag of roasted almonds, admiring a stall of secondhand books, passing a few rupees to the beggars as I shuddered at their deformities. And then the train guard would deliver a long, ear-splitting blast on his whistle, and I would rush back with the rest of the family to jump aboard the train for the next leg of the journey.

Finally, we arrived in Khokhrapar, a dusty town at the edge of the Thar Desert. At this time, there were only two locations where people could cross legally into India, and this was the nearest one for our family. We piled off the train and gathered our small mountain of luggage. Then we had to file through the large customs shed and stand in line to be searched, interviewed, and have our paperwork inspected. The customs officers, like everyone, were surprised by our large wedding party and unprepared to deal with us efficiently. One by one, our persons and bags were searched carefully. There were government restrictions on how much money could be carried into

India (no more than fifty rupees), what valuables could cross the border (none), what types of medicines could be carried, and more. Naturally, people took to smuggling. People hid money in the soles of their shoes. They stashed gold jewelry in tubes of toothpaste. They changed the labels on medicines so that they looked innocuous. Our hope was to simply overwhelm the customs officers, if not with our sheer numbers, then with our volume, confusion, and enthusiasm. One of my cousins did not do a good job of hiding her gripe water, and the customs officer found it in the bottom of her suitcase. "What is this?" he demanded.

Gripe water was a popular English remedy for colic in babies, but it was illegal in India since India banned most imported goods. My father could get it, of course, and my cousin was trying to deliver this medicine to a desperate family member on the other side of the border. But it looked like it was about to be confiscated. That's when Zohra Bahen, a lady in her midtwenties burst forward and cried, "That's mine! Don't take it! I need my medicine!"

"You take this medicine?" the customs officer asked, looking suspicious.

"Yes, of course. It's for my stomach."

"Let me see."

She did as she was instructed and took a careful dose of the gripe water. The officer still looked suspicious, but he finally let it pass. We all had fun teasing Zohra Bahen after that. "How is your colic? Are you feeling all right?" we would ask for months to come.

When it was my mother's turn to pass through the inspection, she stepped up to the table with her suitcase and turned her eyes toward heaven. She mumbled and prayed to a saint named Abimbola and prayed for the customs officer to be temporarily stricken by blindness, just long enough for her to get through customs. This was her way of both teasing the officers and setting them slightly on edge. They moved her through the line quickly.

Meanwhile, on the other side of the customs hall, the train was waiting. And waiting. And waiting. This was the Monabao connection, the train that would carry us to the Indian side of the border, but only if we could make it through customs in time to catch the train. My father and some men from our party had made it through the long line already and were pleading with the train security officer. "You must wait! Look, we are almost all here."

"The train is already late," the security officer replied, looking at his pocket watch. "We must depart."

My father pressed some rupees into the man's hand. "Just ten more minutes, and we'll all be aboard."

"Ten more minutes," the man agreed as he pocketed the money. "But no more."

"Of course, of course," my father and the other men replied.

At last, the whole wedding party cleared customs and made it onto the train. The Monabao connection was a short train, only a few cars long, and it was already full of people, many of them unhappy about the long delay. By the time we arrived aboard, most of the seats were taken, so I stood and watched as we set off through the no-man's-land that separated Pakistan from India. This desolate stretch of desert was all that separated the two armies which were on high alert at this time, and our little train was built to travel back and forth through this tense region. The slow, bumpy ride would take just less than an hour, but it was the strangest part of the journey for sure, passing out of Pakistan and watching the machine gun-wielding soldiers fade behind us along with their high fences and coils of barbed wire. We knew that somewhere ahead of us, the Indian army awaited in a similar show of tense preparedness. As we chugged out across the desert, it occurred to me that Pakistan and India were a lot like my father and his brother. They were family, but their relationship was complicated and riddled with tensions.

We were just about two miles from the station when one of the elders of the Jupiterwala clan, Mamajee Abdulhusein, leaned to my father's ear and told him, "Hasan Bhai, I have left my passport back at the station."

"What?" my father asked, alarmed.

"I must have left it with the customs officer," the elder said. He looked terrified.

This was bad news, and I could see the gears of my father's mind begin to churn rapidly. For a Pakistani to arrive in India with no passport, no visa, and no traveling papers would be a nightmare. If this gentleman wasn't arrested outright, he would be detained indefinitely, and who knows how long it would take to sort out the identification and legal paperwork. My father, desperate to avoid that situation, reached up and yanked on the emergency brake chain that hung from the ceiling of the passenger car. The entire train jerked heavily, and the brakes screeched on the metal wheels as we came to a stop in no-man's-land.

The security officer quickly appeared again. "What is the problem?" he asked.

My father explained the situation.

The officer was clearly annoyed, but even he understood the consequences of landing in India without the passport and paperwork. "What do you propose?" he asked. The train couldn't return to the station backward. How exactly were we going to retrieve that paperwork?

"I'll go," said Tahir Bhai. "I can run."

We quickly arranged a small group of younger men who could run two miles to the station and back. Everyone felt the urgency of the situation. They laced up their shoes tightly It was going to be a grim run through the dry sand which blew like dust in the wind. Just as they were about to leap off the train and begin their trek through the desert, however, Mamajee Abdulhusein leaned back down to my father's ear and said, "Hasan Bhai, I have found my passport. It was in my other pocket."

"What?" demanded the security officer when my father informed him of the good news. He was furious. My father and the other men quickly pressed more rupees into his hand. "Look," they said, raising their hands into the air. "No problem. Let's get this train moving."

We arrived at Monabao station, and once more, we had to climb off the train, pile slowly and loudly through customs, and then race to catch the next train. As my family looked around, they noticed many red-turbaned coolies and quickly tried to hire them to help move the mountain of luggage from one train to the next. These exchanges quickly turned heated and burst into yelling matches, however, before we realized that Malwaris wear a traditional red headdress, and these were not coolies at all. My family were accidentally grabbing other travelers and locals and trying to press them into service for a few rupees. The gesture was not much appreciated.

We made it onto the connecting train and continued another two days until we arrived in Ahmedabad. Mamajee Dawoodi, my uncle from Ahmedabad, was at a rail station near the India border, ready to receive us. At long last, we had made it! Now we could reunite with Indian family and friends. We could begin the wedding celebrations. We could eat, drink, and play cricket or *gilli danda* in the lanes outside. There was only one problem, and that was Shirin Bahen's family, the family of my father's first wife. When Shirin Bahen left India to come to Pakistan, her situation was growing tense here, and now that side of the family had united to oppose the marriage. They called it a bad match. They claimed it was forced upon her by my father. They refused to grant their blessing, and what's more, they intended to disrupt the ceremony. They were determined to stop the wedding.

The open family warfare quickly cast a cloud over all our enthusiasms. Traditional Indian weddings are sprawling, days-long affairs of meals, teas, drawing room concerts, parties, henna painting, and other ceremonial events and gatherings. Everyone had been looking forward to this, but now there was an icy tension in the air that no one could escape. Shirin Bahen was depressed by the news and became anxious. Could all her plans and dreams really be ruined after the amazing journey to be here? My father called an emergency meeting with the heads of families that were friendly to the wedding. They quickly decided that there was only one thing to do: marry the couple. Right now. Forgoing the schedule of events, they proposed that Shirin Bahen be married right away, and then the celebrations could ensue for the rest of the week. They would need the blessing of the Syedna though, the religious and spiritual head of the community.

As my family always did, they rallied together in a time of need or family urgency. My mother enlisted the help of Mamajee Dawoodi, Mamajee Ismail, Mami Khadija and Mami Fatema to make everything happen. We needed a venue, a cleric, and notification for dozens of family members, just to start. My mother's family did so much to see that this wedding, which meant so much to my dad, went smoothly.

Fortunately, the Syedna had arrived in Ahmedabad that evening. After learning more about the situation, he offered his blessing.

Just before midnight, we all gathered in secret for the *nikah*, the formal, traditional Muslim wedding ceremony. That night turned out to be magical for me, but not for any of the reasons I might have expected. It was not the clandestine nature of the midnight gathering, not the smile on my sister's face, not the beauty of the ceremony, not the happiness of the family that surrounded me. All those things were wonderful, but what struck me most about that wedding was the beautiful dark-eyed girl sitting across the aisle from me. Isfana. I had known her for years, of course. Our families were intertwined, and I saw her when my mother brought us to India. But I had never seen her quite like this. She was no longer a child. We were both in the bloom of teenage adolescence, and I couldn't help feeling a mysterious connection. As I watched her, I looked forward to the days of celebrations ahead. I had no idea what I was feeling at this moment, but I knew that I wanted more of it. I knew that I wanted to see much more of this beautiful girl.

CHAPTER 12

Keeping the Homefront

The war seemed inevitable. There was such a buildup to the conflict in the newspapers and the national mood. By then, President Ayub Khan had implemented his American-style electoral system and reestablished some semblance of democracy in the country. This allowed him to claim victory in a presidential election and reestablish a civilian government while at the same time install himself as the field marshal of the army so he could keep an eye on any activity that might be threatening to his rule. To bolster his support domestically, he began to stoke nationalist fires and build a case for military action against India over the disputed territory of Kashmir.

People ate it up. Pakistan was a nation on the rise, and it deserved to claim its territorial integrity. I, too, was swept up in the tide of emotions, and I energetically supported Ayub Khan as he ranted about how it was time to take back this stretch of our homeland from the occupying forces of India. We listened to the radio addresses. We devoured the articles as they appeared in the morning and evening papers. We attended nationalist rallies in the parks. Even my satirical newspaper, the *Gupistan*, took on a more serious tone in support of President Ayub Khan and Pakistan. It seemed like such a significant and historical time that I went so far as to create a scrapbook with photos and newsclips about Ayub Khan, his policies, and his propaganda. Looking back, I was probably one of the most enthusiastic cogs of Ayub Khan's unpaid propaganda machine, and Venus Medico was filled with my passionate declarations.

The only people I did not share my fervent political beliefs with were Isfana and her family back in India. The tensions between our two nations might have been building to a breaking point, but I was careful to avoid that topic in my letters to her family. As strange as it might seem now, in those days, it was inappropriate to write letters directly to a young lady. Any hint of impropriety could tarnish both the girl's and the family's reputation, so the older family members acted as careful gatekeepers, restricting access to their young women. Thus, if I wanted to woo or flirt with Isfana, I had to woo the whole family. So that's exactly what I did. Eager to contact her, I sent long letters to the family which were riddled with subtle mentions of our thriving family business, of my success at Karachi Grammar School. I wrote in English, knowing that Isfana would be asked to read them aloud to the family. She, like me, was the most fluent speaker of the language in her family as her education, like mine, was delivered in English. I made a habit of using the most eloquent words I could muster. I would never write *dinner* when I could write *feast*. *Beautiful* became *breathtaking*. A feeling of excitement was *electrifying*. I didn't just think fondly of my visit to India. *I reminisced nostalgically about the magical occasion.*

I also made my motivations clear with not-so-subtle asides meant for Isfana. "Please tell your beautiful daughter I say hello," I might write, and I would get a thrill thinking of the blush that might creep up her cheek as she read that sentence out loud to her family.

Then in August of 1965, the letter writing was abruptly interrupted. Just as I was finishing my last year of O levels at Karachi Grammar School, hostilities finally erupted between Pakistan and India, and all communications were shut down between the two nations.

Pakistan had been sneaking infiltrators into Kashmir to start an internal uprising while the military planned to move on the territory. Only it didn't go exactly as planned. Ferocious fighting broke out across the region, but India repelled the forces in Kashmir and squelched the popular uprising. The two armies then engaged in a complex series of attacks and counterattacks involving infantries, heavy artillery, armored tank divisions, and even the air force.

Thousands of casualties began to pile up on both sides. India fought their way into West Pakistan, but it wasn't until they were on the outskirts of the Punjab, capital city of Lahore, that Pakistanis began to seriously worry.

Of course, back in Karachi, that's not what we heard in the news reports. We received news of Pakistani heroics. Clutch victories against all odds. Brave defenders of the homeland fending off the Indian hordes. We heard about vicious tank battles and running skirmishes through the beautiful, but brutal, mountain terrain. We retold anecdotes of soldiers demonstrating incredible bravery and sacrifice by hurling themselves beneath Indian tanks blowing themselves up to stop the advancing armor. We sang national anthems and songs of victory. As the evenings set in, we would get ready for the air raids, close our windows tightly, and listen to the patriotic songs over the radio and the emotional speeches of the PR machine. Out in the streets, there was total darkness of blackouts, and we would wake numerous times in the night to the sounds of air raid sirens as Indian Air Force bomber flew sorties nearby. Occasionally, we would hear the bombs falling when they struck at Karachi directly, trying to target the local military bases or destroy some key infrastructure, such as the port.

Even when the reports of casualties started trickling in, we never challenged what was happening, and when the exuberant protégé of Ayub Khan, a young man named Zulfiqar Ali Bhutto, went to the United Nations Security Council and pounded his fists on the podium, announcing that Pakistan was no small Humpty Dumpty pariah, I and the rest of the country stood up with him.

It wasn't until years later that we learned more details about the war or the losses that Pakistan suffered. All we knew at the time was what the news reported: we were winning! We were defeating our much larger adversary.

The war lasted less than a month, however, before the United States and the Soviet Union came together out of fear that the fighting would draw other countries into the conflict. Both Pakistan and India were part of numerous international treaties, and the bloodshed was quickly spiraling out of control. The two world superpowers brokered a ceasefire which led to the Tashkent Declaration, a peace agreement which basically returned Pakistan and India to the exact positions they had before the conflict began. The ceasefire arrived in the nick of time for Pakistani forces. Many experts agree that India had gained several strategic victories and was poised to strike much more serious blows against Pakistan. As it happened, all hostilities were ceased, diplomatic channels were reopened, captured territories were returned, and prisoners of war were released.

Only when news of the peace agreement reached home, people were stunned. If we had been winning the war, then why did we have nothing to show for it but thousands of coffins returning home? If we had been winning the war, then why didn't we have Kashmir back in the embrace of Pakistan? The government deceptions became obvious, and the nationalist passion that President Ayub Khan had stoked was suddenly turned against him. People felt betrayed. Thousands of people who had been unflagging patriots one week ago took to the streets for anti-government demonstrations. Riots erupted in many places helped further by the entry of Fatima Jinnah, the sister of Quaid-e-Azam Mohammad Ali Jinnah in politics.

I didn't participate in any of the street demonstrations, but I was as disappointed as anyone in the failures of the government. It didn't help that President Khan decided to go into seclusion for several weeks before finally addressing his nation.

Despite the war and the political turmoil that later followed, I was fast approaching my final exams for the General Certificate of Education—basically the equivalent of a high school diploma. I had to focus. The exam scores were incredibly important to a student's prospects for future education. Based upon that score, students would fall into one of three groups: the first division, the second, or the third. Each of those classes offered different opportunities as students moved forward. I had been traveling all over the city with Shirin Bahen, from one tutor to the next, in hopes of improving my scores.

I had also been spending a large amount of time working in the shop while my father had been engaged in his legal battle, and I hoped that wouldn't have too much negative affect on my exams.

There was nothing I could do but help my family in his time of need, and I did my best to balance all these competing priorities and challenges. But now it was time to dive back into my studies with a new effort, and I spent every spare minute studying.

When the week of exams arrived, I walked through the arched doorway of the school as if it was any other day. Instead of going to classes, however, I spent my hours hunkered over test booklets in various designated testing rooms around the school: biology, Latin, humanities. The classrooms were filled with tense, hushed rows of O-level students concentrating on these paper booklets that would shape the futures of everyone in the room. The soft, scratching sound of scribbling pencils filled the air, punctuated by the crinkle of turning pages. The occasional cough or the scrape of a chair on the polished floor seemed to violate the solemn hush.

I did my best, but I was nervous when I finally closed my exam booklet and turned it in to the teacher. Was my best going to be good enough? All my dreams were riding on this test, and there were certainly some questions that I was making educated guesses on. There was nothing for me to do now but wait though. Our tests would be sent to Cambridge University in England to be graded, and there was no exact time frame for when the scores would be reported.

It was a dull, dreary morning when I received word that the exam scores had arrived from Cambridge. I walked alone through the streets toward the school building. My feelings were a combination of excitement and apprehension. One half of me wanted to hurry and see the result, and the other half of me wanted to slow to a crawl, afraid of what I might find there.

The scores were posted publicly, of course, on the wall outside the principal's office. They were arranged by score, not by name, so it took time to find your result unless you were at the very top of the list. Or the bottom. I jockeyed for position in front of the wall, among a large group of students all looking for their scores. I started in the middle and worked my way up, hoping and praying that I would find my name closer to the top. I passed the names of many of my friends as my gaze traveled up the list. Then I saw it. My name. I had scored a twenty point, which barely placed me in the first division. But still, I was in the *first division*. I blinked my eyes in amazement and looked at the score again. It did not change. It was right there in black and white. It was just barely enough to squeak into the first class, but it was enough. Many students shouted with joy as they found their names, but I kept my excitement quiet. I'm sure I must have been smiling from ear to ear though.

As I walked briskly home, I was overtaken by a moment of nostalgia as I reflected on how Karachi Grammar School had been such a good place for me. It was hard to believe these days were almost over. I knew I was privileged to have passed through that institution, to now be peers with so many smart students in high places. My father had made all this happen, but I was also proud of my own part in the success, and I was thrilled at the thought of making my father proud too. I loved the notion of rewarding my mother's prayers and of earning the adoration of my sisters.

At the same time, I knew that my journey was far from over. Already, I was contemplating my next big decision: which academic track to pursue as I entered the next phase of schooling. It was the first major life decision that was completely up to me, and I was worried about choosing unwisely. Up until now, my father had steered all the major decisions of my schooling and my life: the Presentation Convent boarding school, the Karachi Grammar School, and even my shelf of elocution and debate trophies. But this time, the decision was mine.

The choice was between higher math and natural sciences. Higher math would propel me toward career possibilities in engineering, economics, or commerce. Many of my friends were choosing this route toward a safe and stable business career. I knew I would be in good company if I chose this track, and my life would be a little easier.

Natural sciences, on the other hand, would move me toward biology and medicine. Natural sciences was a more challenging track for several reasons. First, I struggled academically in some of my science subjects. Secondly, my family had no *panga*, meaning that we had almost no connections or help in any of the medical programs around the city. Finally, Pakistani medical schools were incredibly competitive, accepting only a tiny fraction of students from the general pool of applications, and it would be critical that I make it onto the merit list. Numerous seats were saved for students with family or political connections, but for working class kids like me who were relying on their grades, test score, and instincts, there were exactly eight seats available each year. *Eight seats.* Students from across the city would be competing for that tiny, auspicious group of openings, and I would be going against very long odds.

As I weighed that decision in my mind, however, I realized just how much I had begun to dream of that very future. Not only had I grown up in an environment closely related to the medical profession, but I greatly admired my father's ability to help people. My father worked magic within his limited means, but with a medical degree, I would be able to become a true healer. I would also bring incredible respect to my family.

Despite the long odds, the decision was quite easy to make once I thought about it over the next days and weeks. I knew that my dreams lay down that path toward medicine.

CHAPTER 13

Eight Seats

It was a dull, hot afternoon with no breeze. The sun shone brightly with almost venomous intensity, and business at the shop was slow. Everything was quiet as my father sat in his chair at the *galla* (cash register). Maulvi Sahib and Tahir Bhai leaned on the counter, waiting sleepily for customers. I was on the other side of the counter space where Wali Mohd, another trusted shop help, was, and we all were anxious because an Adamjee Science College professor was to come anytime to discuss whether he could give me private instruction in physics. The Adamjee Science College was known across Karachi for its prestigious premedical and science programs. This professor was very accomplished in his subjects, and even better, he assisted students individually and had an excellent track record of helping them achieve higher marks and test scores. Good grades and test scores meant a possibility to be on the merit list, and this was critically important. If I had any chance to get into medical school in Karachi, it was going to be based upon my position on the merit list. That was how students were chosen to fill the very few open-enrollment seats for medical school. That merit list loomed before me, and it also loomed before my father. We both knew that once more, we were trying to beat long odds to get a shopkeeper's son into one of the prestigious institutions of Pakistan. I had barely squeaked into the first class when I completed my O levels, and now I had to get even better if I had any chance of squeaking into medical school. Advanced physics was still my Achilles' heel.

Finally, the professor walked in, just about the time when we are getting a little busy with late-afternoon customers. He was a slender, severe-looking man in a dark suit and tie. He was not tall, but he gave the impression of a man who commanded respect in a room. He approached Maulvi Sahib who, knowing the importance of what was at stake, rushed over to my father excitedly. "Master Sahib is here," he said.

The professor was in earshot, and he immediately corrected Maulvi Sahib rather loudly, "Don't call me Master Sahib. Address me as professor."

Master was considered a title for junior school teachers, and thus it was not an accurate title, nor as prestigious as the professor designation.

A hush swept across the shop as my father and all the staff turned to the man we had been waiting for. We were all almost shivering in our pants. Professor Waheeduddin came and took a seat at the *galla*, facing my father, and the two men started talking softly. I continued my work helping a customer diagnose the cause of a particularly persistent sore throat but kept my ears open as my father and the professor exchanged pleasantries. Soon, the conversation turned to the business at hand, and my father told him how he wanted me to be tutored in physics for getting my marks up to speed. At the tail end of the conversation, I could hear nothing as the dialogue came to a chilling stop. Later, I would learn that this was the moment that Professor Waheeduddin announced his price: one hundred ten rupees per month. This was a large sum. My entire school tuition had been less than that, and my father routinely informed me what a large sum *that* was. With all his children, my father spared no expense when it came to our educations, but he wanted us to be aware not only of their intrinsic value but also of their actual financial toll. Every class counted, he would say.

What he never said directly was that the whole family was sacrificing to make these educational opportunities possible, but we all recognized that we lived in relative squalor—stepping over sewage to climb dingy stairs to our apartments where we shared a communal bathroom and sleep six to a room—in order to achieve these longer-term goals.

At that moment, I didn't know exactly what had just occurred between the professor and my father, but based upon the dramatic silence and the look on my father's face, I knew it couldn't be good. I looked at my dad, then back at the professor. I let my eyes fall to the floor as the awkward silence hung over the shop.

For the first time, I wondered if I had made the right decision when I chose to pursue the natural sciences and premed track. I wondered if I had acted rashly in making my decision. Perhaps I should have given it more consideration and sought more counsel. Maybe the odds were just a little *too* long this time.

Then I heard my dad stand up. With an almost theatrical melodrama and a genuine fire in his eyes, he unbuttoned the top of his shirt and pretended to take it off. He then leaned toward the professor and made sure that each of his words was clearly emphasized as he said in clear Urdu, "Professor Sahib, for this purpose, for my son's education, if I have to sell this shirt on my body, I will. I accept your fees. You teach him all you know."

After my father won his legal battle and earned himself an honorable discharge from the charges against him, his reputation as a battler grew even larger. Not only did people across the neighborhood seek his advice or guidance now, but people across the city now also thought of him as cunning and effective advocate. He was a man who could get things done in a place where the bureaucracy could be incredibly challenging, especially for working people. So it was not a complete surprise when my father's uncle in India called for some assistance. What was surprising was just how much faith he had in my father. "You want me to what?" my father asked over the telephone in the shop.

It turns out my great-uncle had lost his property during partition nearly twenty years ago now. As a Hindu, he had been part of that bloody migration, but he had moved in the opposite direction, away from Pakistan and into India. The Pakistani government had seized his home and property, classifying it abandoned and then sold it to another family. Unfortunately, this was a common story among the millions of migrating families, and people had largely been forced to accept this fate as collateral damage from the chaotic transition time. There was even a common name for it—evacuee property. There had never been a legal case made against the nation, however. There was no official channel for complaints of this nature. There was no legal precedent for a suit such as this. No one was even sure who to sue in the new civilian government, the third national government in the last five years. It was an outrageous, ill-timed, and possibly even dangerous idea.

"Absolutely," my father said. "I'll do it."

So went our days. I went to classes during the days and studied with Professor Waheeduddin on our designated afternoons. My new school was not nearly as warm and welcoming as Karachi Grammar School had been. In fact, students who attended Karachi Grammar were often looked down upon based upon the school's longstanding connection to England. Instead of being an asset for us, it became a label that we were forced to wear, at least socially. There were a few of us attending Interscience Premedical School, and we were referred to as the English kids. The DJ science pre-medicine classes were a great transition into active independent life on one hand and keeping anchored to the family on the other.

Academically, on the other hand, Karachi Grammar had prepared me well, and I plunged into my new studies. This is what I was here for. So much was riding on my work now. If I succeeded in getting into first class once more and scored very well on the cumulative exams, then I could earn a spot on the merit list. I had to get one of those eight seats. I had never felt as focused as I did right now even as the classes became more challenging and blew open new worlds for me. As we delved into more advanced biology, for instance, I realized that the human being was its own universe, filled with interrelated systems, perfectly timed events, and mysteries beyond the grasp of man. I was a rapt explorer of these new worlds.

In this way, time seemed to fly. My father and I both had days so full of activity, imaginations both engaged by our projects, and sights set on these lofty goals. While I was discovering new worlds of biology, chemistry, and medicine, my father was discovering everything possible about my great-uncle's evacuee property: the date of sale, the sale price, the new owners, the appraised value, the legal status and liens on the property, and so on. He used his widespread contacts to assist him, and in his spare time, he helped his four children with schoolwork and cajoled them into massaging his legs as they recited times tables and periodic elements or recited verses from history and literature classes.

In my spare time, I continued to work in the shop. As I was growing older, my father and I were developing more and more of a symbiotic relationship. My father never stopped encouraging me to shoot for the moon with my education and ambitions; he wanted so much more for me than a small pharmacy and a hardscrabble life that could be so easily buffeted by whatever political winds or whims blew through the door. At the same time, it was clear how proud he was to have a son who could step into his role and run the family business. That family business was thriving now too. After my father's great victory against the government, his import license was renewed, and slowly but surely business picked up again. Then it picked up some more. My father had always been a popular man, but now he was even more so, and it worked to grow the customer base even further. People came from across the city to acquire rare imported requests. More businesses hired our services to stock their pharmacies and supply their doctors and employees. It was a very good time for the shop.

If my father had a passion that was rival to my love of cricket, it was his affection for the card game rummy. He loved playing cards with his friends, and a game of rummy was likely to break out any time there was a combination of two ingredients: a moment of down time and some friends nearby. Games spontaneously in the house, in the café, even in a jail cell on that occasion when my father went to help his friend who was arrested. He had a regular game that he liked to attend, and I loved to see him take a break from work and relax sometimes so I would work the cash register, so he could go to his game.

One night, as I arrived at the shop, a regular customer stopped by to introduce us to his new Japanese car—a Hino Contessa. Cars were rare to begin with, but this was a special vehicle, like something out of a dream. It was black and shiny, compact but elegantly curved. The polished chrome glimmered in the streetlight. We all walked around it, admiring the car and peppering our friend with questions. *How long have you had it? How fast does it go? Where did you find such a car?*

The Hino Contessa had been known for its compact reliability all around the world, but in the mid-1960s, it went through a stylish design overhaul. Now it came in a sleek, handsome coupe version with water-cooled 1,251 cc engine in the rear compartment. It could hit top speeds of over 130 kilometers per hour (80 miles per hour), which, at the time, seemed like stupendous velocity. Bear in mind, we had no American muscle car culture in Southeast Asia and largely prized our vehicles for their abilities to maneuver tight spaces, adapt to multiple uses, and endure all manner of hardships.

But the Contessa, she was all that and a stylish beauty. My father fell in love immediately.

We all saw that look in his eye, and very quickly the conversation turned to how good he would look in a Contessa of his own. If he was in love with the car, we were in love with the whole idea of him owning one (and taking us for rides around the city).

As practical and cautious he was, it took some time and much cajoling from both his friends and my sisters before he finally decided to purchase one for himself. The shop was doing very well right now, and he figured the Contessa could only add to his image of successful businessman. It would certainly set him apart from most people in Karachi, including his own peers; car ownership was still common only in the upper classes. Plus, my mother's family, the Jupiterwalas, had a car now. Perhaps it was time for my father to join that elite club of Karachi *drivers*.

In those days, there were no car lots where you went to purchase a vehicle. Rather, there was a ream of paperwork that you filled out to have the vehicle imported directly to you. It took months to get all the applications and payments submitted and then to have the vehicle delivered. But finally, it arrived via steamship, and my father went down to retrieve it from the import shipping office.

The whole family was waiting when he rolled around the corner in that elegant shining beige beauty with the four doors and aerodynamic design. Looking back now, I must smile at the modesty of that small vehicle, but at the time, we thought it was as glamorous as a limousine. We piled in for our first drive around town. Father took us down Elphinstone Street, out through the suburbs, and all the way to the beach. And it was so fast; it was like we were there in no time!

That became one of our favorite things to do as a family—drive to the beach or out to the nearby promenade to picnic amid the beautiful gardens. Having the Contessa was like a breath of freedom that we had never known, this ability to pick up and transport ourselves to any part of the city or travel easily a day trip, out to visit family or some beautiful bungalow that belonged to one of our father's friend's. He never stopped surprising us with his friends, these people that he had met—and was continuing to meet—through all his adventures, tribulations, and business dealings. Pakistan was a land of hospitality, and they often rewarded our trips to visit them with wonderful afternoons of yard games, cookouts, patio meals, and, of course, gin rummy. As busy as I was, I tried to participate in these family outings as much as possible. Often, I would lug a textbook or three along with me so that I could spend some quiet time studying, but they were magical afternoons nonetheless.

Of course, these outings weren't always picture-perfect. It wasn't uncommon to spend hours packing a picnic, making plans with family, and getting completely prepared for a beautiful beach trip only to break down halfway there with a flat tire of one of the cars in the caravan. The Jupiter Wala's car was notorious for this mishap. The car was packed full of family members, who all piled out into the grass on the side of the road. We soon realized that these adventures could be almost as fun as the actual destination as we watched the family rally to fix the tire. It was quite a production in those days.

The Jupiterwala team had turned fixing a flat tire into a science of precision logistics. Each one of them knew exactly what to do. First, a proper rock was required to anchor the car in place and make sure it didn't roll right off the jack. Then there was the lifting of the car, analyzing the cause of the problem, the myriad ways to repair a flat tire depending on what the cause was, the pumping of the tire to refill it, or, in the case of last resort, using the spare tire. Someone had to direct traffic passing by, and everyone else knew to select a good spot for a picnic blanket and then start pulling out baskets of food and get the party going while the tire was being fixed. Nothing could phase this group.

Ma would open the thermos with tea and pass around a package that had snacks, and of course, I always waited until the boiled eggs came out. A little sprinkle of salt and pepper. A dash of cumin and coriander. I was in heaven. In those days, pepper, of all things, was very difficult to come by and often expensive. To this day, a dash of pepper tastes like a luxury to me and sticks to the palate.

Once my father had done all his leg work on the case of the evacuee property, he hired another attorney to assist him. Together, they began to build their legal case and decide how best to proceed through the Pakistani courts. My father and his attorney submitted their case, and to everyone's amazement, the courts accepted it. It would be considered on its legal merits. This meant it would at least get a hearing in a lower court, and we were all thrilled by the prospect.

In the meantime, my high school certificate, also called inter-science final exams, were looming on the calendar. I had been through this process numerous times by now, but never had so much been rising on a single set of exams. My grades at school were excellent, which meant that if I could score high enough on the cumulative exams, then I could earn a high position on the merit list. I just had to be in the top eight results to make it into one of those seats.

Over the next months, my father and I both redoubled our efforts. By now, my baby sister, Akila, was so used to seeing her older siblings with their noses buried in books that her favorite game became "teacher." We would pause to humor her as she walked around with a ruler and made all kinds of outlandish "rules." No humming while you wrote out long division. Books should be arranged by color. All sweets should be handed over to the "teacher" promptly. She provided excellent study breaks, and we often found ourselves doubled over with laughter as we attempted to comply with her directives or, worse yet, tried to appeal them. "Very bad!" she would say, aiming her ruler at the offender.

The week of my exams arrived much faster than I would have liked. The first part of the exam schedule was like many others—the hushed rows of students working carefully in test booklets and scribbling answers to groups of questions of chemistry, physics, biology, English, Urdu, and more. The second part of the week was an intensive series of laboratory practicums. We had to conduct successful experiments, create solutions, dissect organs, and provide detailed analysis at every step of the process. The third part of the week was the most nerve-racking: the *viva voce*. This is when students had to stand alone in front of a panel of professors and answer challenging questions in the subjects of chemistry, physics, and biology. Even worse were the follow-up questions that probed the very depths of both a student's knowledge in the subject and their ability to analyze and calculate quickly, on their feet, and under pressure. In a way, my entire life had been designed for this moment: my careful instruction, the best schools, the tutors and hours of studying, the debate societies and elocution contests, even the fun-but-fierce competition on the cricket field.

Now if only I could draw on all these elements at the same time and use them in concert to pass the scrutiny of this stone-faced panel of professors.

It would take weeks to find out the results. To make the pressure even worse, the results would not be delivered directly to the students; they would arrive in a special supplement in the evening newspaper and would be delivered throughout the city. Karachi had a fascination with its professional class, and results like this were widely published and scrutinized. Every evening, as I worked in the shop, someone would race to the corner the moment the newspaper truck dropped off its tied bundles. We would search for that special insert section, and when it wasn't there, we would settle back into the shop routine and wait for another day. Years later, this citywide fascination with the professional class would take a dark turn, but for right now, I simply longed to see my results.

Finally, it arrived. The special section. All the premed students were ranked by score. We began to scan the results. "Look!" Tahir Bhai shouted. "Right there!"

There was my roll number in the first-class list. Once again, I had to blink to make sure it was real. I could feel the hands of my friends as they shook my shoulders in celebration. I could hear their voices. I had done it! I would be accepted into medical school. I would claim one of those eight seats.

I heard my father shout with joy, something he rarely did even in the best of moments. "Salwaat," he directed. "And someone buy some sweetmeats! Tonight, we shall celebrate!"

PART II

The Dreamers

*I will remember that there is art to medicine as well as science,
and that warmth, sympathy, and understanding
may outweigh the surgeon's knife or the chemist's drug.*

—from the Hippocratic Oath

CHAPTER 14

Rendezvous with Destiny and Fate

Entry into medical college then became the next step that propelled me in a different environment, but this environment was a mixture of academics and career path on one side and the political chaos on the other. The political chaos around us gave me an unusual opportunity of a unique nature. The college classes were sporadic to begin with and then degenerated into total suspension. I took a break from this and convinced my dad to let me visit India.

The visit to Ahmedabad was indeed momentous. I remember traveling by train from Bombay and thinking of my visit and meeting Isfana. The evening I reached, I sat next to her in the movie theater, watching *Gone with the Wind*, and then the evening never ended. By early morning, we had chatted and talked and committed. It was chemistry that met physics and evolved in a mathematical equation. We were in love. There was never a doubt and the struggles we were in for, the challenges we would face were not our priority list, and these challenges were not on our radar or horizon. But we were committed and the emotional passion with which we both moved forward was considered by some as unprecedented and almost impulsive. The families were shocked at our speed, but our commitment was so deep at one level and logical in time sequence at another level that our relationship became more and more cemented.

The events following further proved how wrong the initial disbelief was as the test of time and events showed. The romance of the time between the lovebirds of two nations was shattered by the sound of war in 1971.

At night, bombs and missiles fell from the sky, wreaking havoc and destruction upon Karachi, especially around the port and along the coast. The air raid sirens wailed in the darkness as the city hunkered in a full blackout and absorbed the heavy blows. Rockets roared in from Indian missile boats in the Arabian Sea. Flashes of light illuminated the Karachi skyline. The air trembled with explosions. Pakistan was at war once again.

In the dormitories of the Dow Medical College, all of us students waited at night for the bombing to begin, and then we rushed downstairs to join the first responders. The college was attached to the Civil Hospital Karachi, and we would race into the ambulances that screamed around the city at night, heading to bomb sites and looking for casualties. Fortunately, the Indian Army was most interested in destroying industrial infrastructure, not inflicting civilian casualties, so they struck the naval base, factories, harbors, and rail yards by night when few civilians were around. In most cases, only a few soldiers or workers were injured in the blasts, and we tended to them carefully and whisked them to hospital when necessary, but this was war, and those Karachi ambulances made many trips to the morgue as well. The body count ticked upward in Karachi even as the frontline fighting raged fiercely to the north and the east of us.

By day, we still had medical classes, and we would pass around the morning papers and read with bleary eyes the accounts of intense fighting on the front lines. Despite the hardships, the nation was proud of its fighting forces that were striking deep into enemy territory and quelling an uprising and rebellion in East Pakistan. The fighting was fierce, and the death toll was rising, but Pakistan was winning according to the morning papers and the evening radio news. Pakistani soldiers were fighting like heroes—outnumbered yet beating back the enemy. Of course, we all remembered the last time we read such glowing of the nation's fighting forces, but we wanted to believe. We wanted to be proud of our nation.

As before, communications had been severed between the two nations. Who knew how long the war would last, and how would I contact Isfana in the meantime? Now I was trying to reach my fiancée. In the intervening months, since we had both entered medical school, our relationship had thrived, we had secured our families' blessings, and we had agreed to be married. It had started with my visit to India during one of the long breaks we had in medical school due to political turmoil and strikes. I had reached Ahmedabad and seen Isfana. We had a wonderful visit, and our connection in person was even stronger than I could have hoped through our correspondence. I spent much time with her family, and her mother had liked me also, and I guess that had reinforced the adage "He who the daughter win would must with the mother first begin." With that commitment came the formal engagement and the maturing of the relationship with its romance, but not without the struggles and challenges the circumstances around us produced. Our nations were at war. Phone lines to India were disconnected. The mail service was suspended. All travel at the borders was shut down. This possibility always loomed for Isfana and me, but now that it was a reality, I longed to reach out to her. I wanted to know if she was safe, but all I could do was hope that her family was unaffected by the raging battles. I could imagine her sitting in her own medical classes in Ahmedabad and poring over the newspapers with her classmates exactly as I was doing.

I focused on my courses as best I could, absorbed as much information as humanly possible, and then got ready to race out at night during the bombing. The rest was out of my hands for now.

Our schedule was so crammed that neither my roommate nor I spent all that much time in our tiny dorm room, and so it seemed like no big deal when we decided to allow a friend of ours, Chacha, as we called him, to move in with us. There were two beds and two desks, and we took turns sleeping between classes or after dinner, and we shuffled easily from desk to dining hall to class. The only problem was that this situation was entirely against the rules. Whenever a school administrator or resident assistant would drop by the dormitory, we had to hide our illegal friend under the bed. He had to scurry onto the floor and lay quietly beneath my mattress through inspections or casual encounters, but that seemed a small problem compared to the war that was raging around us. We hunkered at night, listening to the news and preparing for a long season of attacks and counterattacks, of strategic gains and night raids.

Until the war abruptly ended.

Thirteen days after full-scale hostilities erupted between the rival nations, it ended when Pakistan signed an instrument of surrender in Dhaka on the sixteenth of December 1971. At the medical school, we were stunned to learn this news. In the streets, people were in shock. Across the country, Pakistanis couldn't believe what they were hearing. If Pakistan had been winning so valiantly, why were we suddenly surrendering?

It was like déjà vu as the truth began to trickle out. Pakistan hadn't been winning the war at all. Our air force had been roundly defeated in a matter of days. Our navy had been outmaneuvered and incapacitated. Our army had been decimated, with more than eight thousand killed. To add insult to injury, more than ninety thousand Pakistanis had been captured and were being held as prisoners of war.

Even worse, the rebellion in East Pakistan had not been quelled at all. With the help of its Indian allies, the rebellion was victorious, and East Pakistan seceded from Pakistan, becoming the sovereign nation of Bangladesh. The defeat was so complete that it was hard to contemplate. In a matter of days, Pakistan had gone from a regional powerhouse to a country that had lost its military, its pride, a huge swath of territory and more than *half* of its population. People were angry at the government again. They had been lied to by incompetents, and they took their anger to the streets. Riots erupted, and the fallout was swift and crippling. Public services went on strike, and the government seemed to crumble in the face of this adversity. Industry shut down. Even schools shut down as students went on strikes and protested in the streets. Within days, my medical school shuttered its doors too. My classmates and I weren't surprised, given everything that was happening, but still, it was a heavy blow to face after we had worked so hard to get there.

By now, some of my fellow medical students had also become Doctor *Saheb* aka *Daksab*. There were a few among us who opened their own clinics in areas where community and primary health services were lacking. They would act like full-fledged doctors, and the patients and clients they served believed in them as true healers. One may call this quackery in conventional terms, but in this environment of poverty, these medical students did bring an abundance of hope and some assistance even as they served their own egos and pocketbooks. In the same vein, I was inspired to do something too. I decided to do it a different way, however. I approached a very well-known and popular medical primary care general medical doctor, Dr. Sadik Alavi. Dr. Alavi was my colleague Munawar's father. He ran a clinic in the neighborhood and in a densely populated midcity area. His style was unique and his following almost cultish. Essentially, he was a healer first and a medical doctor second. His patients would wait for hours in front of his clinic; before he came driving his small car, swinging his stethoscope casually and greeting everybody in a jovial manner. As soon as he entered his main office and sat down, there would be an onrush of people around his desk and his patient stool. Everyone wanted to talk to him, to get his attention and get examined.

I knew his reputation well, and I stopped by to ask him for an apprenticeship. He did not know me personally in any special way. When I asked him that I be allowed just to be with him and shadow him at the clinic, he smiled and then laughed. "Juzar Ali," he said. "What in the world would you, a smart medical student from a medical college, gain out of what I do?"

I insisted that I would learn just by the exposure and experience. I pressed my case eagerly, and he agreed to let me learn from him.

Dr. Alavi had two outcome pathways for his patients. If the patient history, test results, or clear symptoms told him that the medical condition he saw was serious, he immediately instructed and counseled the patients to visit a specialist or hospital. If he understood that his patients had a self-limiting illness of a transient nature he would either prescribe the appropriate medicines or mix a prescription for them right on the premises through his rudimentary pharmacy run by a compounder.

The crowd around Dr. Alavi's desk would remain rotating for hours and hours until Dr. Alavi got tired in the latter part of the evening and got up to leave. Then he would be approached by another few people who would have been waiting for this time. These people were those whose family members could not come to the clinic either because they were too sick or too frail.

Dr. Alavi and I would go to these homes in every corner of the neighborhood, wherever they may be, climbing three or four stories through slums, poor neighborhoods, and dilapidated structures and do what he could to help and guide his patients.

This was a unique situation. Those who had the monies and resources could pay and get the health care they wanted. They could afford to go to the most sophisticated health systems in the world or the elite care in Pakistan even for a sneeze and common cold. The others relied on the public safety net free system, and then there was a hybrid pathway depending upon the situation and need. You would get what you pay for. I saw the extremes of these.

I would sit next to him and watch and interact as he went through his daily routine, treating his crowd of patients who had come in to seek hope, care, and cure. As long as he had me sitting there, he would send more complicated cases to me to see if my medical college training could help diagnose or detect specific problems. "Juzar Ali, see what you think of this," he would say, and I would try to listen carefully, take a more complete medical history, and do a more comprehensive physical exam as best the space allowed. I also accompanied him on his house calls. It might have been a very tumultuous time in Pakistan, but to this day, I cherish what I gained out of that exposure and experience with Dr. Alavi.

I learned that medicine is as much fine art as science and the importance of humility. I gained the awareness and appreciation of the triad of listening, empathy, and care and realized that cure will follow if one starts with the triad first. To this day, the value of history taking and letting the patient talk holds me in good stead most of the time. I keep telling my students that is why it is called history: *his story*. Please listen.

With medical school (and the hostels/dormitories) closed, I returned to my family to ride out the storm of social and political upheaval. No longer were we living in a small flat, however. By this time, my father had managed to earn and save money and build a bungalow in the suburbs, no small feat, and a story unto itself. At home, things felt familiar despite all the national upheaval. Mother and Father. Work at the shop. The rotating cast of friends and family who swirled around. It was comforting amid all this chaos, but I was up at nights, worried about the future. What would happen to Pakistan? What would happen to my family? What would happen to me? I had worked so hard to get to medical school, and who knew how long this trouble would last? As I understand, these are questions, ironically been asked over and over again through the years. Yet life goes on and Pakistan survives and will survive despite the pessimism!

I began to turn my sights outside of Pakistan. Over the course of those long nights, I realized that I needed to get to the US for my education and training. It would be much harder all around, but they had the medical expertise. They had international prestige. They had the political stability that I needed to make this dream come true. With a US residency on my CV, I would have the skills and opportunity to thrive in any situation. I would be able to help my family. I would make my dreams come true.

One other thing appealed to me greatly about this decision: I could start right now, on my own. I didn't need my Pakistani medical school to be open to start studying for the Educational Commission for Foreign Medical Graduates (ECFMG) certification. I simply had to pass the exam.

"This is no ordinary exam," Iqbal, whom we called Daksab, said when I discussed my plans with him over tea. We sat in a café in the suburbs near his family home and dreamed of our futures. We soon discovered there were more than a few of us elitists who wanted to travel abroad for our educations and training. In a class of two hundred, about twenty-five or so of our classmates also wanted to take the certification degree for opportunities to study advanced medicine abroad. We bonded together to help one another through the arduous preparations. Our school might have been shut down, but this was one thing we could do for ourselves. Our decision to pursue this option was met with either admiration or open disdain. Everyone recognized the difficulty of the exam, but many of our classmates and instructors who we kept in touch with considered it the path of egotists or, worse, people disloyal to Pakistan. "What's wrong with your own country?" they would ask.

"I love my country," I would reply. "But there are opportunities out there which we cannot get here."

"So you will turn your back on Pakistan."

"I will never turn my back on Pakistan," I said. "I will bring my skills back to Pakistan."

"That's what everyone says. No one ever returns."

It was true that most people who studied medicine abroad then took professional opportunities abroad also. Who could blame them? We knew of several students from our own college who had gone abroad and become international stars in their fields. When these doctors returned to Pakistan, they were like visiting dignitaries, flush with certifications, awards, international respect, dual citizenship, and wealth. They lived in a whole new stratosphere. Between the technical difficulty and prestige, that foreign degree was my ticket to success. With that degree, I wouldn't have to worry about my lack of political connections at the hospitals in Karachi. I was serious about returning after all. I loved my country, I loved my city, I loved my family, and I would do everything I could to be a part of this vibrant place.

One evening, as I walked back into my family home, I spied a stack of new mail on the stand next to the door. Mail service had been frequently interrupted, but it must have arrived today. I couldn't help but feel a small thrill at the sight of the unopened envelopes. Perhaps a letter from Isfana was in there.

But no, of course not. Everyone knew that after weeks of strikes and upheaval, there still was no indication of when communications with India might be resumed. The only thing that seemed certain was that it would be no time soon. It felt like ages since I had spoken with Isfana or traded letters with her, and I still didn't know if they had been affected by the war. I realized that I was going to have to do something out of the ordinary to communicate with her. I couldn't just sit and wait for the two states to make their political amends before I could communicate with my fiancé. But what could I do?

I flipped through the mail, and there were two letters for me from my pen friends around the world. One was from Daniel Zaidi in South Africa, and one was from Abdul Kadir Mohammed in Kenya. In those days, it was quite common to find pen friends in other countries and to establish these social connections via letter. It was social media 101. The English-language newspaper had an entire classified section dedicated to people seeking pen friends from around the world. In the days before internet or high-speed communications, these were wonderful ways to explore regions and cultures that one otherwise might never visit. Right now, I was lost in the irony of the situation. I could freely write to Africa, Europe, America, but I couldn't send a letter to the nation right next door. I'd be better off in Africa, I thought, as I turned over the letter from Kenya.

Suddenly, I froze in my tracks. *Kenya. Of course.* If I sent a letter to Kenya, then Abdul Kadir might be able to mail it to Isfana from there. I might be able to create an entire international web of letter senders out of pen friends across the globe. Can this postal network work? I sought their approval. The idea was so romantic. I raced to my desk and began to fire off letters at once. The following weeks were agonizing as I waited for the replies, but one by one, my pen friends all replied, and nearly every one of them agreed to the plan. I was in business. This would be the start of an international grid created through the pen-friendship network.

I sent my first letter to Isfana through Abdul Kadir in Kenya. He seemed like a generous man, very kind and eager to help. It took weeks for the reply to arrive, but my heart nearly jumped out of my chest when I finally saw Isfana's distinct penmanship arrive in the mailbox. It had worked! I tore the letter open and read. She and her family were safe, and no one had been harmed during the fighting. Things seemed to be much more normal in India than they were in Pakistan—no riots, no strikes. She was attending her medical school classes as usual. I couldn't help feeling a pang of jealousy when I read that, but I was eager to share my own news about the ECFMG exam and my plans to travel to the US for a residency.

We soon formed an elaborate system of communication. Instead of burdening one or two friends with our correspondence, we split it up over numerous connections around the world. We made spreadsheets and worked through our friends in an orderly fashion. It was like an excel program before it was known as such! We carefully dated and numbered our correspondence so we could tell which routes were most efficient and if any of the letters went missing. If I got letter number four and had not received number three, I knew I had to track it down somehow. Our letters were a mixture of love, issues, and idle chatter. It was wonderful. We were so young and still falling in love with every letter. Our missives were filled with dreams and poems. We shared our ambitions, wondered how long we would be apart and mused about our wedding day. I think of those letters as if they were love songs being sung around the world and back.

With that problem temporarily solved, I could throw myself into my studies once more and focus on the exam. By now, I had taken enough high-stake tests to know both the pressure and the strategies for beating them. It wasn't a matter of willpower. It wasn't a matter of time or focus. The only question was very simple: did I have the capabilities to master this much material at this high a level? I had come a long way since that first test to get into Karachi Grammar, and this new material was challenging in myriad new ways. More than rote memorization of biology, chemistry, or medical texts, I had to grasp advanced conceptual ideas and apply them to incredibly complex problems. One thing I had learned over these hard years was to enjoy the challenge. I had inherited that from my father. No problem was too complex to unravel if you had the time, energy, focus, and assistance that you needed. I joined my small coterie of classmates, and we drilled one another in preparation for the exam.

The gang of friends at Dow was a great gang. All of us had unique personal situations with a common professional goal. Our headquarters was our hostel room 57 for all the studies, strategy sessions, fun, frolic, and pranks. Daksab, Chacha, Babujee, Munnu Rafi, Athar, Ramazan, Liaquat and Jamal, Shabbir Poloo, and Shafi brought in a different perspective of humor, passion, wit, mischief, and serious commitments to life's challenges. What happened in 57 stayed locked in 57! We were a mixture of different backgrounds and yet homogeneous in most aspects. By now, we had also become well-known among the medical students all over Karachi. We were the upstarts shooting for the moon and formed one of the two main groups trying to get to USA by preparing for ECFMG. We were trying to follow in the footsteps of those medical superstars who had gone before us.

Isfana and her family didn't quite understand my obsession with the exam and the opportunity to study in the US. Isfana was in a much more stable situation in India with a clear path to professional success in India, so she couldn't fully understand my sense of urgency. Not yet, at least.

Months passed like this, with me studying diligently and our international network of pen friends and postal cupids assisting us with our love letters. Finally, the day of the exam arrived, and once more, I settled into a stress-filled room with my classmates to do my best. The exam was everything we had expected: technical, detailed, drawing from the most intimate depths of medical knowledge. This is exactly what we had prepared for. And sure enough, most of us passed the exam. I was ecstatic when I finally received my result. This piece of paper was like a golden ticket. It practically guaranteed that I would at least have the opportunity to go abroad for advanced training. The last thing standing in my way now was receiving the degree from my own medical school.

Dow Medical College had finally reopened its doors, and students were churning through their coursework, labs, and practicals once more. By now, I was in my final classes and could see the light at the end of the tunnel. I would have a degree in one hand and my ECFMG certification in the other. I would be able to travel abroad. I would be able to see Isfana again. It had now been years since we had been in the same room together, and we longed to see each other again.

I was thrilled when the final exams arrived. I had been preparing for this moment for years now, and though I knew it would be challenging, I felt prepared. The first part of the exams was the written portion which I plowed through methodically. The second part of the exams was the *Viva*, or the oral portion. This section was far more challenging because professors had the discretion to throw especially difficult questions or situations at a student if they felt like pressing the student harder. I knew that several of my professors resented the fact that I was part of the international student group, so I prepared myself to be nimble during their questions. We were literally introduced as the ECFMG students when we went before the panel.

The questions from our examiners came fast, and they grew in complexity. The resentful professors tried to throw me off my game with their harsher tone and their challenging line of interrogation, but I did my best to remain professional, fast, and accurate in my answers.

Finally, the exam was over, and now came the dreaded wait for the results. I felt good though. I felt on the cusp of something big in my life. Then I ran into Athar. "Have you heard?" he asked.

"About what?"

"The conscriptions?"

"What are you talking about?"

"The army, man. They're conscripting all the graduating medical students."

"What?" I exclaimed. "That's not possible."

But it was possible. The government had passed a decree, and all graduating medical students were to go into mandatory military service for a minimum of one year. They would be instated as captains in the army.

"How? How can they do this?" I wanted to know.

My father shrugged. "It is the government. They do what they want. They must rebuild the army."

"With me?" This was devastating news. The more I thought about it, the worse it seemed. How did anyone know if they would release the doctors after one year of service? Who knew where the army might send me or what ill-conceived fight they might engage in? Most importantly, how would it be possible for a Pakistani army officer to marry an Indian woman? After everything the nation had just been through, how were we supposed to trust the government?

Many of my classmates felt the same dismay. We had all been so focused, so ambitious, and so close to success. It seemed the government was suddenly trying to rip that out from under us.

"Did you hear about Ali Hassan?" Athar asked me one day as we met for a meal. Ali was one of our ECFMG gang.

"What about him?"

"He has left Pakistan and he is not coming back."

And so it went. One by one, many of our classmates began to quietly leave the country, and we would only learn of their travels after the fact. The idea was simple: leave while you can before our test results were returned and the conscriptions were officially ordered. From abroad, students could pursue their residencies in whatever country they chose. It was a desperate measure, sure to create arrest warrants back home for the offenders, but people felt that strongly about defying the government orders. My personal situation was even more complicated by the fact that I wanted to marry Isfana, an Indian citizen. The pressure was building with every day that passed—no, with every hour that passed. I wasn't sure about much, but I knew three things: I would marry Isfana, I had to get out of Pakistan to pursue my academic career building goals, and I had to do it quickly.

CHAPTER 15

Learning to Fly

"That is not a plan," my father said. "That is insanity." I had just informed him of my plan to flee the country for East Africa where I could marry Isfana. My father never shied away from challenging authority and redefining what was possible, but at heart, he was still a conservative family man, and romantic rendezvous with young women in foreign countries where we had no family or friends save for a pen pal was not his idea of what good people did. "Absolutely not," he said. "You will stay right here."

The problem was I didn't just want his blessing for the excursion. I needed his financial support. For years now, I had been a full-time student with no income or personal savings. Even at my father's shop, I was never paid a salary; I simply worked for the family, and the family provided for me in return. Now I needed the family to back my desperate plan. "I cannot even speak to Isfana from here," I replied. "How am I supposed to marry her?"

"You will just have to wait. Relations will thaw eventually. They always do."

"That could take years," I replied. "And who knows what they will do with me in the army."

My father was not pleased about the new orders for conscription either, and he sympathized with my situation, but not enough to fund what he considered an illicit adventure that could and would bring shame upon both our families. "Enough of this talk," he said, waving a hand in the air, and he returned to his porch to drink chai with his friend, Shahjee.

Shahjee ran the construction company which had helped my father build his dream bungalow. My father had spent immense amount of time pouring over every step of the construction, and he became very good friend with Shahjee in the years it took to build the house. Now that it was complete, Shahjee still showed up every morning for tea. He had built the house, and now he seemed content to enjoy it with my father. Semiretired and full-bellied, he reclined on the porch with a cup of tea and talked with my father about everything under the sun. Both men had reached a place in their lives where they could step back from the day-to-day operations of their businesses to a certain degree, and they enjoyed their relative leisure immensely. I could hear my father explaining my situation to Shahjee and the sounds Shahjee made when he expressed his sympathy or his disdain. As he learned about my plight, I was pleased to note that the sounds of sympathy escaped his lips, a sort of soft clucking with his tongue. If he expressed full-on disapproval, I knew that my plan would be near impossible, but if he expressed sympathy, there was still hope. He and my father conspired over many subjects, and he had my father's ear.

My window of opportunity was very small, and thus my campaign was relentless. Whenever I had the chance, I would bring up the subject. Over supper, I would deliver news from my Kenyan pen friend and use it as a segue to talk about my plans to escape to East Africa. When the newspaper or radio delivered a story about hostilities with India, I used it as an opportunity to remind everyone of my situation. When a conversation turned to medicine, I would use it to talk about the accolades that Isfana and I would earn for our families once we had escaped and married.

"Enough, Juzar!" my father shouted. "We have heard too much about your plan already."

But I couldn't give up. Every night I went to bed with dread, fearing that the exam results might arrive the next day and I would be whisked away by the Pakistani army, never to see Isfana again. Every day the exam results did not arrive I considered a blessing, a chance for me to try again.

Finally, however, I realized that my father had truly reached the end of his patience. I could not keep needling him at dinner or ambushing him during our conversations. I needed to make a serious proposal to him. My mom and Rashida and Akila (whom by now we had nicknamed Cheeko and Mukha, respectively) were my silent supporters but were not going to cross my dad and did not want to deal with his anger and opposition. I would try one final time to change his mind, and if that did not work, then I would accept my fate. I prepared my arguments carefully and thoroughly. I asked for one final meeting on the topic, and my father grudgingly accepted, knowing this would be that last time I would bring it up. I arrived at the bungalow to find him drinking tea with Shahjee, exactly as I had hoped. Part of my argument was designed for my father's good friend in hopes that he might align himself with my cause. Almost like the old days of public speaking challenges in college and Jamaat/community-sponsored debates and elocution contests or campaigns for offices of the Jolly Cricket Club, I gathered myself and launched into my presentation. "You are the one who taught me that no obstacle is too large, no dream is too ambitious," I said to my father. "Isfana and I are separated by a border. I am not asking to go on an illicit adventure. I'm simply trying to overcome an obstacle to achieve my plan for our family."

My proposal was detailed, including the logistics of travel, all the safeguards for Isfana's propriety with emphasis on maintaining dignity in relationships, and the way I would handle the cultural sensitivities of being with Isfana in a foreign land. I proposed conducting the adventure in phases. "Let me go first, and then we can consider the next step of getting Isfana there. The second stage will not happen unless it is proper and agreed upon by everyone concerned in the family, including the host family where I could be attached."

When I finally finished, my father and Shahjee sat quietly. They each retreated into their own thoughts to consider my argument. It seemed like an eternity as I stood there, and finally, Shahjee cleared his throat. My father glanced up at him, and Shahjee stood up from his chair, almost theatrically. "Juzar has grown," he said, commanding our attention. "He is not a boy any longer. He is not a student. He is a doctor! He is a man! He has a destiny!"

My father stared at Shahjee intently and with bewilderment. "Your boy has grown his wings, Hasan Bhai," Shahjee continued. "It is time to let him fly. Let him loose," he wrapped up in superb Urdu.

*****

Somewhere over the east coast of Africa, the nerves began to flutter in my stomach. Not only was I descending on a continent where I had never set foot, but this was the first time I had ever traveled alone in my life. I watched the majestic landscape of Africa unfold out the window of the jetliner—the wide green plains, the dark ridges of mountains, and, finally, the sprawling metropolis of Nairobi. I looked once more at the photo in my hand. It was a snapshot of Abdul Kadir, whom I had never met and seen in person and which he had mailed to me. It was all I had to recognize the man from thousands of other people at the airport. Luckily, he was waiting at the gate when I stepped into the terminal. He gave a wide grin and welcomed me with a warm handshake. "We meet at last," he said. He seemed very excited about the whole adventure which was nice to see. He had always been supportive in his letters, but still it was a different thing to show up at a friend's house for an undetermined amount of time and bring the adventure into his kitchen. We stayed in Nairobi for the evening before making the drive back to the coast. Abdul took me out on the town. Nairobi was a sprawling, gritty, energetic city, filled with characters from all over Kenya and the continent. International businessmen strolled down the streets alongside peddlers. Sidewalk cafés were crowded with eclectic clientele, and police lingered on street corners, keeping an eye on foot traffic. Women wore vibrant-colored outfits, and traditional clothes from the countryside mingled with city fashions to create a visual mosaic.

After dinner, we went to a cinema and watched an Indian film, *Sathi*. It was wonderful; in all my years, I had seen very few Indian films. They were banned in Pakistan, and I was delighted to see the quality of the cinematography and acting. The Indians brought a unique and colorful style to the screen, more familiar than American films but much more professionally produced than the Pakistani movies I had grown up on. As we traveled around the city, I could tell that Abdul Kadir was not only excited about my adventure, but he was also excited about *me*. He seemed very proud to inform people that he was hosting a foreign doctor. In many cultures, there is a social status or prestige that comes from being a good host, and the higher the social status of the guest, the more prestige is visited upon the host. Clearly, my friend was impressed with my being a foreign doctor with dreams of the US, and he wanted to make sure others were impressed by it too, which was both flattering and a little embarrassing. It also gave me some cause for concern: who exactly was I staying with?

That night, we checked into a *musafir-khana*, a traveler's lodge of community living at the edge of downtown. A narrow room was filled with bunks which ran in long lines down the walls. Bare light bulbs dangled from the ceiling, and the room was stuffy and filled with the chatter of drifters and low-wage working men. I settled into the hard bunk and listened as the men drifted off to sleep, one by one, and fell into a loud snoring rhythm. Fear came slinking through the darkness and touched me with its cold hand. What was I doing here? Had I made the right decision? I felt incredibly vulnerable in this strange nation with no family, but I thought of Isfana and told myself over and over, *Stay the course. You're here for one very good reason, Juzar Ali.*

The next day, Abdul Kadir and I piled onto a huge bus and squeezed our way toward the back where there was still some room to stand as the rolling village lurched through traffic and then bounced down the highway toward Mombasa. Covered in luggage and packed to the gills, the bus ride was like nothing I had ever experienced. People talked loudly, laughed, and unpacked entire meals while babies wailed and children climbed over legs and crawled between feet. With every jolt, the standing passengers tumbled into one another or spilled onto the seated passengers who complained loudly, and the bus stopped constantly to drop people off, pick people up, and lash new cargo to the roof. To make the experience even more disorienting, I could barely understand a word anyone said. Even when Abdul Kadir tried to stick with English, our common language, he fell into a very quick manner of speaking in Swahili riddled with local slang, and I couldn't keep up with the group conversations at all even when they were clearly directed at me. Once more, I just smiled and tried my best, hoping they were laughing with me and not at me.

Meanwhile, out the windows, I could hardly believe what I was seeing. As we passed through this rural landscape, herds of antelope appeared in the fields and wild elephants strolled alongside the road with their huge gray bodies caked in mud. No one looked twice as we bounced past these sights, but I couldn't help remembering those maps I used to study in Karachi Grammar when I would dream of the world outside the classroom. For better or worse, here I was.

Finally, we reached Mombasa in the early evening. Two of Abdul's friends met us at the bus station, and we set off for home. "How far is it?" I asked.

"Just down the street here," Abdul replied.

Man, was it ever down the street. By the time we walked all the way through town, full darkness had descended over the countryside. We left the edge of the city behind and plunged into this darkness. This was *dark*. No streetlights guided the way as the paved road turned into a rural lane and we trudged through fields with my luggage. Houses and huts appeared occasionally with windows glowing like candles in the distance. After two more miles, a small house appeared in the midst of the darkness, little more than a shack with a single yellow light shining from the window. Once more, the cold hand of fear reached through the dark to touch me. Was that Abdul's home?

Sure enough, he exclaimed happily, "Here we are!"

Abdul's wife and children met us at the door. They were kind and welcoming although clearly curious about this foreign, big-city doctor who was staying with them. The house had one main room, and a very small side room which was normally used for storage but would now be my sleeping quarters. A small cot was erected, but when I tried to store my suitcase underneath, I discovered that is where the eggs were stored. A sheet had been strung across the entrance to offer me privacy. I took a deep breath and tried to make myself comfortable as Abdul's wife set out tea, and everyone settled in for a welcome celebration of sorts. I joined the party, presenting the small gifts I had brought for the family and talking long into the night until I was past exhausted.

Abdul walked two miles to work every day where he served as an accountant at a popular local bookseller and stationers. Of course, Abdul wanted to show me off at work, and he eagerly introduced me to his colleagues and the shop owner, Mr. Dungerwala, and his son, Moez. The Dungerwalas, like Abdul and many of the folks in this part of town, were the descendants of Indians who had come to Kenya during the days of the British Empire. These forebears had established trading hubs, and generations later, many of these Indian descendants still ran import businesses, such as this shop, which served a cultural center as much as a business. In addition to selling books, stationery, and cards, they distributed the English-language newspaper and served as a gathering place for the local community. The shop quickly became an invaluable resource for me, providing me information, news, entertainment, and, most importantly, connections throughout the Indian and Indian-Muslim community of Mombasa.

Mr. Dungerwala was a big, friendly man and not a little surprised to hear I was staying in the two-room shack with Abdul and his family. He offered me a room in his house here in town, and it was an incredibly tempting offer. The problem was I knew it would crush Abdul if I bolted his hospitality for a better offer. Despite his meager means, Abdul had been a good friend, and he was so proud to be hosting me. I politely declined Mr. Dungerwala's offer, but soon his generosity would be offered again and next time I would accept wholeheartedly.

One of my first goals was to secure a post office box at the local post office, and I immediately began writing Isfana to let her know I had arrived. Phase one of the plan was underway, but we still had to get her here too, and that would be no easy task. If my family had been skeptical, hers was downright hostile to the whole idea. What kind of family sent an unmarried daughter alone to another country to meet with a man? Like me, Isfana would need the support of her family to make the plan work. Like me, she had numerous logistical hurdles to overcome—travel visas and government documents. International trips were still uncommon for average citizens, and the government kept strict control of people's movements across borders. If there was a silver lining, it was that Isfana and I could finally contact each other directly. She and I resumed our long-distance romance through letters, and I checked my mailbox three times a day in hopes of finding her mail.

On one excursion to the post office, I found another letter waiting from my father. He included a clipping from the Karachi newspaper announcing that I had passed my exams and was officially licensed to practice medicine in Pakistan. This was a bittersweet victory for me and certainly not how I had envisioned receiving this news when I began medical school all those years ago. Instead of celebrating with family and friends, I was an exile in Africa, imagining the Pakistani military police hunting for me through the streets of Karachi.

On a practical level, however, this meant I could begin my own hunt for medical internships in the US and Canada now, which was a wonderful change of pace for me. Until now, I had very little to do aside from lingering around the bookshop, but now I could throw myself into a new project. I had to track down internship programs at the local libraries, contact hospitals and universities, and work on securing visas and permissions. These were long before the days of Google or internet databases, and here I was in a remote corner of Africa, trying to conduct this research on world-class medical programs and submit these applications.

In the meantime, one of Mr. Dungerwala's good friends announced he was going on a business trip to Pakistan. I was thrilled. This would be a chance for me to introduce someone from this very warm African community to my own family. I knew this could reassure my father greatly, and that, in turn, might offer some assurance to Isfana's family, especially her uncle, who was her guardian after her father passed away. I wrote my father and made all the arrangements for a family visit, and Mr. Dungerwala's friend was wonderful. As a traveling businessman and upstanding member of the Mombasa community, he made a strong impression. He assured my father that I had attached myself to a respectable community and there was nothing to fear, which my father then conveyed to our family and friends in India. Isfana and I kept up our relentless lobbying to convince her family that our plan could be executed without compromising the honor of our families.

Finally, after months of writing, scheming, and dreaming and after months of introducing people, providing references, and planning logistics, I received a letter from Isfana that nearly blew me away. "It is done!" she wrote. "My uncle has agreed to let come to Kenya." I blinked and read the lines again and again just to let them sink in.

She was coming.

*****

I took the bus back to Nairobi and stood in the airport waiting. After being separated for six years, I would have imagined that a day-long bus ride would be nothing, but it seemed to take forever. Then I waited for the plane to land. I waited for the passengers to deplane. I waited for Isfana to walk through that boarding gate and into the terminal. And then there she was, walking toward me with that smile that I knew so well from my dreams. She hugged me tightly, and I squeezed her back. Six years melted away like nothing. We were together again.

We walked hand in hand through the streets of Nairobi, and we talked endlessly. I had wondered if we would have anything to say to each other after so many years of writing letters. What topic hadn't we covered already? But we fell into easy conversation, and it never stopped. Isfana loved movies, and she slipped into songs from her favorite films as we walked and walked, happy to be in each other's company. While in Nairobi, we stopped at the US and Canadian consulates so Isfana could fill out the same applications which I had already completed. We wanted to be ready if we got a chance to go. That evening, we checked into adjoining community lodges for men and women, and once more, I could barely sleep. This time, however, it wasn't the crowded conditions and fear that kept me awake; it was knowing that Isfana was so close and I would see her again as soon as the sun rose. I could hardly wait that long.

Back in Mombasa, we got her settled in with a nice local family, and I introduced her to everyone that I had met so far. It was a warm welcome for her, and there was a great enthusiasm bordering between curiosity and gossip at times about our adventure and our wedding, which we now began planning in earnest. The local priest was initially awestruck at our plan, then very respectful at our intentions and methodology and then amused at our enthusiasm.

Under the most normal of circumstances, a wedding is an important event, linking two people and numerous families. The social and religious aspects must be carefully navigated. The ceremony and celebrations are planned with great care and attention. In this case, I felt even more pressure. I wanted to do everything exactly right to make sure that no one had any grounds to question our relationship or cast doubts on Isfana's character. Today, these kinds of improvised events are more common as families have spread over many continents and travel has become far easier, but at the time, conservative traditions were the norm and were strongly enforced within families. Here we were having a destination wedding before there was such a thing as a destination wedding was prevalent!

We set a date with the local priest and issued invitations to our families. We knew that it would be difficult for people to attend with all the restrictions on travel, and we prepared for a very small wedding. Still, our event became the talk of the town as people around Mombasa heard of our crazy adventure to be married abroad. Isfana's uncle refused to attend the wedding but sent her younger brother, Iloo Bhai, to come and give the bride away during the ceremony. My parents also secured all the ridiculous paperwork and travel documents and arrived soon after. By now, the Dungerwala family had taken us fully under his wing, and he was kind enough to host the entire wedding party in his spacious home. Isfana and I were ecstatic.

This was not going to be one of the grand affairs we had known in India or in Pakistan with dozens of relatives and friends and hundreds of guests, but some of our most important people were gathering. Our dreams were coming true. There was just one problem now: my father. Now that he was here, he suddenly seemed to realize that this was really happening. This wasn't just a harebrained idea he was entertaining for one of his children; this was about to be the wedding of his only son.

"We need to celebrate," he announced.

"We are celebrating," I replied.

"No, we need to *celebrate*," he said with flourish of hand gestures. "We must have guests and a proper wedding feast."

"What guests?" I asked. "We only know a few people here."

"I will print one hundred fifty invitations," my father replied. Clearly, he had already made up his mind before we even began the conversation.

"All right," I said, smiling at his newfound enthusiasm. I had no idea who would receive these one hundred fifty invitations, but I was certain they wouldn't go to waste.

Mr. Dungerwala printed them at the bookstore, and we passed out clutches of invitations to the people that we knew. "Please invite your friends," I told Abdul Kadir and his coworkers. The Dungerwalas, of course, were offered numerous invitations, and they spread the word too. We had the hottest ticket in town, and strangers met me on the street with big smiles. "I'll see you at your wedding!" We might not know our guests, but we were doing it right. We were the talk of the town, some in awe of what we were up to, some in amusement, and some enjoying the gossip that always accompanies such a situation.

I wasn't quite sure how I felt about being married in front of strangers, but I was looking forward to my big day. I couldn't wait to be wed to Isfana. Our life would begin together, and no one would be able to separate us again.

On the day of our wedding, the sun rose into a hot, clear sky over Mombasa, and I nervously began my preparations, dressing in traditional wedding garb. I wore a sherwani, the long tunic, and a *feta* upon my head. I would not see Isfana again until our ceremony. When the hour arrived, we went to the mosque where all our friends, family, and new neighbors were gathered. It was a beautiful mosque in the historic district of town along the seashore. It was strange to see so many unfamiliar faces at my own event, but there was a joyous energy in the room which immediately set me at ease. Weddings might be very formal and reserved by nature, but people still shared in the thrill of the occasion. My family and I processed to the front of the ceremony, and that's when I got my first look at Isfana in her wedding garb. She was stunning—so slender and beautiful, wearing a bright red sari which intensified her dark hair and eyes. Her hands were painted with henna, and she was adorned in gold jewelry. She took my breath away.

Ours was a traditional ceremony, and the *nikah* began with Isfana sitting on her prayer mat behind the beautiful curtain, just as my sister had sat so many years ago when I first fell in love with Isfana. It was hard to believe it was all happening again, only I was the one being married this time. The official read from the Holy Koran and led prayers for the blessing of the couple. He delivered a short sermon where he couldn't help acknowledging our unique circumstances and how well our families had done under these strange conditions. Then he turned to the two men before him: Iloo Bhai and me. "Do you freely give your sister to this man, Juzar Ali?" the priest asked.

"I do," Isfana's brother replied.

"And do you agree to accept this responsibility?" the priest asked me.

"I do."

The *mehr* was given—a small jeweled sculpture. The *nikah nama* was signed. We were married. The priest would be referring to this unconventional process we had adopted yet sticking to a traditional wedding according to Islamic tenets in his future sermons. We were the talk of the town. The wedding feast was a grand occasion. My father had done very well. We had chicken on the menu, and this was considered top class then in that society. We enjoyed ourselves immensely, but I couldn't help noticing that my father was a little under the weather. His jubilant mood was somewhat subdued although his pride still shone through. He had thrown a wonderful wedding for his son miles away from his hometown where this man of societal impact in his own land knew only a handful few. But he was not saying anything. It wasn't just a lack of words, for he could be a man of contemplative moods. It was his mannerisms and mood and nonverbal language that gave me pause. Something seemed amiss. *It's probably nothing*, I thought as I rejoined the celebration.

CHAPTER 16

Letters from America

Isfana and I were in heaven. At last, we were married. Not only were we living in the same country for the first time, we were also living beneath the same roof. We spent time visiting with new friends as we basked in the first days of our new married life. Soon, however, people began returning to their respective homes. Isfana's brother and Mom returned to India. My father still wasn't feeling one hundred percent, but he decided it was time for him and my mother to continue their journey as well. As long as they were out of Pakistan with all their hard-earned travel papers, they were going to make the pilgrimage to Iraq and Mecca; it was another one my father's life goals, right there alongside seeing his only son get married.

Isfana and I escorted them to the airport and said our emotional goodbyes. My dad was not much of showing and soft emotions. "Good luck and God's blessings for you both," my father said before he turned and climbed onto the jetliner. Then Isfana and I turned and looked at each other as we stood in this international terminal. *Now what?* We were thrilled to finally have our life together, but this was not exactly how we imagined it. We couldn't just climb onto a jetliner ourselves. Technically, I was AWOL from my military conscription in Pakistan. We couldn't return to India because our two governments still had a travel ban. We had no prospects in any other country right now. In many ways, we were stranded here in Africa. "Let's go for a walk," Isfana said brightly, as if she were reading my mind and knew I needed a pleasant distraction.

As long as we were in Nairobi, we would take a stroll through the bustling city, holding hands and window-shopping as we dreamed our future and planned our next moves. As always, Isfana was enchanting company with her sing-alongs and her quick laugh. If I was feeling pensive about our current predicament, she was feeling thrilled by the adventure and up for the challenge. We had already submitted visa applications for the US and Canada. All we could do now was wait. "And work," I said and Isfana agreed. We were determined to put our hard-won skills to good use here in Kenya. "We did not become doctors just to sit on our hands," she said, and she was right.

We took a small room in a house in Mombasa. It was all we could afford. It came with breakfast, but it was only for the evenings, so by day, we packed our belongings back into a suitcase and left the house. We stashed our suitcases at the bookstore with Abdul and walked to Mombasa General Hospital where we waited to speak with the director. "We would like to work," I told him when we were finally admitted after hours of waiting.

"We cannot hire any more doctors," he replied quickly.

"We will work for free," Isfana countered. "We will volunteer wherever you need assistance."

He looked up at us, and I could only imagine what he thought as he examined the two skinny young foreigners who had wandered in off the street with no introductions. "I'm afraid my hands are tied," he said as he leaned back in his chair. "I cannot let you work, not even volunteer, without permission from the Ministry of Health. You must have work papers."

Once more, we took the rollicking bus ride to Nairobi. The ministry building was miles from the bus stop, and we drifted past countless cafés, restaurants, and hot food stands as we made our hungry way to the office. The whole world seems made of food when you're hungry and penniless.

Once more, we announced ourselves and waited for hours. The health secretary whom we needed to meet had his secretary who tried to turn us away, but one thing I had become skilled at over the years was strategic perseverance as I tried to weasel my way through bureaucracies with a smile and a sense of determination. I had learned from the best: my father.

"The health secretary's schedule is full today."

"We don't mind waiting, just in case there is a free moment between appointments."

"He does not see people without appointments."

"May I make an appointment now? These are our résumés."

We made ourselves kindly, benign presences and waited. And waited. And waited. People went in and out of the office, casting curious looks our way. Isfana and I sat there with our stomachs grumbling until, finally, the secretary announced, "He will see you."

We jumped to our feet and entered his office. The health secretary seemed very busy handling several people inside his office already. He was a lean but fit-looking man, wearing a sharp suit and leaning back in a leather chair behind his massive mahogany desk. He was surrounded by his entourage of cronies who all smirked as Isfana and I walked up to the desk.

"What brings you to my office?" the minister asked.

"We are doctors," I began to explain.

"I know who you are," he replied. His secretary must have passed along our résumés.

"We would like to work in Kenya."

The minister leaned his big head back and laughed. "You stroll in here and want me to issue you work visas?" His cronies burst out laughing at this.

"We only need permission to volunteer," Isfana said, ignoring the insult. We explained our situation, how we were simply waiting to be accepted to internships and wanted to work in the meantime. We did not need complicated visas to do what we were asking. We simply wanted permission to work at Coast General Hospital, and we wanted to help people there while we waited for our US and Canada visas. The minister listened as we made our case. He looked at us with skeptical eyes, but slowly a smile formed on his face. "You guys are nuts," he finally said. I could sense him thinking, *Why? why?* I was becoming used to this accusation by now. It seemed everywhere I went these days, I was off the beaten path, trying to do things differently, often the more difficult way. People didn't seem to appreciate others who worked outside the firmly established routines or norms. Perhaps they felt it compromised their authority in some way if someone came along and tried to do something outside their system, but they often seemed to relent when they realized our intentions were true. As we would learn many times over in the future, when Isfana and I confronted an issue head-on, somehow, we seemed to break barriers.

To our surprise, especially after the initial reaction, he agreed to give us permission. The minister acted bored as he signed the papers and sent us from his office.

"Enjoy your stay in Africa," he said.

*****

Mombasa General Hospital was a small regional medical facility housed in a concrete building built like a square wedding cake. Despite the relative newness of the facility, it was still equipped with old and rudimentary equipment, from the World War II-era gurneys to the very basic EKG machines. The doctors and nurses who worked there, however, were a passionate group, made up of Christian missionaries, foreign medical workers, and local physicians and nurses. Their mission largely consisted of dealing with the effects of crippling poverty. Being a small city surrounded by very rural—and very economically disadvantaged—landscape, the hospital became ground zero for malnutrition, smallpox, tuberculosis, poisonous snakebites, farm accidents such as impalements and severed toes, and mining accidents such as mangled hands and crushed legs. Since the hospital was often a daylong journey or more for people, minor wounds and illnesses were often, unfortunately, left to fester into much more serious conditions.

On a happier note, it was also where most local babies were born.

With our lack of experience and complete deficiency in Swahili, the primary local language, Isfana and I were a bit like square pegs trying to help in a hospital full of round holes. The administrators tried to find very selective roles for us. They sent Isfana to the urology department, but it was such a limited assignment—mostly checking vitals, inserting catheters, and the like. It was work, but it soon became extremely repetitive and dull. I landed in the orthopedics department where I spent my days wrapping patients' arms and legs in casts and plaster wraps. It, too, became very boring after a short while.

In the meantime, we were called in for an interview at the Canadian embassy. After a long meeting, they promised to review our visa applications, and it looked quite promising. That was incredibly encouraging news for us. We felt a little less stranded and desperate just knowing that there was some progress in our goals. Isfana decided that she would stop volunteering at the hospital to focus on her US exams. She would also need those credentials to work in Canada.

I had already taken my foreign qualifying exam in Pakistan, so I returned to the hospital but asked for a new assignment outside orthopedics. They had a great need for skilled help, but they thought long and hard about where else to place a doctor who spoke not one word of Swahili. Finally, we found the perfect fit for me: the obstetrics delivery room. The reason would soon be obvious.

Most of the women who came through our doors had never visited for prenatal care, had never arranged to see a doctor, and had never informed anyone outside their village that they were pregnant. They simply showed up at the emergency room in the full throes of labor, and we had to whisk them off to birthing tables. It was often a chaotic but thrilling environment as nurses swirled around the expectant mother and we raced the medical staffs into place. As any expectant mother can tell you, every pregnancy is slightly different, and every delivery is too. There are a million variables, from the size of the baby to the health of the mother. Some deliveries proceed smoothly, and some require more serious interventions. These variables made the delivery room a fascinating place to work, and for the most part, it was a joyous environment too. I quickly learned one important Swahili word: *sukuma*. Push. And that was the only Swahili word that I needed to know!

Sukuma! Sukuma! Or *no sukuma!* I would shout as the women battled bravely and often loudly through their contractions. I monitored the medical progress of the delivery, and the nurses translated important information from the patient—any abnormal pain, fatigue, or other factors that might need to be addressed. I delivered dozens of babies like this, and it was a wonderful feeling to lay a new infant in a mother's arms. I soon became a valuable member of the OB-GYN team then headed by the MD from the Loyola School in Chicago, and she proved a good reference for me.

It was not all joy, however. The cruel hand of poverty often struck at the most vulnerable people in a population, including the unborn and new mothers. Malnourishment, coinfections, eclampsia, and hypertension were, unfortunately, common, and I delivered heartbreak as well: stillborn babies and infants so sick they didn't last more than a few hours. We managed to save most of our mothers when they suffered complications, such as hemorrhaging or amniotic embolisms, but we also lost mothers to killers like sepsis, puerperal fever, or preexisting heart conditions. At times, we had to do Caesarean sections, and with the help of my senior resident doctor, I became a very good first assistant. That led to my being then asked to cover for him and especially at night and then I was the main surgeon! That was an exhilarating experience that sends shivers to this day when I think of it.

Our stay in Kenya was a mixture of romance and excitement on one hand and the reality of the situation on the other. It was not only a destination to arrange a union of bliss among ourselves but also a stark reminder of the challenges people face around the world, including us currently. After months of living and working and forming our married synergy, Isfana and I received two simultaneous pieces of news, one good and one bad. The Canadian embassy informed us we were in line to be approved. We soon would be free to travel to the country to seek medical residencies, work, and even citizenship! Isfana and I were overjoyed to receive this news, but our excitement was cut short by the arrival of a letter from home just days later. My father had grown gravely ill. Unbeknownst to us, his condition had never improved since our wedding day, when I had seen him subdued. He had, in fact, grown worse. His health was now deteriorating at a more alarming rate, and my family was worried that he was looking at the end of his days. As I read these words over and over, all the joy was sucked out of me. Just moments ago, I had been on cloud nine. Now I felt the whoosh of a plummet. I was falling into despair. *My father…*

*****

Two family friends met us at the airport in Karachi as Isfana and I stepped onto Pakistani soil with all our belongings packed into two suitcases. I was home again—with my wife. We had made hasty arrangements to secure travel visas and a Pakistani passport for Isfana as we both concluded that our returning to Pakistan was what was needed and what we wanted. The time and situation dictated that decision. My medical school friends in Karachi had helped me secure government permission to return without penalty. The military conscriptions had proved to be so wildly unpopular that the government had abandoned any pretense of enforcing them aggressively and offered waivers to prevent their skilled graduates from fleeing the country in even greater numbers.

The small victory was a hollow one for me, however, as I stepped into the terminal and saw the looks on the faces of my father's friends. They greeted me warmly, but the concern was clear in their eyes. "Take me to him," I said.

In the car, on the way to the hospital, they warned me not to be alarmed when I saw him. "He is weak," Munawwar said.

"His color is off," Iqbal added.

My father had contracted hepatitis during his travels. The disease would have been in its infancy during the wedding in Kenya, and it slowly took root as my father traveled to Saudi Arabia, to Riyadh and Mecca, and Karbala and home again. It pained me to think it had been right under my nose and I hadn't noticed in time to prescribe more preventative care. By now, the cascading health effects were beginning to ravage his body, the worst of which was cirrhosis of the liver and its complications. In those days, this was a death sentence.

Sure enough, he looked ill. He appeared tiny in his hospital bed, stick thin, and his skin was a dark shade of yellow. The strong-willed man who had been the bedrock of our family, who had dominated my imagination for so long, who had overcome so many obstacles in his life was now wasting away in a hospital bed, and it nearly broke my heart to see him. "Juku," he said when I stepped into the room.

"Hello, Daddy."

Instead of revealing my strong emotions, I leaned upon my training. "How do you feel?" I asked, calculating his pulse rate. I checked his vital signs and asked about his urine output.

"It's good to have you home," my father said with a smile.

Isfana and I sat with him for a while before we went home to the bungalow to unpack and settle into our new room. I had to admit, it was a very nice feeling to know we had a permanent room in this house. We wouldn't have to abandon our quarters by seven o'clock in the morning and shuttle all our belongings around the city until evening as we had had to do in Mombasa.

The next day, we returned to the hospital. Three of my med school classmates worked in the hospital, and they were taking the lead on my father's care, making sure he had everything they could offer him. I was glad to see them and introduced my new wife as we greeted each other warmly. "Your father's responding well to treatment," Munawar said. "He'll be able to return home soon."

Dad was on a diuretic, an ammonia reducer and a beta blocker. The long-term prognosis was still grim, but in the short term, he appeared to be doing well. "He will be much happier in his own house," my friend Iqbal said.

"You can say that again," I replied with a laugh. Everyone knew how much my father loved his bungalow, including his doctors and nurses. It was one of the great prides and joys of his life, and he would love nothing more than to be installed on the porch, sipping tea with his buddies and neighborhood friends with whom he could discuss politics.

After a few more days, his wish was granted, and my father moved back home. Isfana and I spent time with the family, and I showed her around Karachi, including Elphinstone Street where we stopped in to visit with Tahir Bhai and Maulvi Saab and the rest of the gang at the shop. They were excited to see us, but it was a bittersweet reunion for me. After spending so many months away from Karachi, it was suddenly clear to me just how much the shop had declined over the recent years. Instead of the bustling pharmacy that I knew from my childhood, this was a dusty, lethargic place. Many of the shelves were half empty, there were very few prescriptions waiting to be picked up, and the window displays, which I once took such pride in, were disheveled and sun-faded, as if no one had changed them in a while. "How's business?" I asked Tahir Bhai and Maulvi Saab.

He shrugged and raised his hands, palms up. "So-so," he replied. "Without your father, we can't get a lot of the specialty items. Many of the old clients do not come around anymore."

"I'll be back at work this week," I told him.

"Excellent!" Maulvi Saab replied. "We look forward to your return."

Isfana and I visited for a while and then continued the grand tour of Karachi.

Within a few weeks, we were settling into our new life. We didn't have much, but we had a stable roof over our heads and medical school connections all over the city. Isfana found a proper internship in psychiatry, and I found one in general medicine. I worked part-time at the shop again, and my father was stable and enjoying his time at home. Things were okay.

That's when my imagination started drifting overseas once more. I had put my North American dreams on hold for now, but they still burned bright in my mind's eye. I knew my deepest ambitions still lay there. I still knew that America was a land of opportunity, and it offered a combination of skills and prestige that would blow open doors for me here in Pakistan. I knew it was important to be here with my family, but I also knew that my destiny was larger than this, no matter the obstacles. My father himself had shown me this. He had spent years of his life helping create this destiny for me.

The next morning, I went to the US consulate and began researching medical residency programs in the United States. The library kept a "Green Book" which listed the medical programs. It was probably as fat as New York phone book and provided details on thousands of programs across America. I selected them in a hierarchy of competitiveness. Ivy League schools at the top, followed by other internationally prestigious programs: Johns Hopkins, Stanford, University of Pennsylvania. Next, I selected my tier two options and, finally, my tier three. I spread my selections geographically across the entire country—from Hawaii and Alaska to New York and Florida.

In many ways, this was a roll of the dice, so I spread my bets evenly across the board in hopes that Lady Luck would smile upon me. Then I bought one hundred aerograms, and slowly, over the next weeks, I mailed one hundred letters to introduce myself, along with one hundred requests for information and applications. One hundred aerograms, filled with my dreams, crisscrossed the planet for weeks, and finally, the responses began to trickle back in on the breeze: letters from Sloan Kettering and the Mayo Clinic, applications from medical centers like the Cleveland Clinic or Touro in New Orleans. In all, twenty programs replied to my inquiries, and now I had twenty full applications to complete. As always, it was a long shot, especially since I had no way to present myself for the typical interviews, but I went to work, diligently completing the forms, essays, and replies. There was no way to succeed if I didn't even try. These correspondences kept my spirits up through the months even as my father's fortunes rose and fell with his health.

He was in and out of the hospital frequently. He would be fine for a few weeks, and then a cold would send shock waves through him and return him to emergency treatments. It was a matter of trying to manage the condition during my father's inevitable slide toward death. "He has a lot of life yet," my good friend Iqbal kept telling me as we hunkered in hospital hallways to examine my father's latest test results or discuss his symptoms.

Then one day, Iqbal came to me with some different exciting news: "I have an interview!" he said. "With a hospital in Chicago."

"That's excellent!" I replied. "Congratulations!" Iqbal and I had worked hard together through medical school and beyond, and it was wonderful to see him get this opportunity.

"There's one problem," he said. "I don't speak English that well and am anxious."

"I will help you."

We spent the next week studying English vocabulary and usage, but it was true that Iqbal spoke very little of the language. "It's no use," he said one night as we sat in a break room of the hospital going over vocabulary. "I'm going to embarrass myself."

"You can do this," I replied. "I'll be right there to help you. I'll give you the words you need if you forget them."

On the day of the long-distance meeting, Iqbal and I gathered at his home and attempted to place the long-distance call to Chicago. We gave ourselves plenty of time; making an overseas call felt like it required an act of congress. We had to go through level upon level of operator, receive permissions and connections to intermediary operators in far-flung nations as our call made its way slowly through the wires and connections which ran over nations, crossed borders, snaked beneath oceans, and finally joined Pakistan to the United States.

When we were connected, Iqbal began his interview. He was knowledgeable and enthusiastic, but very quickly he began to struggle with the nuances of the American English language. Most of the time I was able to guide and prompt him to ask questions and answer as appropriate. The interviewers understood that I was present to help Iqbal with his English, and at moments, I simply leaned in to attest to his work ethic, his skill as a physician, and his admirable qualities as a human being. All these things were true, and I did my best to convey them to this invisible panel of interviewers on the other end of the phone line. When the interview ended, Iqbal and I had no idea if it was a success or not, but within weeks, he had received confirmation. "I'm in!" he said, waving his letter of acceptance.

"You're going to the United States," I said, giving him a warm handshake.

"You're going too," he replied. "You just don't know it yet."

I hoped he was correct, but I had received nothing but rejections so far from my applications. Either that or the deafening silence of indifference. But really, what was I hoping for? Could I even leave Pakistan now with my father in such poor health?

From the second-floor window of the bungalow, I tracked the postman as he made his rounds through the neighborhood. The bell on his mail cart rang out, and I could place him from blocks away and track his progress toward our house. Months earlier, I had waited impatiently for letter from Isfana. Now I waited impatiently for letters from America.

For some of the applications, I had used the shop address also, so there, too, I waited on the mailman to make his rounds down Elphinstone Street. The route the postman took through the lanes was familiar, and I knew exactly when and where he would appear. Delivering the mail was a very social occupation, however, and it took an agonizingly long time for the postman to have his conversations, to accept his cups of tea, and to finally turn the corner onto our street. I could tell by the angle he took that he had something to drop off.

"Salam, Dr. Saheb," he said as he strode up to the front of the shop in his belabored fashion. He liked to give the impression that it was a wearying job, and he could use all the fortification and rest stops he could get. "Here you are," he said, handing me a small stack of mail. Right there on top I could see a letter from America. By now Tahir Bhai and Maulvi Saheb knew exactly what I was waiting for, and they seemed equally enthused. My pulse quickened when I saw it was from the National Resident Matching program. I knew not to get my hopes up too high as I looked at the letter. But still.

As soon as I was alone, I opened the envelope, read the documents, and jumped in joy. Lady Luck had shined on me after all. I had been matched with Touro Infirmary in New Orleans as part of the Touro-Tulane University program in New Orleans. Tulane had not been one of my top choices, but they operated a good teaching hospital. The committee at Touro was impressed enough by my application that they weren't even asking for an interview. They were offering me a residency. I just could not believe this. It was not unprecedented in those days, but for me it was a game changer.

My father was back in the hospital, and I stopped to visit him after my shift ended. "What's the news?" he asked. "Any word from your American hospitals?" He kept track of my applications the way a sports enthusiast follows the scores of his favorite cricket team. I couldn't help smiling even as I debated telling him.

"I've been accepted," I finally said. "They want me to go to New Orleans."

"New Orleans!" he exclaimed. He had no clue where that was except that it was far away in America. My own knowledge of New Orleans was slim. Something about music and jazz. My father was not a Western music fan, but he was thrilled about the residency.

"But, Dad," I said, "how can I leave now? I can't leave you." I looked at my mother. She was a rock of strength. She was dealing with her sick husband and still managing to support the dreams of her son.

Any son would be hard-pressed to leave his father in this condition, but in Pakistan, the pressures were even more intense. It was not only customary for sons to stay near the family in the best of circumstances, but it was the moral and ethical thing to do. It would be something like sacrilege to leave now. My father sat quietly for a moment in his bed, and then he said to me, "You are going. This is your dream. This is my dream for you."

"But what about…"

"You are going," my father said, "and I'll be fine. You go."

CHAPTER 17

That's Not How It Works Here

Wednesday, June 4, 1975. That's the day I finally laid eyes on the United States of America. The jetliner approached New York City from the Atlantic, and the wide expanse of blue ocean came to an end at this magical island where skyscrapers rose up and glittered in the sunshine. After all the dreaming, all the work, all the years I had spent trying to achieve this moment, it was hard to believe I was finally here. I stared out the small round window filled with joy, curiosity, and apprehension. Such a strange combination of emotions, but not completely foreign to me. I had felt something similar as a boy on my train ride to Murree and the Presentation Convent School. I had felt it standing outside the prestigious gates of Karachi Grammar School and on my first day of medical school. Now I felt it once more, only it seemed to have grown in scale to be like these high-rise buildings and this huge nation.

When the plane landed, I retrieved my belongings from the overhead bin, including a heavy winter coat. Having no idea what to expect from American weather, my father and his friends had alarmed me into preparing for icy, subzero temperatures and unpredictable storm fronts. Before the plane even reached the gate, I could tell how over prepared I was as I watched the runway marshals and baggage workers stand outside in the heat wearing sweat-stained short sleeves. I had to laugh and wonder what else I was about to learn about America.

Banu Bahen, a cousin from my mother's side of the family who lived in Queens, picked me up from the airport. She and her husband, Shabbir Bhai, were the pioneers of the American dream and migration. She couldn't help teasing me even as she welcomed me to New York. "Good thing you brought your jacket," she said as we stood in the eighty-five-degree heat. "You never know when a blizzard might hit."

She drove me back to her apartment in Queens. The neighborhood looked a little rough and tumble, but her apartment was very nice. It was smaller than I expected, but it had a doorman at the ground floor who kept an eye on the place. I had one month to get acclimated to the United States before my residency started, and I planned to spend some time here with my cousin and some time with my friends from medical school who were in Chicago for their own residencies. They would come to pick me up in a car for an American road trip. I had one week to explore before they arrived.

My cousin and her husband invited some other Pakistani friends over for dinner to introduce me to some people and help make me feel comfortable. They brought a carryout pizza with them, and we sat around the living eating a very casual meal. Even more than the skyscrapers, this pizza seemed alien to me. I had been in large cities before, but I had never been anywhere where people carried food out of restaurants and then sat on sofas to eat. Everyone else seemed very comfortable with the arrangement, so I tried to relax and keep my large slice of pizza from spilling as I pulled at the amazing layers of cheese. What was this thing? Again, I was familiar with pizza, but I had never seen anything quite like this—the size of the slice and the myriad toppings baked into the mozzarella. It was delicious.

After another day of entertaining me, my cousin and her husband returned to work, leaving me to explore on my own. What I found most fascinating wasn't the typical New York City attractions, not the Empire State Building or the Statue of Liberty, however impressive they might be. Instead, I was riveted to daytime television. The game shows, soap operas, and even the children's programming were incredible. *The Price Is Right. General Hospital. Sesame Street.* These were fascinating peepholes into American culture. Rather than venture to museums, I could spend half a day just exploring TV channels. I would walk down the street, investigating the small shops in the neighborhood. They seemed familiar in style, but businesses themselves were so different. Beauty parlors and racks of fashion magazines. Music shops full of rock and roll posters. American clothing styles that hung in window displays.

Even the tiny bathroom in my cousin's apartment seemed to hold elements of interest at that time. What were all these things for? Magnifying mirrors and mysterious bottles of lotions, powders, rinses, and colorful liquids. American tubes of toothpaste, ointments, and conditioners. And Q-tips? What on earth did the average citizen do with something like this? Just wait until Isfana saw all these things; she too would be amazed, I was sure. She would be arriving in a few months, and I was excited to see her again. These were days when the world seemed like a huge place and distances felt very far indeed. Cultures were more foreign and unique. Isfana felt much too far away right now, but our world was brimming with possibilities, especially with our first child on the way. I couldn't wait for her to arrive.

But first, I needed a bath. The hardest thing to get used to was having the toilet featured prominently in this compact space. In Pakistan, the toilet would be in the water closet, or WC, far removed from the bathroom, which was typically a large tiled room with little more than a couple water spigots and a big drain in the center of the room. Buckets and washcloths were nice options for a more robust scrubbing. Alone in my cousin's apartment, I was determined to take advantage of the privacy to relax and bathe. Despite the cramped quarters, it did seem luxurious to have a shower and bathtub built into the same unit, and I took advantage of both as I scrubbed and sang and prepared myself to go out and see more of the city. There was just one thing I hadn't yet noticed: the lack of a drain in the bathroom floor. This was such a ubiquitous feature of bathrooms back home that I never even imagined that a person was supposed to keep all the water inside the bathtub or the sink. Scrubbing was a messy, soapy, flailing business after all. Only when the doorbell began to ring frantically did it occur to me that anything was wrong. That's when I noticed the inch or so of water just standing on the tile floor.

I dressed quickly and answered the door. It was the superintendent of the building, and he wanted to know if any pipes had broken in the apartment.

"Pipes? No, I don't believe so," I replied.

"Well, something happened," he replied. Water is pouring into the apartment beneath you."

"Oh, it is?"

"Yes, may I please check your bathroom?"

"Do you need to check right now?" I inquired.

"Yes, immediately. Water damage is a serious business."

He was not impressed by what he found in the bathroom— soap and water everywhere, standing on the floor, leaking into the walls. He turned and gave me an incredulous look. "What the hell were you thinking?"

I just shrugged and smiled with a lot of embarrassment. "May I offer my sincere apologies?"

"Offer away, buddy, but also clean up this mess and don't do it again," he snarled back.

A week later, my medical school friends arrived to whisk me away on my first road trip. I thanked my cousin and apologized once more for all the trouble and then packed myself and my luggage into the old Chevy Impala, and we rode off. Once more, I was struck not so much by the scenery as I was by the actual road. I had never seen a highway like this. Four paved lanes were raised onto higher ground as they wound smoothly through the city and into the countryside. To get on and off the highway, people used these well-designed entrances and exit ramps. The architecture of highway bridges was immense and impressive. And infrastructure which had sprung up along these highways was just amazing. You could pull off nearly anywhere and find a gas station, convenience store, a restaurant, a motel, or all these things right beside the road. This nation was clearly built to span great distances and its people traveled well.

We drove to Niagara Falls, which was beautiful. I had never seen a waterfall so huge and majestic, and we enjoyed learning the local history too. My friends wanted to visit the Canadian side of the falls, but we were all afraid of complications crossing the international border with our visas. Despite any assurances, we were all accustomed to the agonizing whims of Pakistani bureaucracy and could not bring ourselves to take the risk. After a few hours, we piled back into the car and drove on.

We took a scenic route to Chicago, driving through lovely countryside and exploring smaller cities and towns along the way: Buffalo, Cleveland, Ann Arbor, Grand Rapids, South Bend, and more. We were on a very tight budget and did our best to avoid staying in hotels by taking turns sleeping in the back seat. With four of us, we could easily ride three across in the front seat and let one person stretch out and sleep in the back in two or three-hour shifts. Back home, it wasn't uncommon at all for men to show physical displays of friendship such as holding hands or hugging, so it seemed perfectly natural to find ourselves squeezed into the small front seat and singing songs from Pakistan. Clearly, this was not a typical sight on the American highway as we noticed people staring, laughing, or even glaring at us three men squeezed into the front seat of the car as they passed by. Now I know what they must have been thinking then. Then I did not realize that the cultural norms were so different.

We spent a fun week in Chicago, enjoying the food and camaraderie with my friends. Together, we tried to make sense of American sports like baseball or basketball, but they seemed utterly strange to me, nothing like the high drama and thrill of the cricket pitch. Finally, it was time to say goodbye and head south to settle in and begin my residency. It was sad and exciting at the same time. For the first time, I would be on my own in this country with no family or friends, but this is why I had come here, and I looked forward to joining my program. After many thanks and an emotional goodbye, I boarded the plane and took off for New Orleans.

On the plane, I chatted with a passenger next to me. She was intrigued to know my background and the purpose of my travel to New Orleans. I had done my homework too and talked about Mardi Gras and the use of the local word *lagniappe*. She was impressed and offered me a ride downtown from the airport. I was impressed too and very grateful.

New Orleans is a magical city, but my first impressions were fleeting at best as I went straight into my residency program. I noticed the beautiful uptown mansions and the streetcar which rumbled beneath the live oaks lining St. Charles Avenue. It was hard to miss the corner bars and sounds of music which drifted from those doorways. But my days of sightseeing were behind me for the moment as I turned my focus to medicine once more and tried to grasp the immense differences between the Pakistani and American systems. For years, I had caught glimpses of the American system through films or television shows like *Marcus Welby, M.D.* or *Doctor Kildare.* The hospital setting itself felt vaguely familiar with its nursing stations and specialized units filled with uniformed personnel. Aside from that, everything was different. The organizational structure, the technology, the terminology, and everything. From the first session of orientation, my head was spinning as I tried to understand what was being said or described. My first assignment didn't help calm my nerves any. Right out of the gate, I was placed with the CCU or coronary care unit on July 1 and was scheduled to be on-call that very day. This is what happens, I guess, if your last name starts with the first letter of the alphabet. This was a serious assignment, treating life-threatening conditions, such as heart failure, myocardial infarctions (heart attacks), coronary heart disease, and more. My background was in general medicine, not as a heart specialist. My hands literally started shaking as I thought about trying to save someone's life under these circumstances, completely unfamiliar with the medical equipment and feeling so bewildered by the environment.

On my first day, I walked into the unit and looked up at the eight heart monitors that were each recording patients' heart rhythms—one monitor for each room on the unit. My first thought was, *Juzar Ali, you are in trouble.* I mumble to myself periodically. Back in Pakistan at this time, it took a special application to the Health Ministry to get hold of a heart monitor and run an electrocardiogram (EKG) on a patient in the civil hospital, so very few doctors had ever used one of these machines. I had never actually seen one up close, and here I was responsible for eight patients! I didn't know how they operated or how to read the results or spot the arrhythmias that would require immediate medical attention. I knew the basic theory well enough and could rattle off the names of arrhythmias and the responses they each required, but in practice, I couldn't always tell what I was looking at. I was in trouble. I turned around and marched myself directly to the head of the cardiology department.

"I cannot do this," I announced.

The head of cardiology was an Indian American named Dr. Dhurandhar who possessed an oversized personality, complete with a wide smile which he gave me now as he leaned back in his desk chair and listened to my concerns. He had confidence in spades, which was evident in his voice that often seemed to boom through the halls or break into an unmistakable laugh. Right now, he said, "Ali, come with me."

I felt comforted by his Indian accent; Dr. Dhurandhar was an immigrant to the US and has spent time in the UK and Canada before arriving here and rising to his respected position. His reputation was of a tough taskmaster with a no-nonsense style, but with a very soft heart. I felt I could relate to him, and indeed, he took me under his wing and, in fact, continued to help me many times over the years. We walked back to the cardiology unit, and he sat me down with the head nurse.

"This is Dr. Ali," he told her, making the introduction. "I want you to teach him everything you know. Until then, he will live, eat, and sleep in this place."

This was an incredibly humbling experience for me and the first of many difficult lessons I would learn here. Back in Pakistan, doctors were treated like gods, and so they acted like gods even when they weren't completely sure of themselves. Never, *ever*, would a doctor follow a nurse around taking notes and lessons. My outward dignity was damaged by this entire exchange, but I realized immediately that I was going to have to change my way of thinking to succeed here and welcomed any way I could learn. I would be in this department for a one-month rotation, and I needed to learn everything I possibly could in that time. I thankfully accepted the head nurse's assistance, and so we began. She showed me how to operate the monitors and how to read the results and identify the rhythms. She showed me the equipment and procedures used to respond to everything from fever to full-on heart failure. As we made the rounds, she showed me how to make specific orders for patients, whether it was testing, treatments, or other medical interventions. Technically, her job was to follow my orders, but she was the one dictating the orders to me so that she could then fulfill them. We had a laugh about that. Once word got around that I was an eager pupil, the other nurses on the unit also pitched in with my education. So in addition to the senior residents who guided me, I had this wonderful team of nurses helping too. To consider the nursing team as a partner, if not a teacher, was truly an eye-opener for me.

Not everything went smoothly, however. One night, I was in my on-call room when I received a phone call from the mental health unit on the eighth floor of the hospital. One of the nurses in my unit needed orders to treat a patient for some pain, fever, and inflammation. I was on call, so I knew to expect middle-of-the-night phone calls and questions like this. Sometimes, they were more serious situations that required immediate attention, and sometimes they were minor predicaments such as this one.

"Tylenol," I advised and gave my instructions and orders in what may have been a perfunctory manner.

She didn't understand me, perhaps because of my accented English or perhaps because she was distracted. "What?" she asked.

"Tylenol," I repeated.

"I'm sorry, what?" she seemed not to understand or hear.

"Are you deaf?" I snapped. "Tylenol," I said in a rather loud voice.

She took the order and promptly got off the phone. I returned to bed and went back to sleep, not giving this another thought.

The next day, I returned to work, not thinking of the phone call at all until I got a call from Dr. Jacobs's office. He was the head of medicine.

This was odd, but I still didn't think much of it. Only when I was in his office did I realize what this was all about. "Dr. Ali," he said flatly, almost like a father, "what happened last night?"

"Last night?" I thought for a moment and then reported, "It was mostly quiet. Nothing unusual."

"Did you get a call from the eighth floor, and how did that call go?"

Only then did I realize what this was all about. "It went fine," I said.

"That's not what I heard," he replied. The nurse had reported my verbal exchange to the head of nursing who had gone to the head of medicine, Dr. Jacobs, and to Dr. Dhurandhar to lodge the complaint. Nothing official or punitive, but she wanted to make it clear that her nurses were not to be disrespected.

"That's not how it works here, Ali." Dr. Dhurandhar explained how teamwork was an invaluable aspect of the US system and that teamwork required courtesy and respect. "You should apologize to Nurse Simpson."

Once more, I was struck by how different this culture was from Pakistan's. Once more, I was humbled and embarrassed but, since I had not meant any malice, was eager to track down Nurse Simpson and offer her my apology. She accepted my gesture with grace, and we moved on to have a good professional relationship for the rest of my time there.

I didn't spend much time socializing outside of work, but I did attend the occasional party with my peers and coworkers where we got small tastes of New Orleans' culture and life. Many of the residents were international students like me, from far-flung places like Venezuela, Mexico, St. Thomas, Cameroon, and Poland. That Halloween, one of the local New Orleans nurses hosted a party for us. Some people dressed in makeshift costumes, but many people, like me, were only vaguely aware of the American holiday and what it represented. There was so much to learn both inside and outside the hospital, but this was a fun and supportive group to study with. One thing I was coming to understand was the racial tension that existed in the United States. Nurse Miller, our hostess for the evening, was

African American, and up until now, I had no knowledge of how that affected the way she experienced the world around her or the way it affected how that world treated her.

This year, 1975, marked the ten-year anniversary of the Watts riots in Los Angeles, so it was on the minds of many people, especially the African Americans whom I worked and studied with. Through conversations, I began to glean bits and pieces of the violent history, the struggle for civil rights, and the ongoing problems of racism. It seemed such a peculiar problem to have in a nation that seemed so advanced and enlightened in so many other ways. But then again, I had grown up around rigid caste systems and segregated social hierarchies, so I knew very well how deeply ingrained they can become in a society. I knew how difficult it could be to escape upward from a less advantaged position on the social and economic ladder.

After the party, many of us returned to the house we shared in the neighborhood near the hospital. It was divided into tiny, sparsely furnished apartments, but it was a tight-knit communal group who lived there.

"Juzar, when is your wife coming?" my neighbor Didier asked me.

"Next week," I replied, and I could hear the excitement in my own voice. I couldn't wait for her to arrive and join me here.

The week flew by, and the next thing I knew I was catching a ride to the airport to meet Isfana at the gate. The first thing I noticed was how *pregnant* she was. At seven months, she was showing much more than when I had last seen her. I have never been especially affectionate in public—such displays are frowned upon in Pakistani culture—but I must have been grinning from ear to ear when I saw her. Her own smile was a joy to see.

Once home, I showed her around the neighborhood as best I could, but I didn't even know where the grocery store or restaurants were. Since I had been on my own in New Orleans, I had barely eaten outside of the hospital cafeteria. She quickly discovered some places and settled in to make the tiny apartment feel more like an actual home. We only had two pots and a small handful of cutlery, but soon the smells of her cooking wafted out of the kitchen, and we began hosting other residents from the house for meals. Suddenly, I had a social life although my world was still very small.

In return, my housemates and colleagues decided to throw a baby shower for Isfana. Once again, something unheard of in the eastern culture at that time. It was very kind, and we were both touched by the gesture. Doctors and nurses from the hospital went out of their way to offer their support if we needed anything at all. People gifted us baby clothes, blankets, and toys. Even the Touro head of medicine, Dr. Jacobs, called Isfana personally to introduce himself to her and offer his services if they could be of any help. This American system could be disorienting, humbling, and challenging in so many ways, but at this moment, I felt embraced by a deeply supportive community that made extraordinary gestures and efforts for its people. The baby shower was a wonderful experience, and Isfana was shy but glowing at the center of all the attention. She, too, was struck by the generosity and the outpouring of affection and support for us and our little family.

We soon fell into a rhythm of daily life. I still spent hours and hours at the hospital, but in my downtime, we would take walks, ride the streetcar to the grocery store, or just wander hand in hand down Canal Street, singing songs and window-shopping, just as we had so many times in Nairobi some years ago. We were good together on these adventures of ours. We were living on the very meager salary of an intern in those days, but we budgeted for a weekly Coke drink which we loved.

It was just a couple weeks later that I received a phone call from Pakistan. It was my mother calling. I knew right away that something was wrong from the tone of her voice. "Is everything all right, Ma?"

"It's your father," she said, and she choked back tears.

CHAPTER 18

Peaks and Valleys

My father was gravely ill. His liver cirrhosis symptoms had surged back, along with numerous related conditions. He wanted to go to India despite his frail health. By now, his regular hematemesis had set in, and he was bringing up significant amounts of blood. Here I was 8,350 miles from home, trying to settle in a new environment, establishing a career and immersed in one of the most intense and important learning experiences of my life. Instantly, my heart leaped across those thousands of miles to be with my family though. How could I possibly give everything I had to this medical residency if I knew my father was dying? After discussion with Isfana, it was settled. I would take a brief leave of absence and fly home. There was just one large problem with this plan: I didn't even have enough money for a plane ticket.

The next day, I explained my situation to Dr. Dhurandhar, and he approved my time off. Another colleague, Arun, whom I had just gotten acquainted with in my residency offered to lend me one thousand dollars to fly home. I wasn't thrilled about being in such a needy position, but what was I to do?

"Juzar, listen," he said. "Everyone begins in this position with empty bank accounts. One day, you'll do fine. For now, you do what you must take care of your family. Pay me when you get back."

Before I caught a ride to the airport, I said goodbye to Isfana. By now, she was well into her third trimester. "I will be back soon," I said to her as we held hands in the doorway. There was another small problem. We only had a few dollars in our account, and the next paycheck was not due for a week. "Hold on to what we have at home and try to manage till you can buy some groceries."

She smiled. "I will manage. You don't worry. Give my love to the family," she said. "And hurry home to me."

Back in India, it was every bit as bad as I feared. I attended the planned surgery, trying to grasp the seriousness of the situation. My father was in stable condition after his surgery, but he was so pale and emaciated in his bed that it broke my heart. The fire was still in his eye, though. "Well, how is it?" he asked. "How is America?"

"It's so different," I replied. "I'm learning so much."

When I look back now on the hours I spent beside his bed, I see this time as a precious gift. We talked about Mecca, the US highway system, and medicine. We debated aspects of Pakistani culture, politics, and business. We visited with family, played games of spades, and pored over the cricket scores in the newspaper. I might have been in the very beginning of my career, but for the first time, my father and I spoke truly as man-to-man. I was his son, but no longer a boy who needed his constant support. We had both been out into the world. We both had achieved some amazing things and tackled challenges our own way. Now we sat here together at what we both knew was the end of his days. My visits seemed to help in keeping my father in good spirits, and as the days passed, it became clear to me that his condition, although stable, was not good and that I was going to have to leave soon to attend to my wife and the arrival of our baby. As I had flown to India, I imagined standing vigil at my father's bed as he passed away, but now I realized that I might have to do something equally difficult—say goodbye again, knowing for certain it would be the last time I ever saw him.

However, Isfana would be delivering our first child any time now, and I had to resume my place in the residency. It was like being torn in two, these competing emotions. On the one hand, there was my obligation to my father and family. On the other, my obligation to my wife, our unborn child, and the future that my father had fought so hard for and given his blessings for me to push forward. I was being stretched between two continents. My father understood though. "Go home," he said. "Your home is with your wife. Your child." I still remember the look in his eyes as he let me go again for the second time around from a hospital bed. It was sunny outside, but there was a lot of gloom in my head. I still break out in tears as I recall that morning goodbye.

Just then, one of my cousins came into the hospital room with urgent news. A phone call had been received from America. Isfana had gone to the hospital. She had delivered our baby. They were both fine, and I was the father of a beautiful boy.

I was stunned. "What?"

"You have a son!" my cousin said.

In a state of shock, I turned to find my father grinning from ear to ear. "I am a grandfather again," he said. Not only that, he knew that a boy from his son would carry his name into the world, and that meant a great deal to him. His smile and the sunshine outside made the arrival of the newborn a blessing to treasure, and he was sure I knew that. My mom was caught up too in a situation, facing the two realities in front of her.

"I have to go, Ma," I said.

"Of course, you do," she replied. "Go! Go!" She was one strong woman.

"Yes, Juku, go," said my father.

My mother gave me a list of customary instructions that she felt we needed to know with the arrival of the baby. I was also acutely aware of the state I was leaving my ma in there. She was with her family though—her brothers had gathered, along with Mami Fatima who had always stood by Ma. Mami Fatima, Isfana's mother, had a very giving nature, and the support she would provide all the family even later earned her, in later years, the title of supermom and cybermom.

*****

Crossing continents was no easy task though. After the first leg of the journey, the plane ran into a flock of birds on liftoff at Istanbul, causing serious problems to the engines. The pilot managed to turn the plane around and land it again, but now we were stranded in Istanbul, waiting for a new plane to be brought from somewhere. For three days, I sat in an Istanbul airport hotel room, counting the hours. Later, the story would be recounted to me about how Isfana spent those same hours while I was stranded on the wrong side of the world. In my absence, all our friends, specially Parveen took turns looking in on Isfana and visiting with her and the baby. She sat in a hospital bed, recovering while our international assortment of new friends and hospital colleagues came to keep her company. Every time one of the nurses came in to discover a new male friend from India, Africa, El Salvador, Venezuela, they asked, "Oh, is this the father?"

"No," was the reply each time. "He is on his way though." It soon became a running joke among our friends and the maternity ward nurses. *Who in the world is the father of Isfana's baby? Is there a father we will see?*

I finally touched down and raced to the hospital. I was overcome with joy to see Isfana again, and to see her looking so well and well cared for. As I held my son for the first time, one of the nurses came into the room. "Let me guess," she said. "You're not the father either."

"I am the father," I replied, confused.

"Really?"

"Of course," I replied.

The nurse laughed. "Finally. The father has arrived!" she announced.

Despite all the jokes and the drama of my travels home, here I was holding my son in my arms, and he was beautiful. Flawless. The whirlwind of emotions and time zones finally seemed to stop, and all my attention was riveted on this tiny entry into our lives. *Murtuza Juzar Ali.* I was as happy in this moment as I had ever been.

But the happiness was soon tempered by the grief which we had all been expecting for months now. Just two weeks after Murtuza was born, the phone rang in our small apartment. That phone rang often and at all hours of the day and night, friends, colleagues or nurses from the hospital, so I didn't think twice about grabbing the receiver and answering cheerfully, "Hello?"

But as soon as I heard the voice on the other end of the line, my heart sank. "Juzar, I have some bad news." It was my uncle in India. "It's your father."

"Yes?"

"I'm so sorry to have to tell you. He has died."

I broke out in a sob even though the news was not unexpected. The sudden impact of news like this can never be overestimated as we all find out sooner or later. "Thank you for calling," I finally said as I hung up the phone and turned to Isfana. She was so beautiful, holding our son, but the look on her face told me that she understood what had just transpired on the phone.

"Juzar?" she asked.

"Dad," I replied, just as the sobs of grief came up through my chest. This moment had been looming for months and months now ever since Isfana and I first left Kenya, but now that it was here, it was as horrible as anything I could have imagined and feared. Even when he was sick, the connection between us was alive. But now. The sense of loss felt impossible to bear, and the sobs seemed to erupt from my chest and out through my mouth. He was gone. I was alone. I felt alone.

Later that morning, I prepared for work like it was any normal Tuesday.

"Do you think it's best?" Isfana asked gently.

"I can't sit here all day," I replied.

She understood. Isfana has always understood me, sometimes better than I even understand myself ever since we were young together.

As I did rounds with my attending staff, Drs. Shames and Dhurandhar, I told them the news. They wanted me to leave and go home, but I refused as I would have been more miserable and made Isfana sadder too. All day at work. I was noticeably quieter than usual. I was known to be rather serious and studious, but I had my lighthearted moments and enjoyed joking with my colleagues. Not today, however. I diligently made my rounds, studied my patients' test results, and issued orders for them, but clearly something else was on my mind today. Finally, Nurse Margaret asked, "Dr. Ali, is something wrong?"

I could have evaded her question, but I answered frankly, "Just got the news. My father has died."

A look of sympathy overtook her face. "I'm so sorry."

I didn't ask her to keep it a secret, and word quickly spread among my friends. One by one, they sought me out to offer condolences. "What are you doing here?" they asked. "You don't have to work at a moment like this."

"But I don't know what else to do," I admitted to them.

That was one of the longest days of my life. The last letter that I received from him faded in the aerogram format remains fresh in my memory as it hangs in a frame in my study.

I spent that night at home in agony, alternately crying and praying as memories of my father played across my imagination like the flickering of a film in the darkened movie theater on Elphinstone Street. I saw him behind his counter at work, laughing with Maulvi Saheb or teasing Tahir Bhai or scolding them for something they had not done right. I saw him sequestered at the top of our apartment building in one of his dark moods. I saw him thrilled as he drove us all toward the beach in his Contessa for a Sunday picnic. I saw him all night long. It dawned on me the vicissitudes of life.

*****

It took a few months to recover from that news, but eventually the winter weather, such as it is in New Orleans, gave way to spring. Work was wonderful and busy as ever. Isfana was doing well, and Murtuza turned three months old. I managed to repay Dr. Shah the thousand dollars he had loaned me. What's more, I was participating in a new American tradition for the first time in my life—tax day. With some help from my friends at the hospital, I filed my very first US tax return and was struck by the orderliness of it. The tax brackets were clear and easy to understand. Uniform data went into the form, and a uniform equation revealed the tax burden. It seemed so organized and fair compared to the haphazard and arbitrary system of taxation that plagued Pakistan, where a taxman might walk in off the street to demand payment for some new or obscure tax. It was unfortunately common to be hit with a bill for back taxes which required a lawyer and untold hours of administrative headaches to dispute. The easier option was often just to pay the bill.

But here in America, everything seemed so straightforward and aboveboard, and to my absolute amazement, the government even gave money back to people if they paid more to the IRS than was owed. *The government gives money back?* Isfana and I received our first tax refund a check in the mail and were stunned to see this windfall. It was an incredibly modest sum, but it felt like a gift from heaven at the time. It also happened to be almost the exact amount of money I would need to place a down payment on a Volkswagen Rabbit. In Pakistan, there was tremendous respect for anything built from German engineering, so it seemed a no-brainer to go with the Rabbit. Soon, we would learn that not everything lived up to its billing, but for now, Isfana and I were ecstatic. For the first time, we could move freely about the city and the region. We weren't beholden to the streetcar schedule or the kindness of friends for rides. We decided to take a vacation. Somewhere nice and sunny. We packed up our small family and drove off to Pensacola, Florida, in our new car. This was amazing.

Pensacola is as old as New Orleans with similar Spanish forts, old quarters, and architecture all perched on the edge of white sand beaches and beautiful blue water. We brought beach towels and picnic supplies. We brought a small camera and sun hats. The one thing we forgot was to check the weather forecast.

By the time we arrived, the entire coast was smothered by a low-pressure system that blotted the sun out with thick gray clouds and dumped rain while the wind whipped in off the Gulf of Mexico. This was not the sunny beach vacation we had envisioned. But it was our first vacation and a new car and our baby and our new parent experience. What more would we want?

We fell back into our busy routines as spring melted into another hot New Orleans summer. It was hard to believe I had already been here an entire year, but here was the annual banquet looming on the calendar. It was a yearly celebration for the participants of the residency program, and people had been talking about it for weeks. Isfana and I found a babysitter for the night, dressed up as best we could, and arrived at the private hotel dining room for the event. It was a beautiful room with hardwood floors, chandeliers hanging from high ceilings and white linen tablecloths. This was a far cry from the hospital cafeteria or the tiny low-budget apartment we were used to be living and eating in.

The evening was one part joyful celebration and one part serious occasion. It was a chance to reflect on the year, to honor people's achievements, and to enjoy each other's company and hit the dance floor with a live band playing for us. The awards ceremony was one of most anticipated portions of the night. This was where individual hard work and personal ambition was recognized, but also an occasion to recognize the collective commitment that we all had made to field of medicine, to advancing this mission, to helping people around us and joining in this time-honored profession. It was no small commitment, and many people in this room had sacrificed so much to be here. The speeches and awards were all very moving, and there was such a wonderful sense of camaraderie in the room. This, too, was a family that Isfana and I had joined. After all my personal struggles this year, I had no illusions that I was about to be singled out for any great recognition, but I felt honored to be in the room with these accomplished doctors and teachers, with these wonderful residents from around the world and their families. Every one of them had inspired me in some way over the previous months.

One of the most distinguished awards of the evening goes to Intern of the Year, and I waited eagerly to hear who would receive it. Dr. Dhurandhar gave a warm speech about what an honor it was to offer this award and how much it meant to the program. "This is recognition not only of individual achievement but also of personal growth. Of professional growth. The candidate who receives this award has not only demonstrated unwavering dedication to patients and to this challenging field of medicine, but he has overcome many challenges to do so. I would like to present this year's Intern of the Year award to Doctor Juzar Ali."

It took a moment for me to process those words. How did my name just appear with that award? The entire banquet was cheering loudly for me. The only thing that felt real was Isfana's hand on my arm as she gave me a slight squeeze.

"Come, Ali," Dr. Dhurandhar said. He always called me by my last name. "Come get your award."

I stood up and realized my eyes had begun to fill with tears once more, only these were tears of gratitude.

Isfana and I returned home that night, and as we laid the baby down in his crib and prepared for bed, I couldn't help thinking of all the things that had happened in just one year. Some of them were wonderful, some were humbling, and some were terrible, but here we were, tired and happy. We were home together and making our way in the world and I could not help but remember my dad. He sure would have been proud to show off all this to his friends and customers at Venus Medico.

CHAPTER 19

Homeward Bound

It was a happy chaos, but it was a chaos nonetheless. I was working intense hours at the hospital. By now, Isfana had full-time work of her own. We had an infant and a Volkswagen Rabbit which always seemed to break down at the exact wrong time. Then again, when is the right time to have a car break down? On the way to day care? On the way home from a night shift? While your wife is waiting to be picked up from her own workday? We did our best to juggle our crazy work schedules with our family life. Luckily, Touro had a good day care, and I often was able to bring Murtuza with me to work. When I had some free moments, I could drop in and play with him. The ladies at the day care were wonderful, but they had a terrible time trying to pronounce the baby's name. It was those ladies who nicknamed him Zee, a name which has stuck with him through his whole life now: Zee Ali.

Very quickly, the time arrived for all the residents to choose their areas of specialization which they would engage in once they completed the three-year residency. My mentor at Touro, Dr. Dhurandhar, was in cardiology, and I had been an eager student under him and other senior colleagues, so many people assumed that's the direction I would go in. It was a prestigious field here in America. The problem was I knew I would be heading back to Pakistan when my next fellowship ended, and in Pakistan, cardiology is not nearly as developed. Despite my strong interest in the field and my admiration for the cardiology team here, I knew that pulmonology was going to be the most valuable specialization back home. Illnesses of the lungs were the scourge of South Asia, and I felt that was where I could make the most significant contribution for my own people. I felt that the complex intersection of medicine, infectious disease, and critical care could best be explored in this field, and I would be able to contribute more comprehensively.

My classmates were incredulous about my firm convictions to return to Pakistan. After all, we had all worked incredibly hard to be here, and once a doctor had achieved an American degree and licensure, he or she could work in a much more lucrative and prestigious system here in the US.

"Why would you return home?" they wanted to know. "You will make peanuts compared to what you can make here. You should stay here and send *your money* home."

But it had always been my plan to return to Karachi. My father had sacrificed so much to be there at the time of the creation of Pakistan and be a part of that new nation, and I would pick up where he left off. I felt my future was there, and I would be glad to be back with my mother, sisters, and family. Besides, as a doctor with international licensure, I would still have opportunities to travel and train in the US and abroad. My convictions were so strong that I had intentionally arranged for a temporary visa instead of the extended immigrant visa that was so easily available at that time. Legally, I could not stay in the US even if I changed my mind. At the time, I was quite zealous. "If you want to do something, do it with passion and determination and burn your boats that tempt you on the alternatives," I said.

Today, I take a more nuanced approach to situations like that, especially having lived with the consequences of my actions.

Work continued, and hectic days turned into months. We were able to take occasional breaks which included visits back to Pakistan and India to visit family. Isfana and I were both in our training programs and had intense on-call schedules which often meant that we barely saw each other in thirty-six-hour periods. It also meant that Zee was sandwiched within this schedule as we relied on day care nurseries to help us navigate this very difficult time. Zee was growing right in front of us, and yet we were missing out on it without much quality time.

On one visit to Pakistan, we decided to let Zee stay with my mother and Mukha. It would be a lengthy separation, which we were not happy about, but we felt it would be beneficial all around. Zee would spend his days with loving family instead of in day care centers; my mother and sisters could spend quality time with the baby they adored, and it gave Isfana and I time to complete our work and adjust our very tough schedule. We were very nervous about leaving our young son on another continent, but we knew he was safe in the family home, and it seemed like the best option at the time as we were in such a transient phase of our lives.

Ironically, the gift of time that my mother and Akila had bestowed upon Isfana and me helped produce yet another fruit of our "labors": a new pregnancy.

"Are you sure?" I asked Isfana when she delivered the news to me.

"Yes, I'm sure," she said with a smile.

I took her in my arms and twirled her around our tiny kitchen. This was wonderful news. Our family was growing right along with our dreams, and yet here we were facing another challenging milestone.

The last months of the residency flew along after that. I was on cloud nine. Isfana was pregnant, Zee would be home soon, along with my mother, and my pulmonology fellowship had been arranged under a world-renowned physician at Tulane, Dr. Ziskind. One of my mentors at the VA, world-renowned endocrinologist Dr. Kastin, had helped me with his recommendation to get that fellowship. Kastin knew Ziskand and put in a good word for me. The conversation was later recounted to me, and supposedly, it went something like this: "Look, Ziskand, if a Jew is recommending a Muslim from Pakistan, it must mean something!"

It was a funny approach, but that vote of confidence seemed to do the trick.

The icing on the cake was that I would have four whole weeks of free time when the residency obligations ended. Isfana and I made plans to take a driving vacation before Zee and my mother returned. We spent time poring over Triple-A travel brochures and plotting our route on a map of the United States. We would drive all the way to California and back. The only problem was the Rabbit. It had not become any more reliable over the months, and I was sure we would never make it there and back. We were constantly having trouble finding parts for the German car. I could imagine us stranded in some random small town in the middle of an American desert waiting for some auto parts delivery. So on the morning we were to leave for California, I drove it to the car sales lot and traded it in for a nice used Chevy. American made. Easy to repair. Easy to find parts. I drove to pick up Isfana, and she didn't recognize me in the new vehicle as I pulled up. "What is this?" she asked, laughing, when she finally realized I was parked in front of her.

"Our chariot," I replied. "Let's go!"

The drive across America is stunning. You can look at those maps all you want, but you will never understand how big this country really is until you take off and see it. The swamps of Louisiana give way to the sugarcane fields and then the rolling prairies of Texas. The Hill Country gives way to the desert, which, in turn, becomes the Rocky Mountains of New Mexico. The stunning sunsets of Arizona are matched by the grandeur of the Pacific Ocean which pounds against the coast of California. The scenery was magical, but the best part of the drive was just spending time with each other. After three years of hectic schedules, it felt luxurious to spend all day daydreaming about our family and trying out names for the new baby. We would pluck names from the surrounding scenery and try them on for a while. Sabine, from the Sabine River, which winds along the Louisiana-Texas border, was a favorite for a while before the baby became Katy and then Guadalupe for a while before becoming Gila, Zuni, Sedona, Mojave, and more.

Once more, we fell in love with the American Interstate system—the smooth roads, the clear signage, and the incredible ease of access with all the well-constructed exits and entrances, not to mention the commerce that springs up at each of these amazing interchanges: food, gas, hotels, sightseeing destinations, gift shops, and more.

Once we reached California, we stayed with family friends from Pakistan. They had a great place, and we thoroughly enjoyed ourselves, relaxing on the West Coast. On the way home, we stayed for a couple nights at the Grand Canyon and even took a helicopter ride down through that geological masterpiece. The view was simply amazing, and the ride was thrilling too as we swooped high and low, looking at highlights of the canyon. At over two hundred-fifty miles long, there was a lot to see. The canyon floor is a full-mile deep in places, and it was a strange sensation indeed to drop that far beneath the surface of the earth in a helicopter.

All in all, it was a wonderful trip. The car didn't break down once, and when we finally returned home, we felt rejuvenated, optimistic, and ready for the next phase of our life.

I had been in Pakistan the last time Isfana had gone into labor. This time it was a different situation. I was the anxious husband as we prepared for our second baby. Isfana, as usual, remained calm and fully under control. This is what she does. It was a long night in the hospital, and we welcomed our new baby, Riaz, around midnight. It was late, but it was a bright new day for us.

We should have known life couldn't stay this easy though. Shortly after we returned home with our new baby, I received a call from my mother who was still trying to arrange her trip to the US with Zee. It was taking a painfully long time to secure the necessary permissions. "What do you mean the visa was denied?" I asked. My mother was stranded in Karachi. We had made all her flight and travel plans, just as we had before, but suddenly there was a problem with her travel visa to the United States. "We already did this," I said. "It should be fine."

But it wasn't fine. The US government saw a widow traveling with a baby who was a US citizen by birthright, and they deemed her a flight risk. In their matrix of criteria, she now appeared to be someone who might try to become an illegal immigrant, so they revoked her visa.

I immediately began calling government offices to explain the situation. "*None* of our family intends to stay in the US permanently," I carefully explained. "Why would my mother?"

But nothing seemed to move the American bureaucracy into action on our behalf. Now as Isfana and I both started work again, we carefully scheduled time to pursue government officials. We had to get our son back. After all our phone calls failed, we made an appointment to meet with Lindy Boggs, the US senator from Louisiana. She was known to be an active advocate for her people, but we didn't know if she could help a couple of foreign students like us. We went to her New Orleans office, and she was very kind and courteous. She listened carefully, and her assistant made notes. She was sympathetic to our situation, but she wasn't sure if she would be able to help. "This is out of my jurisdiction," she informed us. "But I'll see what I can do."

The next time we had an opportunity, we visited the State Department office in New Orleans. After that, we dropped in at the office of our House representative. We called the governor's office, and the Pakistani embassy in Washington, DC. Anything we could think of. We even wrote to Rosalyn Carter, First Lady of the United States, and then we waited.

Finally, after three weeks of this, my mother received a call from the US consulate in Pakistan. "You can come get your visa," they informed her. "It has been approved."

We were thrilled to get the call from her. We had no idea how it happened. No idea who might have helped us. But someone, some-where along the way, must have put in a good word for us, and once more were amazed by this American system of government. Yes, it was a bureaucracy, but at some level, it was responsive to people. It worked. No bribes or personal connections or backroom maneuvering was required to receive help here.

*****

With the salary from my new pulmonology fellowship, we had a good steady income now, so I decided it was time to get out of our small apartment. There were now five of us beneath one roof. When I had free time, I began to house hunt. A real estate agent took me around during my lunch breaks or when I had an afternoon off before a night shift. One day, she walked me into a house in New Orleans East that looked fine from outside, but nothing exciting. It was a modest one-story, ranch-style house in a suburban neighbor-hood, but when I stepped in the door, I knew this was the place. In the wide, open hallway was a beautiful mosaic floor of small hand-laid tiles in a pattern very reminiscent of the ones back home. I took this to be a sign. Isfana liked the house too when I took her for a visit, so with no further ado, we were homeowners.

Now we really felt like we were living the American Dream. Before, we were tourists to the American Dream, but now we owned a piece of it.

As always, life was crazy with a newborn in the house, but my mother was a lifesaver. She helped with the cooking and cleaning and looking after Zee. Without knowing a word of English, she navigated grocery stores, post offices, and shopping excursions. She became friends with all the new neighbors on the block.

One day, the pipes beneath the sink burst, spraying water every-where and beginning to flood the kitchen. My mother ran to the neighbor's house and somehow managed to explain the problem in a combination of Urdu and frantic hand gestures. The neighbor came to the rescue, helping to turn off the water. Then I received a call at the hospital. "Dr. Ali, this is your neighbor, Barbara. You need to call a plumber." It was always an adventure, and it was amazing how my mother, despite not knowing conversational English except a few words, would always manage to take care of herself, her children, and any crises.

Isfana was able to return to practicing psychiatry and her train-ing, and in this way, the three years passed by quickly and produc-tively. My mother was long since home in Pakistan, but Isfana and I had been able to establish more traditional and workable sched-ules. Suddenly, it was time to prepare for board exams. This was the final step in my long journey to becoming a full-fledged doctor and American-certified specialist. All my colleagues signed up to take boards in the US, but I took the extra step of signing up to take boards in Canada as well.

"Why on earth are you flying all the way to Toronto to take Canadian boards when you're not even staying on this continent to work?" my friends asked me.

"I need the alphabets and letters," I replied. "The more, the better."

In Pakistan, appearances were very valuable, and board certifications were a commodity that would pay dividends. They brought prestige, whether they were particularly useful or not. It might be expensive and stressful in the short run, but the extra letters at the end of my name would pay for themselves: "Juzar Ali, MD, was not going to be enough. A *diplomate* (diploma) in Pakistan was earned with less than a full degree, and therefore, the Pakistani eye was trained to seek out the degree and certification lettering, like the Canadian FRCP. I made a twenty-four-hour trip to Toronto to appear for the Canadian Boards (FRCP), and the race was on. I studied in airports. Hotels. Cabs. I was on my way to be a board-certified physician in two countries.

One of the final things we did as a family in the United States was take a trip to Disneyland. Over the years, it had been pressed upon us what a quintessential American experience this was, so we felt we had to try it before we left. We knew it would be expensive, but it seemed like a perfect way to cap our extended stay in this wonderful nation. We flew to Orlando, stayed in a hotel, spent a long weekend exploring the amusement parks, and had a ball. Then we climbed back on the plane to return home.

"So what did you think?" I asked Zee who was now five years old.

"It was good," he replied thoughtfully. "I like City Park New Orleans better."

City Park! He was more entertained by a one-dollar ice-cream cone and bag of stale bread to feed the ducks than he was by the fancy rides and his photo with Mickey Mouse. I laughed all the way back to New Orleans.

*****

We sold the house. We sold the car. We donated most of our belongings. We were going back to Pakistan. We mailed home the things that would be useful: some clothes and sixty boxes of medical equipment, textbooks, and supplies. Over the years, I had been scrounging for used medical equipment, especially anything I thought might be difficult to acquire at home: spirometers, peak flow meters, pulse oximeters, inhalers, nebulizers, oxygen therapy systems, chest drainage units, bronchoscopes, emergency crash cart kits, and volumes of specialized medical texts. I practically had an entire library by now. We had all that shipped. There were no fancy gifts or luxury items to take home. We had meager few thousand dollars in cash. But I had two important investments that I hoped to build upon when we arrived home in Pakistan. The first was the training, education, experience, and credentials I had received in the US, and the other was a medical office space in Karachi where I would practice. I had been paying a small monthly instalment for years now, and finally I was going to take advantage of it.

It was a bittersweet moment, looking back at our American Dream house for the last time as we drove away. We had achieved our wildest dreams so far, but we were sad to say goodbye. New Orleans was the only home our boys had ever known up to now, and it had been good to us. We would miss it dearly.

CHAPTER 20

Trouble with the Law

Karachi even smelled like home, that combination of sea air, spices, and pungent alleyway. I loved watching the city glide past us as we made our way from the airport to my mother's bungalow in the northern suburbs. For me, this was a joyous homecoming with family, school colleagues, and childhood friends, but I recognized that for the rest of my immediate family—Isfana and the boys—this place was new and mysterious. Isfana and Zee had both visited, of course, but this would be different. For Isfana, having mostly lived in India and US, this was going to be a significant cultural and social adjustment. I was thrilled to think of showing them the things that I had cherished so much as a boy: picnics at the beaches, cricket on the Polo Grounds, or films at the Elphinstone Street movie house.

My mother greeted us warmly, and over the first weeks, we had beautiful meals with the family and friends who all came to welcome us home and hear our tales of living in America. Everyone wanted to see what treasures we brought back from the Western world—what clothes, what modern electronics, kitchenware, entertainment, and more we might have brought with us—and they were universally disappointed to learn we had brought almost nothing except medical equipment. "You went all the way to America, and this is all you brought home?"

"Yes indeed," I replied while Isfana could only smile.

It took awhile to settle back into the rhythms and life of Karachi. It was so different from the United States, everything from

191

the language to the food, from the religious traditions to the very conservative social customs. In the United States, we had seemed like the reserved types, but here in Pakistan, we quickly realized we were more like radical progressives compared to most everyone else. We knew this wasn't a culture that looked favorably on radical progressives, however. They were often treated more like threats than like leaders. Still, I longed to bring some of the First World advances to my nation. I wanted people to see there were better ways to practice medicine.

Before we could do that, however, we had to get the kids into school. Like my father, I knew just how important and challenging it could be. Getting into a good elementary school in Karachi was something like applying to Harvard University. Even my own alma mater, Karachi Grammar, required an elaborate, months-long application process. Many people began the process the moment their babies were born, and here we were showing up in the middle of the school year with children from the American school system which didn't line up age-wise or skills-wise. The American school system focused more on developing the young individual and less on rote memorization and specific bodies of knowledge. South Asian school systems were just the opposite. They focused more on conformity and specific bodies of knowledge in areas like history, civics, mathematics, writing, and so on. After weeks of hunting, we finally discovered a Parsi-affiliated montessori school where we might have a chance. Many Parsis migrated from the same region of India where Isfana was from, so she went to the meeting in hopes that their shared history might create an opportunity for us. Before we went in, I reminded Isfana to converse in Gujrati and not English or Urdu. Language is a greater bond.

It worked. They instantly hit it off, speaking the common language Gujrati, and the administrator was receptive to our family. The power of language and communication. The administrator had one burning question for Isfana when they learned that we had moved to Karachi from the United States: "Why did you come back? Are you in trouble with the law?"

"Of course not," Isfana answered.

"Is the FBI after you?" they asked in bewilderment.

"No," Isfana replied again, trying not to laugh.

"Then why? We don't understand why anyone would choose Pakistan over the United States."

"This is our home. This is where we want to be."

The administrator grudgingly accepted that answer, and the boys were admitted into the school.

Next, we had to find work for ourselves. We started with Isfana, knowing it would be a challenge to find a position in mental health. All our initial inquiries were met with blank stares. "You want to work in mental health?"

Mental health care and psychiatry were still quite stigmatized in Pakistan, reserved most often for those considered criminally insane. Isfana's specific field of childhood psychiatry simply did not exist. Once again, we set off to meet the department heads of various institutions to sweet talk our way through security and past protective secretaries. Once again, we found ourselves standing in front of a hospital director pleading our case together. He ran the Jinnah Postgraduate Medical Center and Hospital, a teaching hospital affiliated with the medical school. He was polite and listened attentively. When we were finished, he asked very simply, "Who sent you?"

"Excuse me?" I asked.

"Who sent you?" he repeated.

"Nobody sent us. We have approached you on our own."

"Do you have any connections in Islamabad?"

"No."

The director let out a bark of a laugh. "Ha!" Then he explained, "Doctor, don't you know in this country, positions don't exist for people, positions are made for people? If you don't know anyone, how do you expect to acquire a position such as this? Especially this. Childhood psychology?"

"No, sir, child psychiatry," we meekly corrected. But the message was clear. We walked out despondent.

We realized that we had no connections left. The goodwill my father had created in his lifetime was limited, and now that he was no more, it meant nothing. So were my own medical school connections after all these years away. It was a rude awakening. After all those years honing our skills and credentials in the United States system, we knew we were extremely qualified to work here, and yet here we stood with the director literally laughing at us. We had known it was going to be hard work getting established professionally, but we hadn't expected the nepotism to be quite this exclusive.

There was no such thing as an entry-level position to apply for, and our direct appeal to the director had been rejected. Next, we went right to the heart of the hospital, to the physicians themselves. This was one of the very few institutions that even had a psychiatry department, and it took awhile for Isfana to arrange a meeting with the head of the department, but finally we managed it through friends of friends of friends. We knew there were no paid positions, so Isfana offered to work pro bono. It didn't take long for the head of the department to accept her offer; Isfana's credentials were outstanding, and he could use an unpaid foot soldier in the department. It allowed him more flexibility in his department. Plus, with another staff member, others would have more time to develop his own private practice in the evening.

This was how most physicians established their careers, through this quid pro quo system. They sought out these positions at prestigious hospitals or universities even though the pay was very low to make themselves known. Then they used that visibility to drive patient traffic to their private practices. In turn, these teaching hospitals could offer the services of qualified physicians without having to spend much on their salaries. Most doctors worked early day shifts at their hospitals and then spent evenings at their private practices where they reaped the profits of their morning labor. Naturally, these physicians were eager for any opportunity to relieve their hospital workloads so they could spend more time on their lucrative side business and other activities. That's where Isfana fit in. We were lucky in that we could afford to volunteer like this to get a foot in the door. At least for a while. We had a roof over our heads and a reliable small family business that was still running after all these years.

Also, this was one aspect of the Pakistani medical profession I had been very clear about. I knew about this quid pro quo system, and for years I was preparing for this arrangement by paying that instalment note on a unit in a medical office building while I was studying in America. Four hundred beautiful square feet of medical offices were mine: one waiting room, one office, and one examination room. We had the space to start a private practice. Now we just needed patients.

I carefully studied my options around the city. I would face the same bureaucratic hurdles that Isfana faced in a public or government institution. These were coveted spots and one could not get in if one did not have *panga*, the local term for inside track and influence. After much consideration, I made my decision and walked into one of the smaller private board-run hospitalsLiaquat National Hospital. It catered to a mixed clientele with its administration more like a foundation board. In that way, it was much like Touro Hospital back in New Orleans. The thing I was most interested in, however, was the sixty-bed TB ward which I found out was being supervised by a Canadian-trained thoracic surgeon. Now that was interesting, I thought.

I had experience of TB management in the US through my comprehensive pulmonary disease training, but the experience was marginal. Here in Pakistan, the disease was much more prevalent. The scourge swept through shanty towns and tenement housing, wreaking havoc and leaving slow death in its wake. TB was often an affliction of the poor and the disadvantaged, although not exclusively. More affluent patients could afford more prestigious institutions where they would receive specialized care, but this TB ward was for the less fortunate, and as such, it was constantly full. In fact, the TB ward was considered so toxic that it was a stand-alone facility located some distance away from the main hospital. Not many people either from the faculty, administration, or staff would visit that unit. It had a single wide-open room filled with rows of beds where TB patients languished, all receiving the same generic treatments and care. Most doctors there, despite the need, would find this a terrible assignment. In fact, for all intents and purposes, a TB doctor fell into a separate category of health-care provider. It was almost like missionary work. How and why a Canadian-trained thoracic surgeon was supervising this was beyond me. His schedule included visiting the ward occasionally, staying in the outer administrative office, calling the ward master (the nurse in charge) and asking him to bring the charts. He would do a cursory chart review, but inevitably, he simply wrote *CT all* on nearly all charts. *CT all* meant "continue treatment all."

I sensed an opportunity to make an immediate difference.

I approached the director of the hospital, and he granted me a meeting. The meeting took place in a typical manner. The director sat at his desk at one end of the room with some sidekicks and subordinates seated on either side. In front of the desk, a pair of chairs were positioned for people to sit, but the entire arrangement was designed to be intimidating, not welcoming, and many visitors would not have the courage or inclination to make themselves comfortable. To make the scene even more exclusive, one *chaprasi*, an attendant, would constantly be circulating, offering tea to the friends. As soon as I walked into the room, I recognized the setup. The friends sitting there originated through the *panga chain*, meaning they had come in either to offer a favor or get a favor. I was offered a chair and a cup of tea. I considered myself honored.

"There's a surgeon already running the TB ward," the chief administrator said.

"Yes, I know that, sir." I had done my homework. "I would like to be the physician in the unit," I told him. "I have some ideas for improvement."

He and his assistants wore surprised looks on their faces. By any normal standard, this was an absurd request, especially for a doctor with exclusive training from the United States with my credentials. "I must ask," the director said. "Why have you come back to Pakistan? Again, the same question came up. "Are you in any kind of trouble with the law in the US?"

"No, sir," I smiled and replied. "I have come back because this is my home and where my family lives."

The director finally accepted that for a sincere answer, and he offered me the position. "Not many people who come back stay here. Soon they get frustrated and run back to the States," he warned.

"I have come back with my boats burned," I replied. "I am here to stay. I have no option."

"I have no budget for this," he then informed me. "There's very little base pay. You will not make any money here. For that, you have to build your practice as others do."

"I understand."

Our arrangement was very straightforward. He would allow me to convert the TB ward into a real pulmonary treatment center, and I would work for a small token base salary. In return for my cheap labor, I could use the position to try and launch my private practice outside the hospital. We shook hands and parted ways.

"Good luck over there," he said.

"Thank you." As I left his office that day, I saw the incredulous smiles on the faces of the director's friends, and I just knew they were probably laying wagers before I even reached the end of the hall to see how long I would last in this position and stay in Pakistan.

The first thing I did was change the name. This was no longer just a TB ward; now it was an official chest unit, and we referred to it as the chest ward. The next order of business in my chest ward was to diagnose the patients correctly. In addition to my training in chest radiology, I had a treasure from the United States that turned out to be the only flexible fiberoptic bronchoscope in the entire sprawling metropolis of Karachi at this time. A quick survey clearly showed that many so-called TB patients had other pulmonary diseases, such as lung cancer, pulmonary fibrosis, emphysema, sarcoidosis, or COPD. I quickly compartmentalized the ward to group the patients according to their actual illness and, thus, their treatments. Many times, these misdiagnoses were based on symptoms and chest X-rays alone (in fact, I have had a pet theory for many years that even Mohammad Ali Jinnah, founder of Pakistan, was misdiagnosed with TB when he was dying of cavitary lung cancer), but I was able to examine patients much more accurately and effectively.

That approach led to the next order of business: establishing rules logical treatment protocol for each individual illness. I spent a great deal of time with patients, seeing them multiple times a day, and my energy and passion must have been evident because a young doctor named Dr. Mosavir Ansarie grew interested in my approach and got himself attached to my unit. As he engaged with my practices, there was an infectious academic buzz around the hospital. It was really working. A change was in the offing. Using an organized methodology and more of my treasures from the United States, such as a portable ventilator, biopsy tools, and resuscitation kits, we were able to establish the first intensive care unit in a small side room of the chest ward, something that was completely foreign to the hospital. No ward at Liaquat had ever had its own ICU. It was very crude by American standards, but it was designed to separate the most severe cases from the general population of patients and offer them more concentrated and supportive level of care. It was the concept and the vision I was striving for. Not unexpectedly, I met some resistance as people resented the change to the status quo. The chest surgeon, for reasons more of ego than actual financial impact, was very vocal and active in this resistance, but I managed to implement my modest change.

One thing that quickly became clear to me was how an innovative approach was desperately needed to address the problems that stemmed from the epidemic levels of poverty in Pakistan. As I could see all around me, health care for the poor and working classes had been neglected and underfunded for decades, but I was sure there could be very modest improvements that could have outsized impacts. Diseases didn't have to be this mysterious, terrifying, and deadly. They could be understood and managed. Correct diagnoses could be a good start. That allowed people the opportunity to become educated about their specific conditions instead of wasting away in these tragic circumstances. In other words, the disease was the weapon, but what was killing people was the neglect and ignorance.

In America, I saw how medicine could be used so much more effectively and not just because of the bigger budgets. There was an ingrained opportunistic approach to medicine (and many things). I knew that I wasn't going to miraculously transform Pakistan into America. I wasn't even sure if I could transform this small ward into a place of more effective medicine and healing, but I was going to try. I was going to hope that it might succeed and grow just a little and then grow a little more.

The nurses and patients were the first people to witness my efforts firsthand, and they went along with my orders even though they were skeptical. I could tell they wanted to ask, *What on earth are you up to?* They weren't sure if I was mad scientist with my approach, gadgets, scopes, and the terminology I insisted upon in clinical discussions.

But it started to work. Almost immediately, the approach began to take effect. The patients with milder ailments began to recover quickly. The patients with more severe ailments understood their symptoms much better and, wherever possible, began to make improvements based upon the new strategy approach and treatment plans. I quickly adapted my practice of medicine to the cultural and social needs of the population also. In this part of the world, it is not the patient alone who is affected by an illness. The whole family is affected. Each patient had an entourage of family and friends who supported him or her—young and old relatives, men and women, friends and neighbors. They were engaged in their own way to help. They also began to talk. Word began to spread that whatever I was doing in my "laboratory" was working. Other colleagues in the hospital became aware of the changes in the chest unit and referrals and requests for consultation started pouring in. Mosavir and I were in business.

It took two weeks for the first patient to arrive at my private practice in my recently completed medical office. I was sitting alone in my quiet office when he arrived, and I put away my medical text. For two weeks, I had been quietly studying alone, day after day, but here, finally, was a patient. I was thrilled but tried not to show it.

"Are you Dr. Juzar?" That is how I was addressed in that part of the world.

"Yes."

"From the Liaquat National Hospital?"

"Yes."

"Oh, good. I have a problem and someone from the hospital asked me to see you. It is for my lungs. I have this X-ray."

I welcomed him in so we could begin a consultation. Little could I know that six months later, there would be a line of people stretching down the hallway just to get through that door. For now, I had one patient, and it felt like a good start.

In the meantime, Rashida, my sister, Cheeko as we called her, worked as a physiotherapist at a private surgeon-run clinic and center, and she introduced me to Dr. Naveed Shah. He was a brilliant surgeon with a keen clinical sense and a passion for merging anatomy and physiology in an amalgam of medicine and surgery. We hit it off, and I asked if I could drop in at his practice just to see if I might be of some service there. He agreed, and soon I became a part of the practice in his center also. On top of that, I also arranged to spend one night a week working at a nearby charitable clinic and shelter. Within just a few weeks, my schedule had gone from completely unemployed to incredibly full. I spent mornings in my chest unit, afternoons with Dr. Shah, and most evenings at my private practice when I wasn't working at the shelter. If I wasn't making much money yet, I was meeting people all over the city and doing my best to make a positive impact everywhere I went.

Despite our growing success, there were stark reminders that we were still working in a different world here in Karachi. One night, a call came to the house at 2:00 AM. It was a nurse from our ICU frantically calling from my chest ward. One of the seriously ill patients had died that night, and his family were now on a vengeful rampage in the ward. They had beaten several staff members, ransacked the center, and taken the house officer (a medical resident) hostage. "Where is the security officer?"

"Right here," she replied. "He won't go in there alone."

"I'll be right there," I said, and I raced to get dressed and climb into my new car, a Honda Civic.

I discovered the family had turned the ICU into a bunker, and they were hunkered there with their dead relative and their hostage. It was half-dozen men armed with sticks broom handles, metal stands, and scalpels. "Should we call the police?" the nurse asked.

"No," I replied, and everyone agreed right away. It was widely accepted that you only called the police as an option of last resort. Anytime the police got involved with a situation in that part of the world, they became their own kind of problem, and it was best to avoid them if possible. "Let me speak with the family," I said.

I approached the ICU very cautiously. "You must understand," I said to the men. "Your cousin was very ill."

"You said you could treat him," one man shouted at me.

"Killer!" another man yelled.

"He had the finest care in Karachi. But he had acute pneumonia on top of emphysema. Sometimes, there is nothing a person can do. Not a doctor. Not anybody."

"It is God's will," interjected the nurse

It took a long time, but the family finally came to terms with their loss. They laid down their weapons, released the house officer, and left the ward, taking the dead man with them.

The families could be as difficult to navigate as the illnesses themselves, especially when the families were so deeply involved in the care delivery. In Karachi's perpetually underfunded, short-staffed hospitals, family members were inevitably converted into volunteer health-care providers. I, too, used this unique system of family support and developed it to patients' specific needs. Wives and daughters might act as bedside nurses while elderly relatives became comforting prayer leaders. Brothers and cousins might take shifts operating equipment or procuring oxygen tanks, changing IV bags, or restraining a patient that couldn't be sedated. Smaller boys would run errands, racing to the pharmacies, fetching food, and the like. I quickly learned that treating a patient often meant caring for the whole family in a way that was very important even if it was distracting and, at times, quite dangerous if not well supervised.

On one occasion, I received a call from another hospital. One of their patients had just emerged from surgery but was having serious post-operative respiratory problems. It was a blazing hot Friday afternoon and a holiday after prayers. None of their physicians were available. I dropped everything and raced over. The surgeon who had operated on the patient put in a request for me to see the patient but then had conveniently left the building and was nowhere to be found. He claimed he had done his part with a successful surgery, but now the lungs were the problem, so he had released his patient to me. Immediately, I tried to salvage the situation. I attempted to intubate the patient to establish an open airway and prevent complete respiratory failure. The family was gathered all around us, as usual. Despite all our efforts, however, the man died while I was working to save him. Reluctantly, I announced the death, and that's when the first punch hit me in the face. Then another. I quickly covered my head with my arms, and the blows began to rain down on me harder and harder as yelling and shoving broke out across the room. The family was trying to kill me. They were outraged and grief-stricken, and they blamed me for the death. They had been told the surgery was successful. Then what was the problem? What had I done?

The hospital staff were able to pull me out the door and whisk me to safety as the melee spilled into the hallway behind me. We dashed down the hall and around a corner before one of the assistants stopped to look me over quickly, checking my face, neck, and head for injuries. "Are you all right?" he asked.

"I'm not sure," I replied.

"You need to get out of here," he said.

He took me through the halls to the back entrance, and I escaped through the alley. For weeks after that, I moved very carefully through the city, always on guard in case the family members were lying in wait somewhere near the hospital or around my office. This also was not uncommon. Everyone in the profession knew a doctor or two who had been ambushed by vengeful family members. Soon, things returned to normal though, and I convinced myself that this was just a minor downside to an otherwise wonderful vocation. This was what happened without a fair legal system that allowed malpractice suits or other proceedings; families and individuals resorted to violent tactics as they sought remedy.

Of course, these events were few and far between. For the most part, need and demand far outweighed the capacity and resources to deliver health care, and this resulted in a very lopsided power dynamic. Doctors were treated like gods. They were literally swarmed by masses of people who praised them, begged for their attention and brought offerings of gratitude. One can imagine the inflated ego a doctor can develop under circumstances like this, and I was not immune from these effects.

CHAPTER 21

Walking with Gods

I was the only US-trained and board-certified pulmonologist in Karachi at that time, and my team was making an impact. News of my chest unit began to spread across the city and the region, which created more and more opportunities for me. My private practice was flourishing now as people came to me with their myriad chest and lung ailments. One of the first things I noticed was the lack of any coordinated care for these patients. Up until now, doctors and hospitals in Karachi essentially worked on their own with very little support or official connection to other physicians or institutions. This culture bred mistrust and competitiveness. Not only was this detrimental to doctors and hospitals, but it also led to disjointed care for patients. As they bounced from one doctor to the next, from one institution to the next, there was a plague of fragmented care, which was only reinforced by patients themselves who were conditioned to "physician shop," looking for the next best thing who might be able to help. This all led to confusing expensive, ineffective health-care delivery, the cost of which the patient would bear.

After working in the US system, I could see just how noxious this lack of cooperation was, and it was one of the first things I decided to challenge. Structured medical record systems were not in vogue, but I established careful records management at both my private practice and within the chest unit at LNH. In addition to the chest ward, we now ran an open outpatient clinic also, and we strongly encouraged all patients to bring their medical records when they came for appointments. I started keeping detailed files and assigning patient ID numbers. Mosavir and I were compulsive about this, and many people ridiculed us, but we were serious. We were good-natured about it, but we also developed penalties for patients who repeatedly failed to deliver required information to us: counseling, reprimands, and in rare cases we used slightly extended wait times consequently. We might have seemed authoritative, and soon we were known across town as those guys who wanted to see every piece of paper and test result. But it worked. With detailed medical histories, we were able to provide much more effective care for patients instead of just ordering repetitive test and sending them off with yet another prescription.

I also made every effort to reach out to my patients' primary care doctors. When patients arrived, one of my first questions was always, "Who is your family doctor?" followed quickly by "What has he said about your condition?" I began reaching out to these primary care physicians to try to establish channels of communication. I created a patient consult form that could effectively transfer important information from one doctor to the next if anyone cared to read it. Not everyone responded to my overtures, of course, and I was accused of being too American, but wherever it worked, it provided much more complete information and seamless patient care.

I was not unique in this approach, and this was not rocket science. This was advanced common sense, as I like to call it. Over the next months, I managed to meet three other US-trained physicians of different specialties who had similar observations and experiences. When I told them about my small-scaled attempts to revolutionize my local systems, they understood what I was talking about. Through this dialogue, we were able to coordinate all our individual efforts to some degree, and before long, the positive results created their own enthusiastic supporters. Patients recognized the better level of care. Doctors and specialists recognized the improved outcomes. Before long, record-keeping systems and patient histories became widespread practices throughout the city. To this day, this is one of the local legacies that I am most proud of in Pakistani health care. I did my small part to introduce and spread this effective, inexpensive strategy for improving care delivery, and it had a great impact.

*****

As Isfana and I began to succeed with our medical practices, our family financial situation quickly improved. We had a good dual income, but we soon found ourselves lacking another critical resource: trusted help. As our lists of patients continued to grow, we both needed not only medical assistants but office workers to manage the scheduling, the paperwork, and the finances. This was sensitive work and not to be trusted to just anyone. It didn't take long to realize that the most trusted and capable people for these jobs were right around the corner—at Venus Medico.

Isfana and I first proposed the idea to my mother and sister, and they agreed. By this time, our two medical practices were more lucrative, prestigious, and valuable to the family than the sleepy old shop on Elphinstone Street. We approached our dear friends at the shop, and they too agreed. Tahir Bhai went to work for Isfana while Maulvi Sahib came to work in my office. The two long-time friends were older now and heads of gray hair, but they were perfectly suited to the work. They were friendly, they were familiar with medical procedures and terminology, they were meticulous, and they were loyal to the family. We all liked the notion of continuing our lifelong association and linking newer generations too. This was especially important to us as Murtuza and Riaz were settling down in their new school. I had finally gotten them into my alma mater, Karachi Grammar School, and Maulvi Sahib and Tahir Bhai became an integral part of their support, growth, and companionship.

The family also made a more difficult decision during this time to sell the old chemist shop. All the old staff were either transplanted to the medical practices or long gone to new jobs around the city. Most of the old customers and Dad's friends had drifted off over the years. It was clear that the future of the Ali family lay in the medical practices, just as my father had always dreamed, but still it was difficult to cut ties with this family business that had been part of our lives for so long. This shop is where all those dreams had begun. In the end, however, we decided the shop should be in the hands of someone who also wanted to build something new and thriving, not a family who ran it out of nostalgia while their real energies were elsewhere. We sold it in 1982, and it is still there to this day, albeit in a different form.

Isfana and I also worked to keep our invaluable US connections with friends intact. We considered New Orleans a second home, especially since the boys had been born there. One spring, our good friends Joyce Ann and Larry Pardue flew over from New Orleans with their son, Loren. Aside from the heat, Pakistan was about as foreign an environment as you could possibly find for this conservative American family. They were wonderful guests though, eager to learn and experience everything they could. They were impressed by our family bungalow which buzzed with family, friends, and servants preparing meals, but it was hard to miss the juxtaposition of our wealth and the incredible poverty which lay, literally, right around the corner. It did not take them long to learn some Pakistani survival skills.

"Saheb, Saheb," a beggar woman implored Larry with her palms outstretched, asking for money as we were walking in the beautiful promenade in Murree. I was about to intervene when Larry, in his quiet way, declined to give her money but waved politely to the woman and said, "Maaf karo, bibi," meaning "Excuse me, pardon me, lady." The open-mouthed amazement on the woman's face was worth photographing, and she burst out in laughter along with the rest of us. Larry knew how to make an impression in his understated way.

In the Punjab, not far from Islamabad, sits one of the great historical sites of the world, the ancient city of Taxila. We spent a lovely day exploring the three-thousand-year-old ruins. The name Taxila is derived from Sanskrit and means "city carved from stone," and the magnificent structures are listed as a United Nations World Heritage Site. Dating back to 1,000 BCE, this had been an important city along the ancient trade routes. As such, it had fallen to many empires over the years: the Achaemenids, the Mauryans, the Indo-Greeks, Indo-Sythians, Kushans, and more. It also happened to be home to what is arguably the first university in the entire history of the world. Not only was this a valuable place of commerce, international trade, and territorial politics, but it was also a center for higher learning as well.

By the time we left, there was no way to catch a cab, so we packed the families onto a public bus, which was also a fascinating study on culture and history. Men and women rode in different sections of the bus, separated by a thin partition. A local villager even climbed aboard with his goat. We were all able to stay close together on either side of the partition, but that didn't stop Joyce Ann from settling in beside a middle-aged Pakistani woman and trying to strike up a conversation. It didn't go very well. The woman was not interested in trying to communicate with this strange white woman who spoke largely in hand signs and a few words of broken Urdu intermingled with English. Joyce Ann was just being friendly, of course, and we all thought it amusing that she couldn't get a smile or response out of this woman beside her. The woman just chewed on her slices of sugarcane and eventually ignored Joyce Ann altogether.

Their son, Loren, meanwhile, was very amused at the amazing variety of colored sodas and drinks available in Pakistan. At one hole-in-the-wall restaurant we enjoyed near Murree, he noticed someone drinking a vivid green colored soft drink. This was a popular local drink called ice-cream soda. Loren was amazed when he saw it, and he called out to his mother. "Mom! Mom! They drink shampoo out here."

We all had another laugh.

That night, back at home, Joyce Ann discovered that the woman on the bus had left her a gift. Joyce Ann's coat pocket was full of chewed up and discarded sugarcane slices. Once more, we all found ourselves laughing together. It was a wonderful visit, and we hated to see it end. But there was always work to do.

By now, I had developed a four-member team, and I mentored these young doctors at the clinic and encouraged them to take these new skills—and even some of this new equipment—back to their private practices. Many of my peers ridiculed me for this approach.

"What are you giving away your secrets, Juzar? You could make a fortune if you guard this practice more carefully."

But knowledge is not any one's monopoly, and I was not interested in fortunes.

Although my focus was not limited, one of my goal was to be a small part in curbing the scourge of TB. There was no direct observed therapy for TB at that time; this is one of the dogma in TB care. There were no field workers, and thus, compliance of treatment was erratic. Patients and family had to deal with numerous other issues which required family resources, so it was extremely challenging to get an improving patient to continue treatment and prescriptions for months after he or she already felt better. But that inevitably led to backsliding and contagion which spread the disease ever further. One of our goals with our careful record keeping was to monitor and curb this behavior, and it worked to a certain degree. When patients knew they were being carefully monitored and held accountable for their own follow-up care, we had much higher rates of success.

With all our energies dedicated to practicing medicine, Isfana and I continued to thrive. Isfana was delivering mental health care that had been nearly impossible to find previously, and I was helping revolutionize the broader concept of chest medicine. By now, we had purchased a separate set of offices for Isfana that were in the same building as mine. She was just upstairs. We had so many patients that we could no longer share the space, a wonderful problem to have. Isfana's work was, by nature, more private and intimate, but my work was becoming more and more public and celebrated. Soon, I was working with international grants. I developed a postgraduate program in chest medicine at the Liaquat National Hospital and University of Karachi. As we were able to reach out to more and more people, we broadened our influence in a positive manner. Our outpatient chest clinic served seventy to one hundred patients per day, which meant patients and family waited all around the clinic: in the hallways, on the steps, gathered upon the green outside, sitting on the mud pilings here or there. Each morning, it was a sight both terrifying and exhilarating. It was so much work and responsibility, but it was also so much trust and opportunity.

It was not unusual for some patients and their families to treat doctors more like gods than people. On occasion, people would literally crouch down and touch my feet, a display of utmost respect, typically reserved for the great teachers and leaders of the world. I hate to admit it now, but that level of adoration and respect went to my head. It wasn't long before I began to feel like I *was* walking on a higher plane. I tried to remain humble, but the environment made it difficult. In addition to the patient adoration, I could find few peers. Very few of us returned to Pakistan. Where were all the people with the same vision and ambition as I had? Even among the doctors who did have international training and expertise, I was somewhat unique in the sense that I was truly Pakistani. Most other internationally trained doctors were there and had dual citizenship at best. They were doing good work here for sure, but they always had one foot out the door with plans to relocate to a more "civilized" destination if and when the time came. Pakistan was like a mission for them, a step in their career paths, but this was my home of final destination. I had no plan B. This was my world. This was my everything.

I felt myself in a unique position. Pakistan might be gripped by poverty and disease, but if I could walk with gods, then perhaps I could lift her up out of sheer willpower. As my professional and social stature grew, I became conscious of the three P's: *paisa, pawaa* and *panga*. Especially *pawaa*, the ability to exert influence and call in favors from hundreds of people connected to government or industry all around the nation.

Health-care delivery in Pakistan was often so rushed and impersonal that most patients were left languishing with conflicting diagnoses, generic treatments, little or no access to specialists, and no follow-up care. The rich, of course, had access to a different level of care, but for most Pakistanis, their interactions with hospitals and doctors were frustrating, time-consuming, expensive, and ineffective. The huge need for medical services, combined with the general lack of health-care resources and combined with the high levels of poverty, created this unfortunate crush. For a physician working in Pakistan, there was no getting around this deluge of patients even for me with my new-fangled approaches and ideas. There was just no way to meet the overwhelming need with the resources we had.

Patients who could afford to follow up with a doctor at his private practice could buy more individual attention, and this is when I would often get to my patients and their families. As much as I disdained this flawed system, I still had to work within it, and I greeted these families, listened to their stories, and accepted the business cards they offered. These cards were the *panga*. These business cards basically said, "You help us now, and we will help you later." They accumulated so quickly that they went into a large ledger, arranged alphabetically by category. Electricity. Police. Construction permits. Taxes. Over the months and years, those cards proved themselves to be invaluable. After a storm, I was able to call in a favor and have our electricity turned back on while the rest of the neighborhood huddled in the dark for days. When we were trying to build a new clinic, I called for building permits that otherwise might have taken months or years to be approved. If I received a citation ticket, it could be taken care of in a matter of minutes on the phone instead of hours at the municipal hall.

I reflected often on the guidance that Dr. Alavi had provided me, and I spent many hours conducting house calls for the frail, the elderly, and, occasionally, the privileged too. It was very taxing after a sixteen-hour day, but most of the time rewarding. One of the most remarkable things about the house calls was the stark contrasts they presented. It's one thing to talk about income inequality. It's one thing to work with both poor and rich patients in hospitals and clinics. But it is quite another thing to meet these people where they live. I might spend one evening in the slums, literally holding my nose as I leapt over moldering piles of trash and stepped around sewerage to reach a patient. I was still quite nimble from my years in the alley off Elphinstone Street. The next day, however, I might be picked up from the clinic in a private car, flown on a private plane, and delivered to the home of a rich industrialist who had heard of my work. These homes were huge, surrounded by stunning gardens, high walls, and guarded gates. The disparity was truly mind-blowing, and it was alarming and a little depressing to realize just how much of the power and wealth of the nations was concentrated in this tiny, exclusive upper class.

On one house call, I was flown in to see a powerful nawab northwest of Karachi. I only knew the man's name and reputation and the reason for his medical request. I didn't know much more about who he was. Of course, nawabs were governors during the Mogul empire, and now the title designated a person of high social and political status, so clearly this was a man of some power and wealth. I was driven to his Haveli, a beautiful, ornate mansion. Right away it was clear that the people around him were extremely loyal; it was in their body language, their tone of voice, their deferential way of speaking. Finally, I met the man. He explained his symptoms, and I gave him a thorough examination, treating him as I would any of my patients. We discussed his condition, and I offered my assessment and my suggestions which he appreciated.

Then it was time for lunch. He provided one of the most lavish meals I have ever partaken of. I was literally being feasted, and there were dozens of people gathered in the dining hall of the mansion with its Mogul style. Out of curiosity, I began to ask the person seated next to me, "Who is that in the corner? Who is that sitting beside the nawab?" Everyone in this room seemed to be some person of power, and many of them looked vaguely familiar although I could not quite place them.

The answers were incredible. "That is the nawab's son. He is leader of the House (leader of the Legislative Assembly). That is another of the nawab's sons. he is leader of the opposition. That man in the corner is the nawab's nephew. He is the commissioner of police. That man there is the nawab's cousin. He is the chief justice." Almost the whole machinery of Pakistani government and power was in one dining room and belonged to one family. And there lay the problem with democracy in Pakistan.

And they were feasting me.

I was stunned, but once again, it was hard not to let my pride swell.

Not all these visits went so smoothly, however. One busy evening, a family walked into my private practice clinic without an appointment. Maulvi Sahib came rushing to me in my office. "I think you should see these people," he said nervously as I was evaluating another patient.

When I was done with my patient, I stepped into the waiting area to meet the family. They had heard of my reputation and wanted a consultation that evening. They introduced themselves, and one of the men handed me his business card. He was with the city department of income tax, the local IRS, and he gave me curt nod and small smile. This was the political favor they were offering—or threatening me with. I remembered vividly from my boyhood days how the taxman in my father's case could sink a business into a legal bureaucratic nightmare, and I was sure that it didn't matter whether it was a small family-run pharmacy or a private practice with a series of pulmonary clinics.

My waiting room was filled with patients and families who had made prior appointments, and I could feel all their eyes on me as I greeted this wealthy, well-connected family who was clearly expecting preferential treatment. My other patients probably expected them to receive preferential treatment too—such was the culture in Karachi. But I wasn't going to do it. I would be glad to work with them, but I wasn't about to bump all my regular patients for this new family just because they were well-connected. I didn't want to set that precedent in my private practice. "I will be happy to see you," I said. "Just as soon as all my regular appointments are taken care of for the evening."

The family became enraged. They felt insulted, and they berated me, flinging accusations and threats. "You have not heard the last of us!" one man yelled as they stormed out the office door.

Almost exactly two months later, the first notification arrived at the office, informing us that we were under audit by the income tax department. There was no way to know for certain that the angry family had anything to do with it, but I have always felt convinced that it was no coincidence.

*****

My mother fell ill in the summer of 1985, and very quickly I began to suspect this was something more significant than a bout of stomach flu. We took her into the hospital where she was treated like a special guest. The test results, however, were far from hospitable. She had cancer of the colon, and even worse, it had metastasized. After further tests, we discovered that the cancer had spread to her spine as well. The whole family was crushed by this news. It was a grim reminder that disease can find any of us and strike with a surprising ferocity.

Despite the good level of care, we simply did not have the most advanced focally directed linear radiotherapy equipment in Pakistan. My mother could receive care, but not the newest treatments that could focus on a more specific location in the body, like the delicate nooks and crannies of her spine. Hers was a very tricky manifestation of the disease, and we had to decide right away how to respond. If the cancer went unchecked through her spinal cord, she would fall into dramatic decline and be dead in months. We quickly decided to fly her to the United States for more advanced care. I still had many connections in the US. In addition to my fellow interns and colleagues from Touro, I traveled there several times for trainings, certifications, and the like. Akila had migrated to California with her husband by then, and that was our destination. Isfana and I both took some time from work, we pulled the body from school, and we flew to California and submitted my mother to the care of some of the world's top oncologists and specialists. While we took care of my mother, we sent Murtuza and Riaz traveling to visit family friend and spend time with the Pardues in New Orleans.

We spent two months in the States. I spent nearly every moment with my mother as she went through her grueling regimen of radiation and chemotherapy. It was challenging for us all, but all the family came together to get the job done, and Ma was a great patient. The treatments were successful.

The trip home was terrible with the usual hassles of air travel: the delays, terminal changes hassles with customs officials, and so on. My mother was still weak, at times carrying her in my arms. I was so concerned about her that I called ahead to make sure an ambulance would be available should we need it in Karachi when we landed. She seemed so small and frail as I helped her into the seat for our last leg of the journey. When we finally arrived back in Pakistan, however, a change came over her. She knew she was home. She straightened her back. She pushed herself up from the chair. She carefully arranged her clothes and walked slowly, but regally, off the plane and to the family car which was waiting for us.

Back in her house, she was surrounded by family and friends who were thrilled to see her restored to health and good spirits. One of our dear old friends took me aside and told me, "Juzar, with this, you have bought your way into heaven." He meant this sincerely, and I considered it a great blessing and privilege that I was able to honor and care for my mother this way. These were good days. At the peak of my career, I felt like I was creating my own small empire here. What I couldn't see—or chose not to see—were the warning signs which had begun to appear on our horizons.

CHAPTER 22

A Gathering Storm

Isfana and I had our private practices in the same building, so often we would coordinate our schedules, so we could go home together. On this particular night, it was hot outside, one of those sweltering, humid South Asian evenings, and growing late. I had finished up all my patient exams and was almost done with the follow-up reports and research, and now it was after ten o'clock. I was looking forward to unwinding with Isfana back at the bungalow and relaxing with a cold drink in a comfortable chair beneath a ceiling fan. I leaned into the waiting room to ask Maulvi Saheb if he would call upstairs and see if Isfana and Tahir Bhai were ready to go home yet. He called but got no answer, which was strange. "I'll run upstairs and see," he said.

"Very well," I replied. "I'll be done soon. We can all leave together."

A few minutes later, Maulvi Saheb returned to my office, and he seemed distressed. "Something is not right," he said.

"What is it?"

"The lights are off, as if they left. But someone is in the back office."

"Tahir Bhai is not there?"

"The front office is empty and dark."

My mind quickly reached around for some explanation that made sense, but I couldn't find one. My stomach tightened as I reached the same conclusion as Maulvi Saheb. Something was not right.

As I began walking, all my instincts told me to hurry. We began to race down the hall and up the stairs. I charged ahead of Maulvi Saheb who was now sixty-five years of age, and when I reached Isfana's office, it was exactly as he had described. The outer office was dark, but a light shone around the edges of the door to the inner office. Muffled sounds came from the office too. My stomach was still clenched in a knot, warning me of danger ahead, and I dashed across the room and threw the office door open. *Isfana* was the only thought racing through my head.

And there she was, tied and gagged, lying in the floor. On the other side of her desk, Tahir Bhai was also tied and gagged. Even worse, he appeared to be having a seizure of some kind. His body convulsed against his ropes, his eyes rolled upward, and his mouth foamed around the gag. Standing over Isfana and Tahir Bhai was a thin tall man with dark eyes that seemed as quick and dangerous as the knife in his hand.

If there was an actual decision made in my mind, it must have been made in a millisecond. Perhaps the sight of Tahir Bhai choking on the floor made me realize there was no time to lose. Perhaps the sight of Isfana bound and gagged sent me into a rage. Or perhaps the instincts that I had developed over the years recognized that there would be only one swift opportunity to attack this disease standing before me. Whatever the motive, I did something that I had never done before: I attacked a man with my bare hands.

He was ready for me as I lunged at him, and he swung the knife viciously. I had no idea what I was doing, charging straight into the blade. As I flew through the air, I twisted my body to protect my vital organs and the strangest thing happened. He somehow swung the knife directly into the bone of my elbow which was clenched against my ribs. My motion combined with his motion did something strange to the physics, and the knife flew out of his hand and clattered across the floor. With that, I was on top of him and we grappled roughly to the floor. He was taller than me, but not much heavier, and I managed to hold him off until Maulvi Saheb finally came through the door and threw himself on top of the man. He was outnumbered now, but he managed to yank himself away from us and bolt out of the office.

"Call the police!" I shouted at Maulvi Saheb as I raced across the floor to untie Isfana and Tahir Bhai. He was unconscious and suffering decorticate seizures often caused by a lack of oxygen. I lifted the tiny man and carried him to the eighth floor of the medical building where there was a hospital, and we began treatment on him immediately. In the meantime, we alerted everyone to the news of the attacker, and the building went into lockdown mode as we all waited for the police to arrive.

It took three hours to find the attacker, but he had never left the building. A security guard finally found him hiding in a bathroom. He was a patient of Isfana's and must have been stalking her before the attack. He knew to wait in hiding until ten o'clock and then come back out to strike. Thank God he didn't know that tonight was a night we were going to ride home together.

Tahir Bhai was stable by now, and we all slowly recovered from the shock. The cut on my elbow was stitched up and appeared to miraculously be only a small flesh wound. We all felt relieved to be alive and to know that the attacker was captured. Little did we know the trouble was far from over.

Due to Pakistan's long history of political upheaval, military coups, and martial law, there were basically two parallel systems of government and law at all times: the civilian and the military. The civilian government was democratic and corrupt, riddled with inefficiencies and officials who worked for bribes rather than the good of the people. The military government was autocratic and severe, but it was efficient. We were now involved with the civilian legal system, and it turned into a nightmare almost immediately. The investigators who arrived to ask Isfana about the attack immediately concluded that it was an attempted rape. Their line of questioning quickly took an offensive turn: "So what did you do to instigate this man?"

"I'm his doctor," Isfana replied calmly. "I did not instigate him."

The investigators weren't convinced.

Meanwhile, the attacker was in custody, but no charges were brought against him, even days later. By now, I had raided my *pawaa* and *panga* file to see what favors I could call in or muster some support, but nothing seemed to work. The police didn't seem to care one bit about the man who attacked my wife and tried to kill me with a knife. Instead, they began to investigate Isfana and me. They would come around our offices during work hours to inform us that they had discovered a delinquent bill, and could we please explain our transgressions. Of course, what they were really after were bribes. This was exactly why no one in Pakistan ever wanted to deal with the police. Once they got on the scent of money, there was no shaking them. Finally, one police officer made a blatant offer. "If you want us to stop coming around, just bribe us. For enough money (paisa), we'll close the whole case."

Isfana and I refused to drop the charges against the attacker, however. We felt it was important to force the legal system to do its job. We suffered the many indignities that the police delivered, and we paid the occasional bride to move the case through the system, and we pressed forward even as our friends advised against it.

Finally, we realized that there would never be a trial or conviction in civilian court. So we turned to the military system. Once again, against all odds, we hounded every connection we could discover until we found a sympathetic ear. It was a military judge. We walked into this office without announcement and presented our case. He agreed to take jurisdiction of the whole case. The attacker finally went to court and was sentenced to one year in prison. We were disappointed with the lenient sentence, but at least there was some sense of closure and justice.

In the back of our minds, however, we couldn't shake the sick feeling we had gotten from trying to work with the civilian police. Their ineptitude and corruption in this case were beyond anything we had already come to expect. This couldn't possibly bode well for Karachi, or for Pakistan. I comforted myself with two thoughts: (1) surely, this situation will get better as Karachi modernizes, and (2) I had the means to stay mostly above the fray. We had learned a valuable lesson from this attack, and I had the private means to keep my family safe without having to depend on the police. After all, I was a god in this town, right? Life was still good.

Not long after the conviction, we received our first anonymous threat in the mail. It was a hand-scrawled note that informed us that the sender intended to kidnap our children. We assumed the note came from the convicted assailant or someone connected to him, and we took every precaution even as we hoped it was all just a hoax.

Pakistan had always had her challenges—her tribalism, political instability, rugged (but beautiful) geography, and more—but throughout the first four decades of her existence, there persisted an overwhelming optimism. The population grew in leaps and bounds. The economy grew on the backs of entrepreneurs and men like my fathers who ran small businesses. A middle class scraped its way into existence. But this felt like something new. Political parties had long been the centers of heated debate, but now there was a menace of violence that seemed to be growing. Of course, the police were little help. Reports of riots and deadly clashes between ethnic groups began to make their way onto the front pages of the newspaper. Violence in neighboring countries also seemed to be spilling over the borders and into Pakistan. Conflicts in Kashmir. War in Afghanistan. The United States had been funneling hundreds of millions of dollars through Pakistan to arm and train *mujahedeen* who were fighting the Soviets and Marxists, and Peshawar, Pakistan, was a staging ground for foreign militants preparing to join the fight.

One of the men running these camps was Osama bin Laden. In May of 1988, when a riot broke out between Sunnis and Shea in the beautiful, mountainous territory of Gilgit Pakistani President Zia-ul Haq authorized Osama bin Laden to lead a campaign of suppression. This became the Gilgit massacre where hundreds of Shia civilians were lynched, burned, shot, raped, and murdered. Thousands more fled from the campaign of terror which included burning farms, destroying crops, and killing livestock. This type of terror hadn't been inflicted on Pakistani civilians since partition. What we knew in Karachi was that this mayhem and bloodshed were seeping into the fabric of our society. To make matters even worse, the nation was slowly descending into an economic recession. As unemployment rates ticked higher, so did violent crime like muggings, armed robberies, and carjackings. It seemed like every week, there was a new story at the hospital about someone being robbed at gunpoint.

I refused to let my optimism be dampened, however. "It is just a phase," I told Isfana. She had been amazing through this whole time. Not only did she bounce back from the traumatic attack on herself in the clinic, but she also continued becoming the anchor of the family, keeping up with my mother's frail health, managing our social obligations, and looking after the boys—all while maintaining her own career.

But she worried about our safety. She had obvious concerns for the boys, especially with their school and event schedules. We knew that the city was becoming a dangerous place and that the police were next to useless when it came to protecting people.

"We'll be fine," I told her. By now, we had employed drivers and guards who would deliver us to our destinations and pick us up at the door. "I'll send a driver with you and the boys wherever you go."

*****

It had been eighteen months since we brought my mother home from her cancer treatments in the US, and she was enjoying her days. Surrounded by grandchildren, family, and friends. But then she took a fall. It wasn't a terrible fall, but it was enough to break her hip, that large bone that becomes so vulnerable with age and cancer therapy. Friends and colleagues and especially Dr. Naveed Shah continued to help her, but her health was on a tragic, final decline. She passed away at home I was there at her bedside, and I said the Azaan in her ears and bid her goodbye. It was a crushing loss, and it rekindled the feelings of loss I still felt for my father too. Now they were both snatched from me.

*****

I worked a lot. It kept my mind busy, and it fed my ambitions as I built my professional empire. Between the hospital, the medical school, the private practice, and the series of clinics, I often worked sixteen-hour days, and I was lucky if I took one day off per week. One of the perks of my position, however, was that I could make an adventure happen by just clapping my hands. If I decided to take an afternoon off, I could have a horse-drawn carriage, a sightseeing excursion, a boat trip, or a huge beach picnic arranged in a matter of minutes. All I had to do was issue the orders, dispatch the invitations, and a wonderful afternoon lay before us. On one such afternoon, I took the family and some friends to the beach for some fun. Everyone had been a little on edge lately, and I knew we needed to relax and remind ourselves of the good things we had here in Karachi.

It was a beautiful day, and we were having a ball on the beach as we swam in the sea, picnicked, and then organized a pickup game of cricket. I was showing off some of my old batting skills to the boys. Everything was going well until I twisted awkwardly and felt a sharp pain in my hip. My foot had been planted in the sand, and I had lunged at a bad angle, and now I was having some trouble hobbling back. What initially felt like a twist turned out to be a freak incident. I had produced enough torque to fracture my own hip.

Surgery, I was told. This was terrible news. This meant I would be off my feet for weeks, not working. That was more disturbing to me than the injury itself. The surgery went successfully, but the recovery did not. I was plagued with one complication after another (the doctor syndrome), including a pulmonary embolism that could have been fatal.

A few weeks bed rest turned into a few months. Then a few months stretched into half a year. I was on medications and physical therapy regimens, and I was sinking into anxiety and depression. The whole episode was stressful for everyone in the family, but we were fortunate to have the support of family, friends, and some excellent colleagues like Dr. Naveed Shah and Dr. Sohaila Ali, who helped us through more than just my rehabilitation but also our emotions, our clinical issues, and other big decisions that had to be made on a regular basis.

By this time, I had reached out to Kakajee Hashim Ali's family and all my cousins, specially Mansoor Bhai and Sajjad Bhai with due respect. I had stressed through my actions that all the previous history of tension and squabbles while we were growing up should be set aside. I always tried to walk an extra mile with our relationship with them, and they reciprocated with their love and support. The relationship with them entered a new phase of family cordiality and support. The same applied with Shirin Bahen and her family and my overtures to be the mediator peacemaker after her falling out with my dad years ago paid off. She and her family became our staunchest allies and well-wishers.

There were also some people, however, who came around who did not have my best interests at heart. Not at all. In my vulnerable state, I did not recognize these people as charlatans, and when I look back now, it's embarrassing to think I fell for their lies, but at the time, I was feeling quite desperate, and that clouds a person's judgment. Both men who conned me were acquaintances I had known for years, and thus, I assumed they were here to support me and my family through this tough time. The first man was deeply religious and preached at mosque. He also worked for the government-run electric company, and we often traded favors. I would look after health-care needs for him and his family, and he would help me restore power to my clinics or my home after storms or outages. As he came around the house, he saw the decline in my physical and mental health, and he took it upon himself to bolster my spirits through religion. "You must regain your spiritual health to regain your physical health," he said. He often led us in prayers and talked to me about the Koran and its many parables. And then he began asking for money. "This small donation to the mosque would shine in the eyes of God. It will bring you peace."

Over the weeks, I consented and gave him several donations for his various religious causes. Months later, I would realize how blatantly he played me for these donations, some of which he kept as a kind of "commission," as if he were spiritual salesman or a *pujari* (religious) trader.

The other vulture was also a man I had known for years. Ahmad Bhai. Again, I treated his whole family, often for free, since he had been a friend of my father's. I was sure the he was coming around now to return the favor and see if he could help our family out in our time of need. He quickly homed in on my anxiety and depression though and saw a way to take advantage of it. "I have a way for you to make money, even from your bed."

"How do you mean?"

"Investment capital," he replied. "If you're smart, you can make your money work for you." He explained that he was helping to finance and manage the building of a new mall in Karachi. I knew the spot he was talking about, and it piqued my interest. On his next visit, he brought blueprints, business plans, financial documents, construction permits, and more to show me how close they were to finalizing the whole deal. "From one friend to another, I tell you: this is a golden opportunity."

I mentioned the golden opportunity to one of my childhood friends, Hunaid. Hunaid and I had been members of the Jolly Cricket Club together, and he still lived in the neighborhood. He also became interested, and he began to investigate the project too. "I think it looks good," he reported back to me, and we decided that we would invest together. We both pulled sums from our savings accounts and turned it over to this investment wizard who had promised us golden returns. Within a month, Ahmad Bhai had disappeared. I couldn't reach him on the phone. Hunaid couldn't find him at his home. He had either left the city or moved to some remote corner of it where he could hide. Naturally, our money disappeared with him. Hunaid and I were crushed, and I couldn't believe what had just happened to us. He was devastated at the loss. I decided to pay him his investment and bear his loss too.

One of the first step I did was to repay Hunaid his share of the investment money he had lost. I felt that I may have inadvertently lured him into that failed investment venture, and although we had participated in it with full disclosure and with due diligence, his loss to him qualitative and quantitatively meant a whole lot to him than my loss to me. I decided to translate the entire episode into a learning experience and reflected on the value of true friendship. I suspected—and I was right—that the future would hold new trials and tests of friendship, and I would be better prepared. Friends remained my focus and one of them, Akhter remained steadfast in his support as I did with him. He was also a sounding board for us as we helped him navigate his personal issues.

As events would later show in different scenarios, I suffered many a financial loss in the future too, not because of bad investments on my part necessarily but because of being tolerant and accepting losses. I would rather do that than compromise on relationships and friendships. A flaw maybe. I do not think so.

CHAPTER 23

Wildfire

Finally, *finally*, I was able to walk again, and as soon as I was able, I returned to work. It was a wonderful feeling to walk through the doors of my clinic. I was thrilled to see the faces of my patients, my students, trainees, and associates. I was greeted warmly by my colleagues at the hospital. And soon, my private practice was bustling again. All the commotion felt heavenly after all those months of illness and immobility. It didn't take long to get back into the routine of things. As my personal anxieties slowly receded over the next few months, it was impossible not to notice that the collective anxieties of my colleagues seemed to have ratcheted up to surprisingly high levels. Over the past year, I had grown accustomed to Isfana's concerns about personal safety, and they seemed perfectly understandable after the attack in her office. What I had failed to recognize, however, was that Isfana also had her finger on the pulse of this much larger situation. Security throughout Pakistan was deteriorating, and doctors were becoming targets of criminals and organized crime.

Another destabilizing force was the war which had been raging in Afghanistan for almost a decade now. Four million fleeing Afghans had relocated to Pakistan, and huge numbers of Pashtuns settled in the cities, including Karachi, where they squeezed in with the myriad ethnic communities like the Punjabis, Sindhis, Siddis, Saraikis, Biharis, Muhajirs, and more. Pashtuns brought with them two iconic symbols from Afghanistan: the Kalashnikov automatic rifle and kilos of heroin which they could sell in the cities. Karachi had never experienced large-scale gun violence or the horrors of rampant opiate addiction, but now she was awash in both, not to mention the organized crime that came with this influx. Ethnic tensions had always simmered just beneath the surface of the city, but now they began to spill out into the open. In the competition for jobs, resources, and territory, communities began to fight openly with one another, especially as Pashtun drug lords and street gangs began to expand. One territorial riot between Pashtuns and Muhajirs in 1985 resulted in over one hundred deaths. In 1986, a Pashtun minivan driver drove through a red light and ended up accidentally killing a Muhajir schoolgirl. Events quickly escalated into another large-scale riot which eventually spread across most of the city, filling the air with the sounds of gunfire the stench of acrid smoke as buses, cabs, and minivans were set ablaze in the lawless streets.

By far, the worst of the riots was the Qasba Aligarh Colony massacre where the Pakistani army turned a blind eye as a huge, heavily armed mob of Pashtuns burned a large Muhajir-Bihari neighborhood to the ground, murdering up four hundred people and wounding hundreds more.

The rise in ethnic violence was accompanied by a rise in political violence too. In the past, political assassinations had been rare and dramatic, but this new era of targeted killings was more chilling because of the casual disregard for life and the cold-blooded carnage. Hit men began to buzz around the city on the backs of motorcycles, pulling up next to moving cars and filling them with bullets. Political organizations began to look for creative ways to finance their legal and illegal activities. Drug dealing, robbery, and carjacking were already a problem, but now they became epidemic throughout the city.

In a span of two years, Isfana and I lost three cars as our drivers were held at gunpoint and, in one case, beaten. Once the car was stolen at gunpoint from in front of our house, once it was taken from the parking area of the boys' school, and once it was taken while Isfana was waiting to be driven home from work. The occupation of family driver or a chauffeur had suddenly become like working in a combat zone. And while neither Isfana nor I ever were forced to look down the barrel of a gun ourselves, these incidents alarmed us. We cared a great deal for the people who worked for our family, and we were scared by the violent turns of events.

Still, I persevered. What else could I do? This was my home. This was my life. I had invested everything to be where I was right now. I was at the pinnacle of my career, and I held out hope that leadership might emerge to curb the violence and to ease the economic hardship. I was still guided by my dreams and by the dreams of my father. Surely, the people of Pakistan had worked too hard to build this nation to simply let it be destroyed from the inside out.

Unfortunately, in this environment, doctors became easy targets. They often earned good income by Pakistani standards, they were private citizens usually not affiliated with the government, and they worked with the public, making them easily approachable. Doctors could be threatened, intimidated, or even kidnapped with relative ease. The police had been playing a version of this game for generations now, extorting brides in exchange for leniency or to simply do their job. Criminals took this tactic to the next level. They began to single citizens out—often doctors, lawyers, or other professionals—and demand money through harassing phone calls or by sending intimidating strangers to a person's office. What did the citizen get in return for this money?

To remain alive.

The first time I heard of this extortion, it sent a chill through my blood. It seemed such a short time ago that my colleagues and I discussed things like cricket scores, conferences, fishing, or family vacations when we gathered together in the break rooms or at a social gathering. Then we found ourselves discussing drugs, muggings, and carjackings. Now we discussed death threats and ransom payments. Fortunately, no one close to us had fallen victim to this new wave of crime yet, but it was almost like feeling the noose tighten slowly around your neck. First it was rumors about a doctor from a hospital across town. He had refused to pay the bribes, and he had been gunned down in his car. Of course, the newspapers and police offered conflicting accounts of the story, so nobody knew for sure.

Next, it was a doctor we knew from the medical school; it was rumored that he was making regular payments to keep himself from being harmed. We scanned the newspapers with new urgency each morning and evening, looking for any bad news involving doctors, and we all continued to show up for work each day to help our patients. Finally, the violence began to creep into our own social circles, and we heard of or received direct and indirect threats time and again.

For months and months, we persevered through these challenging circumstances, but finally came a day when I realized that my situation might be untenable. I was at work when another riot erupted in one of the neighborhoods and quickly ignited across the city the way a forest fire might sweep across miles of dry and combustible timber. The whole city seemed like it was constantly on the verge of fiery destruction. Isfana was on her way home from work, and it took her and the driver hours to navigate around the mobs, the burning buses, the blockades, the platoons of riot police and army reserves pouring down crowded streets. Finally, Isfana and the driver made it back to our bungalow. Meanwhile, the riot continued to grow. Isfana called me at the hospital and told me not to try to come home. "It's everywhere," she said. "Stay in central city tonight."

My eldest sister, Shirin Bahen, whose family we had now become very close with, lived near the hospital, so I decided to stay with her, but I was really thinking how horrible this situation was for a doctor who needed to travel all over the city—from hospitals to clinics to a private practice where patients would be waiting. There was simply no way to work in conditions like these. For days after a riot like this, roads would still be shut down and traffic would be a nightmare.

Later that evening, I was commiserating with a colleague and friend, Dr. Salahuddin. He was an ENT surgeon and one of few other American-trained doctors in Karachi. We were both complaining about the insanity of the situation and how challenging the problem was for the government to deal with. That's when he said, "Well, if the government cannot come up with a plan, I have one of my own."

"What's that?" I asked.

He opened his doctor coat and plucked something from the inside pocket. I recognized that document in an instant: his US passport. He had been one who took advantage of the visa opportunities to gain US citizenship while he was doing his internships and residency. Now he was carrying the passport around with him like a lifeline, even at the hospital.

"You will show that to the looters?" I joked, but I knew what he was about to say.

"When it gets too bad, I will walk out that door and go straight to the airport."

That was the moment when I realized just how naive all my optimism had been. I had declined the US green card and passport. I had invested everything into Karachi. I had "burned my boats," and now I had no plan B.

As if to drive this point home to me even further, I had to pass the US embassy that night on the way to my sister's house. It was nearly dark, and the embassy was closed, but a line of people wrapped all the way around the block, waiting to get an interview the next day in hopes of obtaining a US visa and a chance to escape the bloodshed and mayhem gripping Pakistan. I glided past those desperate people in my car, and that image was forever emblazoned on my imagination—people fleeing toward that American flag in moments of terror and crisis. I knew my kids could leave, and that brought a little peace of mind, but Isfana and I could not.

That night, I lay awake in the dark, listening to the sounds of sirens in the distance, and I thought of my family. I thought of my sons having to sneak out the back door of their school after we received threats of kidnapping. I thought of the fear in Isfana's eyes every time we left the house. I thought of our family drivers, cooks, and staff being held up, trapped in their neighborhoods, and even beaten. *Juzar Ali*, I thought to myself, *something has to be done, no matter the price.*

PART III

Starting Over. Again.
The Perpetual Migrant

God, bless America,
Land that I love.
Stand beside her,
And guide her
Through the night with a light from above.
From the mountains
To the prairies
To the oceans white with foam,
God, bless America,
My home, sweet home.

—Irving Berlin

CHAPTER 24

Mayflower II

July 5, 1991. We told almost no one that we were leaving. Not our colleagues, not our friends or neighbors. There was too much at stake, and there was so much that could go wrong. We only trusted a tight knot of our closest family and friends with our true plans of escape. To everyone else, it simply looked like the Ali family was taking another trip to America, just as we had each year. These plans had been in the works for months, as they were each year, so nothing seemed suspicious. Or so we hoped.

We had no idea what lay in store for us in the US. We didn't know if this was going to be a short holiday or an extended stay, but we knew one thing: we wanted out of Pakistan. We each packed a suitcase, like always, and we said goodbye to that close group of friends and relatives. I now had the nerve-racking experience of driving my family and all the cash I could withdraw from the bank clear across Karachi to the airport.

It had taken months, but I was able to secure visitor's visas for Isfana and me. It helped immensely that we had a long history of professional travel to the US and back, so while thousands of people were being denied visas, we were very fortunate to receive ours. The boys, of course, were US citizens from birth and carried those blue passports with the eagle and shield emblazoned upon them. Now we made our way through the ticket lines and then checked our luggage. We waited by the departure gate, making small talk and daydreaming about what foods and shops and sights we wanted to see in New

York. We pretended to be patient. We boarded the plane in a calm, orderly fashion when our time came.

The flight was uneventful, which is normally exactly what you want in a flight, but the quiet time allowed my brain to spin with anxiety and questions. As we glided over the clouds, I asked myself over and over, *What was I thinking? Was I doing the right thing? Could we possibly succeed?* I had no immediate job offers or prospects and no plan beyond landing in New York and starting to call people. No one even knew what we were up to. Neither did we. Would we stay in America? Was it even possible? My head was full of doubts even as the land beneath us dropped away and the deep blue expanse of Atlantic Ocean glittered as far as I could see to the horizon. I knew this that I had to try to explore what was out here for the sake of my family though. From thirty-five thousand feet, I peered down on the earth and thought about the cycles of adventure and exploration in my family. I thought of my father's fateful journey during partition to find his new life in Pakistan. I remembered my 1973 venture to Kenya to make my own path with Isfana. Or trip to the US for our residencies. The journey back home where I was able to launch such a remarkable career. And now this.

In Karachi, I could easily lose myself on the cloud of my ego, content amid my professional and societal success, happy with the wealth and prestige I had accumulated. But I had to do something about the pain my family and my wife feel living in that toxic environment. I had always believed that life moved in mysterious or cyclical phases, and that dictated one's most pressing priorities. Here we were now back in USA. I could see the mainland come into view through the small window of the jetliner, and I began to feel an old familiar feeling that came from being in a new land: that of the perpetual migrant.

When we touched down at JFK airport in New York, it had been almost exactly ten years since we left the US in 1981 to return to Pakistan with our boxes of books and some used medical equipment. Almost immediately, I knew that I had to give this next cycle of migration my best shot. I knew this from the expressions on the faces of Isfana and the boys. I knew this from their body language, which had transformed in between Karachi and here. In Pakistan, we lived in a constant state of tension. Even in our own home, which was secured and filled with luxuries both small and large, there was always such fear and somberness as the violence from around the nation weighed upon us. We lived with death threats and carjackings and the specter of kidnappings and ransoms. Public spaces had become unsafe for us. With all those fears and fetters behind us, Isfana and the boys laughed and played and moved freely without worrying about what the people around them were thinking.

They appeared taller and brighter than just hours before. I had seen this transformation before, of course, when we came for visits, but this time was different. It made me realize just how long it had been since I had witnessed my family in a state of true happiness. We were here to try and make this beautiful place our home, and my family positively radiated joy. To make the occasion even more joyful, my sister Cheeko and her husband, Bhai Yusuf, and their boys greeted us at the airport. They had recently migrated to the US themselves, and it filled us with hope to see them. We felt like pilgrims to the New World, only this was our second time landing here in as many decades. We were the *Mayflower II*.

We spent the first few days enjoying the city and visiting family and friends who lived in the northeast. Even now, we only trusted our closest people with the truth about our plans. We couldn't risk having someone send word back home. In the meantime, I kept in touch with my Karachi clinics and colleagues via phone to receive updates and make management decisions, just as if this were a normal business trip. The subterfuge began to weigh on me quickly, but I had no choice. If people in Karachi knew that I was actively considering staying in the United States, my medical positions would be eliminated, my clinics clientele could be affected, and my private practice would be shuttered. Then if things didn't work out in the US, I would not only be trapped in a terrible legal limbo, but financially, we could be ruined. There was so much on the line.

Slowly, tentatively, I began putting feelers out to see about job prospects. I made calls to my close American friends and colleagues. I had many professional connections from my residency days and beyond, but none of them had connections I needed in the Northeast or on the West Coast, the two areas I thought would be most appealing and possibility rich. It was going to be like jumping through the eye of a needle to figure out how to stay in the U.S. legally, and that was very important to me. We had come in legally and we were determined to stay legally. All my friends and connections recommended the same thing: *find a teaching hospital system or university*. That would be the most likely institution to offer both employment and a visa sponsorship. After more calls and conversations, it quickly became clear to me that I needed a professional connection to get an introduction. I wasn't going to be able to walk in off the street like some kind of refugee and be taken seriously as a physician and teacher. There was only one US city, however, where I still had those kinds of connections.

When we landed in New Orleans, Joyce Ann Pardue greeted us at the airport and took us back to their home where we stayed for few weeks, until we were able to find a short-term apartment of our own. They were incredibly welcoming and supportive although there was some culture shock as we settled into their lovely Uptown New Orleans home. First, we had to get used to Cupcake, their lovely dog. That was a new adventure and experience for all of us. In Pakistan, as in much of the Middle East and Southeast Asia, dogs were not considered household pets, so this took some getting used to. Then of course, there was New Orleans cuisine, music, and culture that were so foreign. Even when we lived here, Isfana and I had often been a step removed from the city we lived in. We worked hard, we cooked for ourselves, and we rarely went out as trainees with two small kids on a limited income. Now we were immersed in the Pardue home with its Southern cooking, its New Orleans music, and its vivacious energy. It was all wonderful but felt very strange to us.

In the meantime, the clock was ticking. Isfana and I were in the United States on six-month visitor visas, so we had a very short window of time and a limited budget to try to start a new life. I went to work calling on all my old connections at Touro and Tulane, looking for guidance or any kind of opportunity. I had some wonderful reunions, and everyone was generous with their time, but no one seemed to know of a position that I could apply for in my current legal status. They all promised to keep an eye out for me.

When I wasn't job hunting, Isfana and I spent time apartment hunting. The trick was we needed a place with a short lease since we had no way of knowing how long we would be here or where our fortunes—or misfortunes—might take us. It took a couple weeks, but finally we found an apartment complex on the West Bank that would accept us without much credit history and no guarantors. Later, we found why we had been fortunate to get that apartment. It was in a complex known for drugs and drug dealers. I am glad we were ignorant of that background.

Next, Isfana and I decided to go ahead and get the boys enrolled in school here. The US school year was about to start now, and no matter what happened, we didn't want them falling behind in their education or opportunities. They both wanted to attend university in the US, and this would be Zee's last year of high school where he would begin submitting applications. Despite the uncertainty surrounding our situation, we had to keep an eye on the boys' futures as well as our own. Once more, this proved to be very challenging. Once more, we found ourselves going door-to-door at the last minute with our two sons who had been in foreign school systems. As before, it took a lot of time and effort, but finally we found a good placement for them with St. Martin's in Metairie, just outside New Orleans. It was a private Episcopal school, but they provided a warm welcome for our sons and our family, and we were grateful to have found them. We had considered public schools, but we were quickly warned off them.

At the time, the perpetually troubled public education system of New Orleans was riddled with corruption and had a reputation for violence and very low college success rates. The choice was clear, but it came with a cost. The first time I saw the high school tuition rates, I nearly fell out of my chair. By the time I converted the rupees to American dollars, one year at this private school costs more than most people paid for an entire four-year university degree in Pakistan. The fees we paid for Riaz and Murtuza depleted our savings and budget for this venture to an alarmingly low level. But then I remembered the day when my dad had enrolled me in Karachi Grammar School and later unbuttoned his shirt to cover my tuition with the Adamjee Science college professor. It was my time to do the same.

Between the apartment, the school and basic living expenses, I realized we were burning through my savings at a rapid clip. It wasn't just the conversion rate that was hitting us hard; it was the cost of living here in the US too. Still, I had brought my entire savings, so I was confident we would be all right. During a conversation with one of our friends who was helping us finding an apartment, I was asked point-blank, "How much money do you have here?"

"I brought everything."

"Have you converted it all to dollars?"

"Yes," I replied. "It's in the bank now."

"And how much is it?"

I knew she was being helpful, not nosy, so I answered her question directly. The look on her face told me everything I needed to know. I was not nearly as well-off as I had imagined. When I sat down and did the math carefully, it was clear that by bringing my savings to America, I had, overnight, become five times poorer than I had been in Pakistan. It was yet another thing that I hadn't calculated all the way through in our determination to escape, and it was incredibly humbling. Not only had I left my prestige and clout back in Pakistan, but I had suddenly plummeted down the socioeconomic ladder as well. I had gone from being an equal with my colleagues and peers to being pet project, living in a bare apartment and budgeting carefully for groceries. I knew very well that money was not the criteria by which you judged a man, but I also knew that it was an important element of providing for your family and living with a sense of security.

The sudden change of fortunes hit the boys quite hard too. In Pakistan, they lived with fear, but they also lived at the top of their social ladder. They wore nice clothes, spent their time in nice homes, were surrounded by family and friends, and could afford to go out to movies, restaurants, or parties. Now they were strangers in their schools and had very few friends their own age, and we shopped for clothes on the sale racks in Kmart. Our apartment had little furniture. In fact, one of the criteria we looked for in an apartment was wall to wall carpeting so we could put a sheet down and sleep on the floor with just pillows. There was one small television, and this was our entertainment.

In the evenings, after office hours, the Pardues allowed me to use their office so I could research, compose cover letters, and send off more and more inquiries about licensure and employment. When it was time to sleep, we retired to two bedrooms and slept on our bedrolls on the floor. For all the challenges, we were still thrilled to be striving toward a new life here in the United States. It was the cloud of uncertainty that hung over my head at night, however, that kept me awake into the late hours of the night. Those nagging questions just wouldn't go away. *What am I thinking? Am I doing the right thing? Can we possibly succeed? Once again, that feeling that the decision I had taken was a fine line between courage and stupidity and only the outcome would determine which it was.*

One of the most difficult things I did during these months was spend time on the phone with my colleagues and employees back in Pakistan, pretending that everything was still normal. There was still a great deal of work each week running the Karachi clinics, coordinating care and consulting with my residents and doctors. It was like straddling two worlds (and two time zones) that were so far apart that I might split in two. But I absolutely needed to keep my options open. If this American adventure fell through—and it most certainly could fall through—I had to be able to return home when my visa expired. The days ticked off the calendar, growing ever closer to that expiration date, and I juggled these time-consuming affairs: managing work back home even as I reached out to doctors and hospitals all over Southern Louisiana, looking for opportunity. One of the major hurdles we faced was that the Louisiana state board had inactivated our licenses to practice in Louisiana due to nonrenewal. To reactivate that, we would need to sit for a fresh recertification exam, but that alone could take months. This tight situation limited any options for even those who were eager to help us. The only route was an attachment with an academic institution in some capacity that would give me some time and flexibility to complete whatever legal and academic requirements were needed to change my visa status from a visitor to a legal resident allowed to work. Isfana faced nearly identical circumstances although she was tapping in with the Department of Mental Health through the state system.

While most approaches were leading to dead ends, I approached my past mentors at Touro, Dr. Dhurandhar and Dr. Shames, who connected me with the section head of pulmonary critical care at LSU Health Sciences Center downtown. Dr. Summer was willing to meet me, and we set up some time for a Friday morning. I was thrilled. This was the first real opportunity that I had been able to find in my particular situation for months now. When that Friday morning rolled around, however, I received a call from his administrative assistant telling me that he was going out of town for two weeks and needed to reschedule the appointment. *Two weeks.* I almost had a panic attack just thinking of waiting that long as my visa expiration date ticked ever closer. I explained my situation and asked very politely but urgently, "Is there any possibility that Dr. Summer might be able to meet with me before he leaves? Even just for a few minutes."

The assistant hesitated, but she replied, "Let me speak with Dr. Summer." She put me on hold, and I felt suspended in midair, practically holding my breath. I needed this meeting.

When the assistant came back on the line, she asked, "Can you be here at 8:00 AM today?"

I glanced at the clock on the wall; that was in thirteen minutes. "Yes, I can," I replied.

I rushed from the West Bank. Fortunately, the traffic on the Mississippi River Bridge was not terrible as it was most of the time. I parked the car we were using, courtesy of the Pardues, and put in twenty-five cents for the one-hour parking spot. I was thinking that I should have gotten change back; this would not take long. I was not even sure if Dr. Summer was meeting me in earnest or just as a courtesy to Dr. Dhurandhar. The sunlight glared, and the August heat radiated from everything: the pavement, the cars, the buildings. I quickly checked my CV and letters of recommendation one more time and then rushed around the building, getting my first look at the LSU Health Sciences Center.

As with all things American, it was big, spanning multiple buildings over four city blocks. A bright red skyway passed over Gravier Street, connecting the main building with its outposts. Inside, I was grateful for the cool air-conditioning as I observed how organized the main building was, with information desks and specialized departments arranged across the many floors of the large glass and concrete building. That made it easy to find the office I was looking for, and I entered right on time for my meeting.

"Very nice to meet you, Dr. Ali," the assistant said. She was very nice woman. "I'll let Dr. Summer know you're here, and he'll meet you shortly."

"Thank you."

It was only a few moments before she showed me into his office.

"Dr. Ali," said Dr. Summer.

"Dr. Summer," I replied. "Thank you very much for meeting me."

"It's all right," he replied. "I understand you're in a tricky situation."

"That is correct."

"I'm familiar with that."

As a large teaching institution, LSU worked extensively with medical and nursing students from all over the world, not to mention the international physicians and professionals on staff. This was exactly the kind of place that I needed to be attached to, and Dr. Summer understood this perfectly. He was a personable man, and he listened attentively as I told him the brief version of my story. I tried not to come across as desperate, but it was clear to both him and me that I was playing high stakes poker with a handful of twos and threes. "I don't care what you pay me, and I'm willing to take on any role," I told him very directly. We talked a little bit about my clinical experience back home, but then he realized the time. He glanced at his watch and said, "Look, I have to go. But I want to introduce you to a couple people before I take off."

We went down the hall, and he introduced me to a colleague before he left. I started all over with my story, but this time, I had a chance to talk more specifically about my work back in Pakistan. My practice. My clinics. My teaching. I met three of the faculty members in that department, one after the other. It was a strange experience to find myself on this side of the desk again after years of sitting on the authoritative side back home, listening to people come to *me*, looking for jobs, partnerships, or other opportunities. I had gotten used to that view from the padded chair that reclines and swivels. Now I was sitting in the straight-backed chair with my back to the door. It was difficult to say where this was going except that all of them, Judd, Ben, and Steve, were engaged and probably curious.

It had all been very friendly and impromptu, but by the time I reached the street again, I felt like I had just been through the longest job interview of my life. I had spent five hours inside, which was exactly how I returned to my car to find a bright orange envelope tucked beneath my windshield wiper and addressed to the City of New Orleans Violation Branch. Inside, of course, was a parking ticket.

Later, I would come to view that parking ticket as one of the best investments I ever made. Now it was a bummer though and just reminded me of my precarious situation.

A few days later, I got a call. It was from Dr. Summer's office, asking me to meet Dr. Bobear at the Charity Hospital Pulmonary Clinic. This was not a job offer, to be clear, but it was an invitation to work a trial session and see how I fit in with the residents, faculty, and patients of the program. I would act as a visiting instructor. No salary. No contract. No visa or paperwork. But this was a huge break for me.

"I'll be there," I said.

I arrived a little early at the charity clinic, and Dr. Bobear was not there yet. The residents were already there, however, so I introduced myself. The students began asking me questions, and I fell easily into the role of instructor. For years, instruction had been a significant part of my portfolio in Pakistan as I had developed the University PG program at LNH. Now I found myself surrounded by these aspiring young residents, and I fell into an easy banter with them. They conducted all the initial interviews and screenings with patients, and I provided guidance, offering suggestions, follow-up questions, insights into diagnoses, and technical skills such as diagnostic imaging or interpreting test results. It was a blast, and I found myself so engaged in the process I didn't even realize that Dr. Bobear had arrived some time ago and had been hanging back observing me. "Things seem to be going well, Dr. Ali," he said when I finally introduced myself.

"We were just brainstorming a course of action for the patient."

"Excellent."

After that introduction, it only took a few days for Dr. Summer to offer me a full-time position. "You can join us as a clinical research associate," he said, and those were the sweetest words I could have possibly heard in that moment. I knew there was still much work ahead of me, but this was a big break. This was a mountain of stress lifted off my shoulders. These were words that could stop that visa deadline from looming in my imagination and keeping me awake at night as if I could hear the sand of time falling through the hourglass. Clinical research associate was a humble, entry-level position, earning seventeen thousand dollars a year, but it came with sponsorship for a work visa, and that was worth gold to me right now.

Years later, when Dr. Bobear and I were good friends, he would recount his own version of these events to me: "I called Warren and told him, 'You'd better hire this guy. He's good.'"

For that, I would ever remain grateful to him. We developed a long professional and personal relationship, and Isfana and I were with him until he passed away.

At the same time, this was also very depressing. It seemed like quite a plummet from the pinnacle of my career which I had been experiencing in Karachi. I had built a small empire and transformed certain aspects of health-care delivery for my nation. I had helped thousands of patients. I had walked with gods, and people bowed to touch my feet. I had been feasted by nawabs.

Now this.

I completed my first official paperwork with the Louisiana State University School of Medicine, and when I left the office, Isfana was waiting outside for me. She was just as relieved and emotional as I was. We walked to a nearby bench, we sat down together, and as we reflected on everything that had happened recently, we cried. Tears of joy. Tears of relief. Tears of exhaustion. Tears of sadness. We were thankful, but I also felt demeaned by these circumstances, by my sudden, dramatic change in stature. We had no words for each other in that moment; we just held hands quietly, knowing how far we had come and how far we still had to go. I thought to myself, *Juzar Ali, this is a phase, this is a phase, and I must pass through this one too. Patience, perseverance and prayers*

When we stood up again, we went for a walk downtown. Once more, we strolled along Canal Street, just as we had done so many years ago when we were younger. We glided past shop windows, listened to the sounds of street performers playing on the corners, and watched the streetcars rattle and clack along their tracks to and from the river. How was it that Isfana and I always seemed to be starting out on these adventures together? As we walked, I realized that the situation might be challenging, but our family was together again and again and safe, and the boys would be happy. We had hope and opportunity. That is the greatest gift and one that America offers in such beautiful abundance.

CHAPTER 25

Tea and Toast

On October 7, 1991, I officially became an employee of Louisiana State University Health Services. I didn't have so much as an office. My job was to travel to different clinics around the region and rotate through with fellows. I paid my own travel expenses, including parking. If it was a larger clinic, or if it was housed inside a hospital, I might be lucky enough to find an atrium or cafeteria where I could sit and do my paperwork. Otherwise, I would work in the car or find a table in crowded coffeehouse somewhere. It was a grind, and there was something intentional in that. An entry-level position like this could be used to evaluate an unknown candidate, like me, over a series of months to make sure I was dedicated to the work and to ensure no surprises emerged. A stranger like me could be running from past legal problems, could have issues with professional qualifications, or be struggling with any number of personal issues that arise in difficult situations like mine. Warren and the team at LSU were willing to take a gamble on me, but I would have to prove myself.

So that's exactly what I did. After all my years in Pakistan, I was used to the life of a road warrior. In Karachi, I traveled all over the city to work with all the different clinics, organizations, and groups. I could easily rack up one hundred kilometers of driving in a single day as I navigated around gridlock and riots. Now in New Orleans, I worked with the same intensity and devotion even though I was suddenly at the very bottom of the totem pole again. I did everything expected of me in my position and then some. I spent extra time with students and residents. I picked up extra rotations. I jokingly referred to myself as a sponge used to fill in gaps of service wherever needed.

The hard work began to pay off. Within a year or so, I had earned the title assistant professor. I was gaining the respect of my colleagues in the section and school, and I continued working hard to form good relationships with the medical residents and the staffs at the clinics. This consistent approach years later led to acknowledgments and recognition for me in my section, department, and school at LSU and was truly humbling. It was also a matter of great personal and professional satisfaction

As I raced around the region, working in all these medical clinics, many of which were public charity or free care institutions, I couldn't help noticing how uneven the access to health care was here in America. Years before, I had been immersed in a hospital setting where I saw only the patients that made it through admissions. But now, traveling from clinic to clinic, I had a front-row seat to the challenges that many Americans faced, and it seemed a strange juxtaposition. The United States had some of the finest medical care and institutions in the world, housed in these beautiful glass and steel buildings, and yet here were huge populations of people who had no way to access that expertise. It seemed like there were two separate systems. One system served the wealthy and the well insured who were able to access more comprehensive care, including primary care doctors, specialists, advanced testing, and diagnostics. Now I was learning more about this system designed to serve the poor, the working class without insurance, and the underinsured. This system ran on a network of free or subsidized clinics. These patients often had little or no access to routine preventative care, so they appeared in emergency rooms and clinics only after their conditions had become much more advanced, debilitating, and expensive. Of course, this was nothing new to me; it was very similar to the dual-level health-care system in Pakistan. I was just surprised to realize how ingrained it was here in America too. The only difference here was that it was a multi-level system.

In the meantime, I had my own house to put in order. With my official status at the university, I was finally able to begin applying for official documents and accounts. A temporary medical license. A Louisiana driver's license. A bank account. A retirement account. These small steps are taken for granted so much of the time, but they carried so much value for us now. With each step of the administrative process, we felt more and more permanent in our new situation and our new home. With each step, I knew I was coming closer to a difficult time. I was going to have to officially cut ties with my institutions back in Karachi and inform my friends, colleagues, managers, staff, and patients that I was not returning. For every part of me that was thrilled about this new life and these new opportunities, there was an equal part of me that was sad to leave my homeland behind and dreading the official breakup with my businesses.

But the time had come. I could no longer pretend that we were on an extended vacation and work trip. One by one, I contacted my people back home and delivered the news. I had been working on transition plans for the clinics, the medical positions, and the academic programs, and I worked very hard over the next few months to create a smooth handoff of responsibility to new group and yet continue to mentor the team I had created there in Pakistan. It felt very important to do what I could to keep the good work going and to keep their opportunities alive even if I was no longer there.

As I made these difficult calls, there was some confusion and outrage, but many of my friends understood the decision and wished me well. It was clear that I would return home as often as possible and that I could still be a resource from the United States. Plus, it was an opportunity for many of the doctors who had worked under me for years to assume their own leadership roles now for which I had encouraged and mentored them. It took weeks of work and many hours on long distance phone calls, but the full transition eventually happened.

Concurrently, Isfana began to hunt more seriously for opportunities also, and it didn't take her long to find a similar arrangement with an outpatient clinic of the Louisiana State Department of Mental Health. She too would be working with trainees and social workers. We were excited to have the additional security—and the additional income. She too noticed the disparity in health-care access although the simple fact that the State of Louisiana had a department dedicated to mental health was a step beyond what we had experienced in Pakistan where mental health care was still very stigmatized and poorly designed. The state-run system in the US might not be perfect, but it was at least there.

We were clearly on our way, but once more, we found ourselves standing at the bottom of a mountain and gazing up at the steep peaks and valleys of legal work, administrative hurdles, and challenging exams. Yes, we had both achieved these invaluable toeholds, but now we would have to climb through years of immigration visa requirements, medical qualifying exams, state licensure requirements once again, and more. Isfana and I held hands, took a deep breath, and plunged forward and upward.

Studying became the routine around the apartment. The boys came home from school. Isfana and I came home from work. We all shared a meal and talked about our days, and then we all retreated to our books. Zee was preparing for school grades and college entrance exams. Riaz was working hard to transition to this new school system and the requirements. Isfana and I studied for our various licensure exams.

The hard work was still being rewarded though. I received a series of small pay raises over the next several months, courtesy of Dr. Summer. Warren was a no-nonsense guy who was also as shrewd a businessman as he was an expert clinician and academician. I was starting to look like a better and better investment to him, and finally, we were able to pay our family expenses without dipping into our savings every month. Zee was accepted to several universities, and he chose to attend Trinity University in San Antonio where he would study premed. Riaz continued to thrive at St. Martin, and Isfana and I passed one exam after another. We were making our way.

Feeling more secure, we decided that, perhaps, it was time to finally move out of this tiny, barely furnished apartment and into a place of our own. We were excited to plant some deeper roots here in our new community and began to house hunt. We had no particular dreams or fantasies about the house we wanted. I was past that phase, having been through it once before here in New Orleans and in Pakistan. All I wanted was a home in a safe locale, modest and comfortable, and not far away in the suburbs. The realtor, realizing that Isfana and I were both physicians, tempted us into considering huge houses in elite areas all over town. The houses were beautiful, but they seemed excessive, and I was getting dizzy trying to keep up with all the far-flung neighborhoods. Finally, I decided on some criteria to help us narrow our hunt. First, I opened a map of the city and drew three points on the map depicting where I was working, where Isfana's clinic was, and where the boys went to school. Our new house needed to be somewhere in the middle. Secondly, I wanted no grass to cut. Perhaps I am a product of my urban upbringing, but I have always held that one of the most useless things a man can do is spend hours cutting grass and then sit back to watch it grow again and then cut it again.

We found our home in a modest middle-class neighborhood in the Broadmoor area. It was unpretentious. It was perfectly located. It was cozy inside, with wood floors, split levels, and arched doorways that led between the small rooms. It had a back patio instead of a backyard. It didn't take long to pack up our old place. We moved in during one hot day in March 1992, and sweat dripped down our faces and our backs as we hauled our very limited luggage through the front door. It was not a palatial palace by any means. In fact, it was an average New Orleans home with small rooms. But it was home, and we were so happy. Until I slipped and fell on the deck. We hadn't been in the house very long before I took this tumble, and it was a nasty fall. Immediately, I had flashbacks to the months I spent in bed back in Karachi after my hip fracture, and that's all I could think about as I waited for the ambulance to arrive. I was taken to the hospital, and fortunately, the injury did not turn out to be nearly as debilitating as before. Still, I was laid up for several weeks. The boys were wonderfully supportive and so were our neighbors, the Caplans, who became surrogate grandparents for Zee and Riaz while I was recovering.

We were back into the swing of things after my recovery when another medical emergency reared its ugly head. This time it struck Isfana. "I'm afraid it's bad news," the doctor said, and Isfana gripped my hand as we sat together in the outer part of the hospital operating theater, receiving the biopsy results. She had discovered a lump in her breast, and immediately, we had it examined. Now we knew the results. "I'm afraid it's cancer."

"What type?" Isfana asked.

"IDC," the doctor replied. "Invasive ductal carcinoma."

"How bad is it?" I asked.

"We'll run some more tests to see if it has reached the lymph nodes," the doctor replied. "Then I can give you a better answer. For now, know this: we can fight this thing."

And fight we did. We traveled to MD Anderson in Houston for a second opinion. We were going to make sure Isfana had the finest care in the world. The doctors there confirmed the diagnosis and planned an aggressive attack on the cancer. "We can't be one hundred percent certain of anything, but it looks like we should be able to treat this," the doctor told us.

We were both comforted by the assessments, but it was still terrifying to think of this deadly disease living inside my wife. I was on one hand numb, on the other determined to do what needed to be done. We used pragmatism, humor, and distraction as we went through the process of treatment with surgery and chemotherapy. It was brutally exhausting, and I stood by helpless as she rapidly lost weight, lost her hair, and spent days in bed, fighting nausea and fatigue. I brought her tea and toast. Tea and toast. Tea and toast, nearly every day.

Isfana was a spirited patient though, and she always bounced back from the chemo sessions. When she was in good spirits, we teased her. With her thin shoulders wrapped in a shawl, wearing her spectacles and no hair upon her head, she bore a certain resemblance to Mahatma Gandhi. As it happened, her maiden name was Gandhi too, so that became her affectionate nickname to close friends and family who dropped by to visit. *Gandhi.* Isfana enjoyed the playful teasing and joking. I think it helped her feel more normal during that difficult time.

Family and friends visited us from India and US with support by Iloo Bhai. Local friends like Seema Godiwala, John Bobear, and others stood by us as we grappled this news and went through the tests and surgery and further tests. We felt lucky. In just a short time, we had managed to develop a wonderful network of friends and colleagues in New Orleans who went out of their way to support us. People brought food, flowers, and cards. Friends came over to play cards and spend time. Even Riaz's high school friends made gestures of support. We were also incredibly grateful for the level of care we received. We were among the fortunate who had access to the world's foremost experts in this deadly disease. Six months after this aggressive regimen of treatment had begun, Isfana's doctor delivered the verdict: treatment complete. And now watchful surveillance.

I was so relieved I almost cried right there in his office.

Isfana's hair was just beginning to grow back in, her healthy skin color was back, and she was putting some weight back on when the mailman arrived with yet another surprise: our green cards. We both stood staring at them for a few moments, as if they might be a mirage that could vanish right before our eyes. We turned them over in our hands and read them carefully. *Permanent resident card.* I made copies and remembered Tahir Bhai. He would have made hundreds. I opened my wallet and placed the card just behind my driver's license even as my heart felt like it might soar right out of my chest. *We were permanent residents of the United States of America.*

"Let us say Salwaat," I said, channeling my father and remembering all those small celebrations we shared in the Venus Medico days of Karachi. We sat down together, talking about the roller-coaster ride that was our life together, and we had a cup of tea. It was one of the best cups of tea we had ever enjoyed together.

Work kept up at its relentless pace, but as the months wore on, I found a special niche for myself in mycobacterial diseases and, specifically, tuberculosis. These were diseases that had been largely controlled in the United States but were making a terrifying comeback in the 1980s, particularly among people living with HIV. Their weakened immune systems became easy targets for the opportunistic bacteria, and American hospitals—and communities—were suddenly beset by a disease they were no longer prepared for. This scourge was older than the Pharaohs, and now plaguing twentieth-century

America like some long-lost curse. Medical students and their teachers passed through years of training without any instruction or studying about this public health hazard. Few had experience treating strains of tuberculosis and its mycobacterial cousins and look-alikes, and I suddenly found myself transitioning from low-level training instructor to invaluable medical specialist.

One of my interests was chest imaging. I had been trained vigorously in imaging techniques during my residency in the 1970s. Because we did not have the more advanced testing facilities or budgets in Pakistan, I often had to diagnose pulmonary problems from simple chest X-rays, and occasionally, I was lucky enough to get a CT scan. Over the years, I had seen thousands of chest images, and as a result, I could read them with a sharp eye and a broad body of knowledge. Suddenly, my old-school imaging skills were invaluable. Peering at the ghostly, lighted images, I scanned carefully for any tiny spot depicting a diseased tissue or picked out telltale signs of trouble in the patterns. Soon, I was a lead instructor, teaching chest X-rays to the medical students in a more structured manner. This experience was invaluable for me and helped prepare the students for these challenges that were resurfacing after many decades.

Much of my work was still conducted in charity public clinics, especially since this is where many TB, HIV, and AIDS patients came for treatment. Disease often strikes at the most vulnerable in a society: the poor, the homeless, the hardscrabble working class. Poverty and socioeconomic status is closely related to health, well-being, and health-care access. In this way, personal and societal health care is intrinsically tied to larger issues in society. A nation which neglects its poor and does not strive for universal easy access to health care will always be vulnerable.

It was during these early months of work that I was sent to Charity Hospital in New Orleans. This was my first time back to Charity since I was a resident in the 1970s. I was here now on a typical assignment to work with LSU residents and take care of these patients with limited access to health care. This was not a typical destination though. I remember peering up at the huge steel mural above the front doors to reacquaint myself with the towering building. In Art Deco style, it was a montage of symbolic images, carefully arranged to depict life in Louisiana, from oil workers to cooks, from engineers to baseball players, from fishermen to children swinging from a tree. The hospital was the one of the largest and oldest charity hospitals in the nation. The 1930s building was sponsored by the Public Works Administration under Roosevelt's New Deal administration. It was a remarkable structure with its central tower flanked by massive wings which housed over two thousand five hundred beds. No hospital in Pakistan was built to a scale this huge. It was like standing in front of a castle. I couldn't know it at the time, but this institution would eventually come to be an important part of my life and my life's work, and the history of the hospital would be ingrained in me since I would become a small part of that long legacy.

All I knew at that moment, however, was I had a job to do, and it lay somewhere behind those big doors. I entered with head bowed, eyes fixed, and spirits high to face whatever challenge lay here. As I strode through the corridors of this iconic institution, I realized with a smile that the smell of the place had not changed since the '70s. I still remembered the Friday cafeteria menu of fried catfish.

CHAPTER 26

Troubling Patterns

Traveling from clinic to clinic and from hospital to hospital might have been a daily grind, but it offered me invaluable new insights into American health care. One thing that became apparent was the incredibly fractured nature of the system. In fact, it wasn't even a single system. What I found instead was that there were some half dozen or more competing structures, and every time I met with a patient, one of my jobs was to determine which one they participated in, which would determine much about their course of care. There were Medicare patients, Medicaid patients, and health benefits from the Department of Veterans Affairs. They each had separate rules, plans, and coverage options. Patients with employer-based insurance had access to certain levels of care while patients in the charity system had very different options. Then of course, there were the people who didn't want or have health insurance. They planned to pay for services on an as-needed basis. They enjoyed the autonomy of deciding their own fate, but they were inevitably blindsided by the incredible expenses they would incur form any serious illness or accident. Financial distress also affected people's options. In each clinic, I might encounter patients from any number of these systems. In fact, even within a single system, one could have fragmented access such that you could see the doctor in one system, get your tests from another system, and be admitted in the hospital in a third.

To make matters even more complex, American health care was being transformed in the 1990s, moving away from patient-driven

care and toward more system-oriented delivery: *manag*
now, instead of tradition indemnity plans, people were b_
en masse into health maintenance organizations (HMOs). Marcus
Welby, MD, was being replaced by a board of directors.

What that meant to patients was that doctors no longer had the
autonomy to deliver complex care without explicit approval from
the HMO. In the conventional indemnity plans, doctors could do
anything they felt was medically necessary for their patients, and
the insurance company deferred to their judgment and paid the
expenses. Now, however, insurance companies were making many
of those calls. No longer could I simply order tests for a sick patient;
they had to be approved by HMO officials. Prescriptions and treatments had to be approved. Surgical procedures and rehabilitations
had to be approved. When these things were not approved, it was
up to the doctor to try to either find a different way to work around
the regulations or to negotiate directly with the HMO and argue for
the care.

These changes made sense from the perspective of cost control
and fraud prevention. The medical profession, particularly certain
specialties, were known to turn a blind eye to some levels of misuse
and abuse of the financial arrangements, and that gave the insurance
companies reason to convert these plans to their benefit. It was all
driven by money, and it had real impact on people.

One of my patients, DD, had a dangerous lung infection, a
mycobacterium avium infection (MAC) that required a specialized
regimen of medication, treatment, and follow-up. She was a lovely
woman, middle-aged, from a working-class background. She was
immunocompromised due to some chronic health conditions she
had been battling for years. An important aspect of her care was periodic sputum tests, so we could accurately determine the levels of the
MAC and ensure that her treatments were appropriate and on-target.
Otherwise, the disease could do irreparable harm to her pulmonary
system and, in its worst case, even cause death.

The insurance company demanded that we use just one lab for
her tests. Normally, this would be no problem, but in this case, the
lab did not provide the in-depth results we needed. They only pro-

vided basic sputum test results. It fell to me to try to negotiate with the insurance company, and I did my best. The lab had a contractual monopoly on this work, however, and the insurance company refused to pay for anyone else to run the test. Working directly with the lab was no better. Yes, they could produce the comprehensive result we needed, but it was not covered by the insurance company, and the patient would have to pay for it herself, out of pocket. DD did not have the funds to pay for this expensive test, so she declined. In the end, we made our best educated guess on how to proceed with her treatments, and she went on her way. She didn't return to see me, and I can only hope that she somehow found a way to receive the accurate care she needed and didn't wind up back in an emergency room with her health in a downward spiral.

As a physician, these circumstances made for a challenging time to enter American health care. Medicine had not changed dramatically. The technology was familiar. Treating patients had not changed, and it was still my greatest passion. But I was having to learn multiple separate complex delivery systems and then try to help many of my patients understand them too.

The frustrations could seem endless at times.

Another patient I treated, FG, was suffering from advanced emphysema, and one part of his care was a prescription inhaler. I wrote FG the prescription, and he went to the pharmacy and collected his medicine which was fully covered by his insurance. One month later, he returned to the pharmacy for his first refill, and he was informed that his insurance no longer covered that medicine in full, and he now had a two-hundred-dollar co-pay. *What had changed in one short month?*

I investigated, and it turns out FG's insurance company had dropped its contract with one pharmaceutical or distribution company in exchange for a contract with another company to reduce costs. The results were uneven, however, and some medicines, such as the prescription inhaler, increased in price as part of the overall deal. FG could not afford an extra two hundred dollars a month, so he stopped taking his medicine. Guess what? He was soon in the emergency room and admitted in the ICU. The insurance company saved a dime on preventative medicine only to spend a dollar on emergency care. We, as a system, did not save any money.

The disconnect is between business of practice and the practice of business. Americans might have some of the most advanced health care in the world, but it is also the most expensive, rising disproportionately in relation to the gross domestic product. It was no wonder that companies were looking for ways to reign in the soaring costs of health care, but there were always two burning questions: are they saving money with these shortsighted decisions? And what is the *human cost* that must be paid to save these dollars? The problems are multifactorial, and the solutions are complex and not easy. How exactly does a nation root out the poverty of the system amid all this abundance of resources?

*****

Within a few short years, Isfana and I were preparing to embark on yet another American phenomenon: empty nest syndrome. By now, Riaz had also finished high school and was getting ready to leave for Columbia University in New York. He was very excited for his adventure, and his mother and I were also excited for him, but we also had our questions about this American rite of passage. In Pakistan, and many other nations, the tradition is to live at home as one attends university and transitions into adulthood. Family provides both a shelter and a sense of balance as the young student journeys through new concepts, knowledge, and experiences. The new, exciting influences of professors and peers are balanced by the familiar traditions of the family. Most importantly, however, the family unit itself remains very tight. I remembered vividly the family meals I had on weekends with my mother and father where we discussed the events of the week. Those were precious times for me, and I felt more balanced and calibrated after those wonderful conversations.

The American model, where the young student says goodbye and disappears for months, or even years, at a time, forces separation upon the whole family. *Distance*, both physical and emotional, is thrust upon them. Many Americans take this for granted as part of adulthood. Even our boys seemed to embrace it. But Isfana and I had mixed feelings about the system, and we had a hard time walking away from Riaz's dormitory in New York City on a hot August afternoon, climbing onto a plane and returning to New Orleans without him. We had had similar feelings when Zee left for Trinity, but we were still in the throes of *so* much transition then that it hadn't felt quite as disruptive. Now those emotions were amplified by the echoes of an empty house. Now we had a family home with empty bedrooms and an empty seat at the family dining table. Isfana and I had no trouble filling the hours with work and social life in New Orleans, but we felt that distance every time we came home, and we never stopped believing that this American tradition of long-distance treks to university was expensive and unnecessary.

I kept thinking of a funny thing our friend Joyce Ann Pardue had once told Isfana and me as we discussed our children growing up. She said, "This is what happens here in the United States: when our children leave for college, they are replaced by aliens. They act like aliens even when they visit home. If everything goes well, you'll get your children back in ten years or so after they finish college."

That being said, we supported Riaz completely. We were proud of his success, and we were thrilled to receive his calls and letters and to hear of his adventures. Whatever our personal opinions were about the tradition, our son was living out the quintessential American Dream, and that made us incredibly grateful.

CHAPTER 27

The Fourth P

Fate seemed to be smiling on us in those years, for as the year 2000 approached, Isfana and I were notified that we had passed all the requirements and tests, cleared all the hurdles, waited through all the bureaucratic processes, and were going to be sworn in as citizens of the United States in a special ceremony. *US citizenship.*

This country had provided so much for us and for our family, and we couldn't wait to be official members of the family and to invest our work and our lives in this place. Both boys were home for the holidays, and on a cold, clear afternoon in January, we all packed into the car, drove to the courthouse downtown, rode the elevator to the third floor, and signed in for our citizenship ceremony. Isfana and I received a small American flag, a certificate, and a clutch of official paperwork tucked into a blue folder. We then sat in folding chairs which were arranged in rows to fill the small room. Soon, all the chairs were filled with immigrants from all around the world: South America, Africa, Europe, and Asia. Everyone seemed to wear the same thrilled look on their face and in their body language. Some displayed their happiness more obviously than others, but the room was clearly full of joy. Together, we all took our solemn oaths of citizenship. We recited the Pledge of Allegiance. We turned in our green cards. We would no longer need them. We were now fully naturalized citizens of the United States of America.

The boys were very happy for us, but they may have thought the whole process was a bit hokey and over the top. As citizens from birth, they had the luxury of taking their citizenship for granted. They did appreciate our journey and our joy though, and it gave them a broader perspective than many of their friends. Zee and Riaz understood the tribulations of the perpetual migrants better than most.

It is well-known that in many ways, immigrants are ideal citizens. They are studious and diligent with a work ethic that facilitates success. They are patient and detail oriented; they have to be. They have the recent memory of their background, know the history of the United States, and appreciate what is around them, taking less for granted. I had to earn America; this was not my birthright.

The question is whether this gets diluted as each generation slides through the years. It has nothing to do with one's race or ethnicity; it has to do with intrinsic values, role models and priorities, and the journey through the generations.

With a US passport, I would be able to travel internationally much more easily. I was less likely to encounter long immigration interrogation or rude behavior than I was used to when I traveled with a Pakistani passport, whether I landed in Saudi Arabia or the UK. I remember one such episode when I landed in London with a Pakistani passport and had to pass through a checkpoint with a stern, burly immigration officer.

"Why are you visiting the UK?" he asked.

"Holiday, tourism," I answered with some sense of joy. It was rare that I got to travel just for pleasure. "I'm on holiday."

That's when the officer leaned back and laughed with a note of sarcasm in his voice. "My dear sir, there is no such thing as a Pakistani tourist," he said. I was offended by the bias in that comment. He would not have dared say that to a US citizen.

Isfana and I were still glowing in our newfound freedom and joy of being US citizens when the telephone at the house rang one evening. "Hello?" I said as I lifted the receiver.

"Juzar Ali," said a voice. I immediately recognized the crackle and slightly distant sound of a long-distance, internationally routed call, but it took me just a moment to recognize the voice on the other end of the line. "You have become a very famous man," he said.

"Daksab, Iqbal!" I said. It was my dear friend from Karachi. "Asalamoalaikum! What is this nonsense about me becoming famous?"

"I'm afraid it's true," he replied. "Only it's not for the right reasons."

It turns out that the government of Pakistan had labeled me a tax cheat and a criminal and published my name and photo in the newspaper. They claimed I owed the Pakistani government 1.4 million rupees, and I was classified as absconded. What's more, they were in the process of confiscating my last remaining properties in Pakistan. One property was a medical clinic, and the other was the last residence that I owned in Karachi.

"They're lying!" I declared angrily.

"You know that, and I know that, but do the right people know that?"

"I'll prove it."

"I hope you can," Iqbal said.

"Thank you for calling to let me know."

"I wanted you to hear from a friend first."

I began that very evening as soon as I hung up the phone. I consulted with Isfana, as always, and we worked to devise a plan. "I'll fly there immediately," I said.

"No," she replied quickly. "That's too dangerous. With these charges, they could arrest you right in the airport. Then we would have a much more serious situation."

She was right, of course. We would have to work from here and try to navigate the situation and solve the problem and clear our name.

It took many more long-distance calls to figure the charges out clearly and to begin assembling a defense team. I sought help from Iqbal, Mosavir, Naseeb, and my legal counsel of the past to get all our files prepared. The authorities did not need to produce no documentation for missing tax payments from years past. They simply submitted a massive tax bill that had been generated mysteriously. I, on the other hand, was tasked with producing all kinds of documentation to prove that they were wrong.

Of course, it didn't help that I had left the country in such a quiet and apparently clandestine fashion. It fed right into their narrative. And that was the real poison pill here. It was more than just my money and property at stake here; it was my name and my good standing with my home nation. Would I never be able to return to Pakistan? How many of my lifelong and cherished relationships could this damage? How many of my professional and medical connections would this sever? This had the potential to be a huge blow. And they knew that. They wanted me to pay dearly and have my integrity destroyed at the same time.

We used to tease Tahir Bhai about his obsessive photocopying and redundant record keeping where the backup files were backed up and then backed up again. But it was exactly this compulsive filing system that saved my case. As my friends and lawyers went through the old file systems, they found copies of absolutely everything— every tax form, every receipt of payment, every detailed accounting ledger. I looked heavenward and said a prayer of thanks for my old companion and friend.

We completed all the paperwork and produced our rafts of documentation, and after the official government inquiry was completed, the results took a turn for the ironic. It turns out I had overpaid my taxes by sixty thousand rupees over the years. The charges against me were dropped, and the ITO sent a notification indicating that they would send a refund for the overpaid taxes. I have been waiting nearly twenty years now, and I still haven't received that check in the mail. I'm sure it's coming any day.

When it was all over, I found myself amazed at how smoothly events had gone with the government inquiry and the hearing, and I learned about an interesting turn of events that had occurred. When the final hearing had been arranged, my team in Karachi that I had assembled remotely had encountered a middle-aged man at the income tax office who was facilitating the logistics. When he saw my name on the case, he generously guided my team through the whole process to make sure there were no problems. It turns out I had met this person many years ago at Liaquat National Hospital when he had brought his very sick daughter to me. I had taken good care of the girl. He held a very low position at the time and had no money to pay for her treatments or my professional fees, and I had told him, "It's okay. Don't worry. I will help you with the cost." He had not forgotten that favor.

Well, he returned the favor.

The incident reinforced what I already knew: if one can help, one should. The reward will be there in some form or the other. If, however, one cannot help, still be courteous and sympathetic about it. It will be counted somewhere, and you never know when that event may come back to you.

I thought my anger at being subjected to this unfair treatment in Pakistan would blow over once the whole episode was over, but it didn't. I tried to let it go as I had so many other times over the years of dealing with Pakistani corruption and bureaucracy, but I just couldn't. More so, my family could not forgive or forget. My whole life, I had loved Pakistan dearly. I had sacrificed so much to return there and work there. I had learned to survive and thrive in that flawed system even as I tried to make small changes for the better. In my small sphere of influence, I had worked tirelessly to transform health-care quality and delivery around me in a positive direction. This was not my doing alone by any means, but it sure was with a lot of personal effort and passion. When I had returned to Pakistan in 1981, I had gone back with a thought that my future and my passing the baton would lie in that land. Even up until now, I had held out hope that the political turmoil might relent, allowing me a chance to work in that world in a more meaningful way again.

But now, after this episode, I now knew that the passing of the baton would occur here in the United States. I was angry and fed up with Pakistan in a way that I had never felt before. For many years, I had given her my all, even when loving that nation became physically dangerous to me and my family. With this episode, I felt her betrayal of me was complete.

Sometime later, we learned that my good friend and classmate from school, college and medical school, Shafi, was coming to New Orleans. This might have been wonderful news, except that the circumstances were tragic. Shafi had been a classmate of mine all the way back in Karachi Grammar School, and we had followed very similar life career paths. We had chosen the same academic tracks and enrolled in medical school at the same time. Where I had gone to New Orleans, he had gone to the UK for his specialized training and residency. Then we had both returned to Pakistan, but while I had gone into practice and teaching, he also did but had the connections to move up into administration with the national Ministry of Health too. He was rich in the three Ps.

But alas, there turned out to be a fourth P that one had not anticipated: politics with violence. I had fled Pakistan for safety, but Shafi remained, and now he had become the latest victim of an assassination attempt. He barely survived, but his gruesome injuries left him with quadriplegia. This shook us badly as it did all our friends and families. Isfana and I flew to London where he was brought for treatment—and for safety. There we learned that he needed specialized brachial plexus surgery which might improve marginally hand function. This was to be performed in New Orleans by a world-renowned neurosurgeon specialist at LSU, Dr. Kline.

As a childhood friend, it was the least we could do to facilitate that and try to help navigate his care while he was in New Orleans for two weeks. Everything went smoothly, and we were glad to spend time with him and help in whatever ways we were able before he returned to the UK to be with his own family. Once more, it left us feeling grateful for America and the blessings in our life.

Life moved on. Isfana and I decided to make a trip that we both had been hoping to make all our lives. We would make the *hajj*, the pilgrimage to Mecca.

The hajj is one of the five pillars, or duties, of Islam, along with the profession of faith in the one God and Mohammed as his prophet, prayer, charitable giving, and fasting during the holy month of Ramadan. Every Muslim who has the physical and financial means is required to make this five-day pilgrimage once in his or her lifetime. Now was our time. Isfana and I made all our travel arrangements, and when the day arrived, we took a taxi to the airport with our packed bags. We didn't need much by way of luggage. This was not a trip for sightseeing or going out on the town. This was a spiritual journey. We had travel clothes, our ihram (simple white clothes worn by the pilgrims), our holy books, and almost nothing else.

Getting to Saudi Arabia was very easy, but once we landed in the land of Mecca, things became much more intense. In the age of technology, where transportation has become so much more efficient and accessible, the crowds which flock to Mecca each year are huge. People come pouring in from countries across the globe. In 2000, Isfana and I joined roughly two million pilgrims. On one hand, it is a logistical nightmare, compounded by the biases of the people around. We talk a lot about racial discrimination in the United States, and our history in this arena is nothing to be proud of. We still must learn from it, and unfortunately, we need constant reminders of our own tainted history.

But we are not alone. There is no society, no nation and no group that does not have its biases, prejudices, and discrimination. The difference is on how they project those issues and, more importantly, how they confront that problem. We had been warned repeatedly about the level of hostility and disrespect the Saudis exhibited for hajjis and non-Arabs. All the pilgrims might be equal in God's eyes, but the Saudis felt free to discriminate terribly. Non-Arab Muslims were clearly treated far worse than Arabs. Muslims from First World countries like the US, UK, France or Canada faced hassles, but nothing like the abuse that was heaped upon Muslim Africans, Muslim Asians or any of the other non-Arab groups, especially if they were from poor or developing nations, like Pakistan. Hajjis were verbally abused, delayed, and searched. Their holy books were confiscated (since they were not as pure or perfect as Arab holy books), and they were held up endlessly in customs. This would have been Isfana's and my fate if we were not US citizens. Every time a Saudi official was about to berate us, he caught a glimpse of that eagle emblazoned on the front of our passports, and he was simply rude to us instead. We had seen the difference through the years when we had traveled for, which is like hajj in many ways but limited in scope and can be performed at any time of the year. Even though we witnessed and encountered this discrimination abroad and the logistical issues notwithstanding, our hajj was a journey of indescribable personal enlightenment and spiritual fulfillment.

CHAPTER 28

Love and Hate

Year 2001 began on a high note. I was sitting in my office when the news arrived in the form of a letter. I saw who the sender was, and I was sure I was about to open up a rejection notice from the Fulbright program. Months ago, I had completed an application for one of their scholarships and academic programs. I had proposed a science and medicine-centric partnership with a university in Turkey. It loosely fit the parameters of the scholarship requirements, but I had doubted all along that it would be chosen from among the thousands of submissions they receive. To my amazement, the letter was to inform me that they had accepted my proposal! I was beyond thrilled. What an adventure this would be. Turkey was a country I had always wished to explore, and this presented a unique opportunity to collaborate with their professionals and health-care system. With His blessings, this was shaping up to be a very productive and successful few years in my career.

I brought the news home to Isfana, and she was excited also. Once more, we began to daydream of travels abroad. That evening, we received a call from Zee who was now attending medical school at LSU. We told him the good news, and then we caught up for a short while. Isfana and I both knew how stressful and hectic a medical school schedule was, so we cherished these moments when we got to speak with him. He told us things were going well with his girlfriend, Kacie, a beautiful girl from Louisiana who was also attending LSU. Isfana and I both had the sense that this was getting more serious than some other of his relationships, and we couldn't help feeling a little nervous about this romantic bridge between the two cultures and religions that they represented. This was the first time in our lives we had to deal with this so directly. Isfana and I had both been raised in very close families who were tied to the same culture and faith, but here were our boys in this wide-open American culture that was much more liberal in so many ways.

Isfana and I had always knew we were navigating this duality, steering between American culture and South Asian culture, balancing the tides of a liberal society and our more conservative beliefs. Most of the time, it was wonderful, like being part of the great American melting pot. Sometimes it was tricky as we tried to keep the boys connected to our Muslim and Pakistani traditions even as they were going out to football games, attending proms, traveling away to college, and meeting girls at dorm parties. In New Orleans, we didn't have much of a Muslim community at the time, just a few other families and a few get-togethers throughout the year. Occasionally, Isfana and I would take the boys to larger cities like Houston where we had friends and could participate with a much larger community. We wanted to boys to see the beautiful aspects of the culture and traditions, the ones that Isfana and I grew up with. It wasn't that we wanted them to stop being American boys in any way; we just wanted them to have and to cherish both aspects of their identities the way that we did.

Zee, our eldest, had always been the most reluctant to fully embrace conventional religious dogma and Muslim tradition. Over the years, he had become more disillusioned by the harder elements in the culture. As a boy, he had chaffed, like his mother, against the strict social codes and norms of Pakistan, and as an adolescent, he rebelled against the stricter interpretations of the religious tenets, leading him to a more agnostic point of view. Many times, we had long discussions, and I tried to persuade him to embrace his culture and religion a little more closely.

I explained there were extreme positions in all religions, and that voices of moderation made more sense. Religious services, houses of worship, and rituals were not to be equated with faith and spirituality, but certain elements of culture and rituals were important because they were a vehicle or a process for the physical body to mesh with the spiritual. In nearly any faith, it is through a certain ritual that a person connects with God even if that ritual is sitting at the side of the bed every morning and closing one's eyes and meditating. The ritual must not overshadow the intrinsic faith and spirituality one needs to achieve and the church or the mosque activities must be thought of as an organizational setup. If that setup impedes the goal of spirituality and becomes a business as many do, then one must remain cautious. One must feel the warmth and not the heat of these organizations and yet have the passion and conviction of one's faith and spirituality. This coupled with the values we grow up with and the ethics that we police ourselves with makes for a firm foundation. Belonging to an organized community has its benefits too, provided it does not become a business with that being its primary goal

Zee chose his own path, however, and while he never rejected his Muslim faith, he kept the aspect of structured organized religion at arm's length. So when we began hearing about Kacie, Isfana and I couldn't help but worry that he might step even further away from his Pakistani heritage, and, thus, further away from us. In retrospect, these fears seem overblown, but that is how it felt to us at the time. We did caution him about the challenges they and their children would face as they navigated their lives to adopt bicultural, bilingual, dual religious path, their own intrinsic faith and spirituality notwithstanding.

In contrast to his brother, Riaz embraced the culture and faith a little more closely. As he was finishing his college years in New York City and beginning work at a marketing company, he decided to date Muslim women, knowing that he would be looking to settle down before too much longer. As soon as he made that decision, the family went into action by playing matchmakers. In Pakistani culture (and many other cultures as well), matchmaking is a joyful preoccupation that family members relish, sometimes to an excessive degree. Cousins and relatives tried setting Riaz up on dates. Friends up and down the East Coast began working their connections, looking for young women in similar circumstances that they might introduce Riaz to. Family members as far away as California began poring through their contacts.

Riaz connected with several young women like this, but nothing really clicked between them. In the meantime, he was living his life in New York and meeting people there as well. Eventually, a family member connected us to a family who lived in Canada. The Canadian family was very similar to ours in many ways. They were first-generation immigrants from Pakistan, they placed great priority on education, and they had a lovely daughter, Sausan, who was close in age to Riaz. The question was how to get them together within the cultural norms to see if they liked each other.

In the past, it was much more common for the families to arrange marriages. The young woman's father and I might discuss our children at some length, discuss our families and faith, and then confer with our own families. As a group, we might decide if the match is right or not. If it was, then arrangements would soon begin for a wedding. This remains a practice in many corners of the world. I did not want that for my sons though, and the Canadian family did not want it either. The motivations, practicalities, and customs were different now, especially in twenty-first century America. I arranged a four-way call so Isfana and I could reach out to Sausan's parents, and we had a very nice conversation about our families, about Pakistan, about our situations and work here in North America. We all agreed that these two people should at least be introduced and have a chance to build a chemistry. If it worked out, great. If not, so be it.

Riaz and Sausan spoke on the phone and began exchanging e-mails. Over weeks and months, they grew closer despite the geographical distance between them. Finally, Riaz decided he needed to meet her in person. With the blessing of Sausan's family, he flew to Canada to meet her for the first time. This was the beginning of their chemistry merging with physics!

Then came 9/11.

It was a wake-up call for many. As Muslim Americans, not only were we reeling from the terrorist attacks against this nation of opportunity that we loved dearly, but we were also watching a series of hate crimes unfold around the nation as some of our fellow citizens, gripped by fear and anger, lashed out at Muslim Americans and people of South Asian descent. Isfana and I begged Zee and Riaz to be careful in their day-to-day activities. The first few hours post World Trade Center incident, with Riaz living and working in Manhattan were agonizingly painful as we hoped that he was not personally hurt and waited for news from him. We, like most of us in our sphere, felt that this was a political issue that had morphed in a religious war. The faith and core beliefs of the faith had been hijacked by extremists. Nothing new. This had happened over centuries before in all religions, and we just had to tide this over. For our part, Isfana and I were in fortunate positions. Within the medical profession, there was very little of that kind of backlash, abuse, or violence. None of my colleagues, students, or patients subjected me, personally, to any kind of anger or fear. But it was out there. I tried not to make any big display of it, but I quietly went out and bought two new American flags that week. One flag was hung on our house, and the other, a smaller flag, was placed on my desk. I've never been the type of patriot who thumps my chest or shouts about it, but in my own quiet way, I wanted to make sure there was no question about where I stood or who I stood with, and it most certainly wasn't with some band of misguided zealots who had an agenda of their own. To me, this conflict is more of a power struggle of dominance and influence than a religious or faith-based divide.

*****

In many ways, the trip to Turkey was timed perfectly. By the time I packed my bags for the trip, the United States had already toppled the Taliban government in Afghanistan and were still beating the drums of war as they began eyeing an attack on Iraq. Politicians raged on about weapons of mass destruction while talking heads debated the merits of preemptive war. My objectives in Turkey were tiny by those standards, but they represented a mission of hope and positive collaboration during a rather violent and anxious season in the world.

Personally, I was very excited too. Going back to the 1960s, Turkey had always been a close regional partner with Pakistan, and I had been hearing wonderful stories about the nation since I was a boy. During the application process, I had carefully researched my options and had arranged to work in Izmir, a beautiful part of the country, just across the sea from Greece, which boasted numerous biblical Ottoman and Muslim historical sites. Prior to this, I had never worked with anyone in Turkey, so it was like a blind date. Only this blind date would last six months.

My Turkish counterparts at Ege University Hospital sounded a little nervous about the date. They had never heard of me until I contacted them one day clear out of the blue and proposed my agenda through the Fulbright program. I wished to focus on the concepts of teaching in the medical arena with bedside clinical instruction, small groups, and with models of the American residency programs. The Turkish doctors did not reply right away, but I kept reaching out until I finally received a specific reply from Dr. Nesrin, a chest physician faculty in the chest department in Izmir, who informed me that she was assigned to my program. I could tell they thought of me as little more than a pest at this point.

My own team at LSU also required some cajoling. "You want to do what?" the lead physicians asked.

I explained my Turkish program, and they offered some skeptical looks. They had little information or details of the Fulbright Scholar Program and were unsure what to do with me. It seems I have that effect on people. Ultimately, they saw the value of the program and the exchange and approved the sabbatical.

Now I was landing in Turkey. A team from the university was there to greet me, and I could literally see the relief on their faces when they realized that I was the American. They had been anticipating some tall, blond swashbuckling white American doctor, but they got a brown one instead. I must have seemed more relatable to them. We had a great conversation as they took on the scenic route to the hospital, and I was thrilled to be in this beautiful city which wrapped along the coastline of the Aegean Sea and had rows of white buildings and houses rising into the green hills all around. It was a lovely combination of the modern world and the ancient.

At Ege University Hospital, I finally met my liaison, Dr. Nesrin, whom I had been corresponding with all these months. She too seemed relieved when she met me, and I made sure that she knew right away I was not here to try to make extra work for anyone, and I didn't expect any special treatment for myself. "I don't even need an office," I told her. "I can sit in any assigned space to do what I need." I was careful to approach the position without a lot of fanfare or demands. Let the efforts and work ethic speak for themselves. Command respect, not demand respect. That was my mantra, as it always had been in the past.

As we talked, Dr. Nesrin and her entourage introduced me to Ayran, a delicious yogurt-based drink that was very refreshing and soon became one of my favorite small pleasures. We all seemed to be getting off on the right foot. As I had done in other institutions before, wherever I had started worked, I spent some time traveling from office to office to introduce myself and ensure that I conveyed due collegial respect from the get-go. From experience, I knew this was an important custom and an expectation in some parts of the world. I explained my goals to each faculty member and sought their cooperation.

In the months following, the program went better than I could have possibly imagined. None of us knew exactly what we were doing since this was all brand-new, but quickly it became a very open collaborative process where we examined the unique approaches of different medical and educational systems. I brought perspective from both Pakistan and the US, and I had a good deal of knowledge about the Indian system from Isfana. In return, I was learning this new medical system as well as the Turkish language. The work felt relaxing and inspiring. For this small window of time, I wasn't working directly with patients, which meant the pressures were not nearly the same. I worked with these medical students, residents, and faculty. In every sense, it seemed to live up to the ideals of the Fulbright mission to foster a great exchange of ideas, education, and cultural awareness and to act as the US cultural and professional ambassador. In the process, I went from being "the pest" to being the guy who brought that really cool program to the university.

Isfana arrived in time for the going away celebration at the hospital. The team threw a very nice farewell party for me, complete with a small ceremony. I gave a very short speech that went something like this: "Here I am, a Muslim born in India, raised in Pakistan, immigrated to US, a US citizen with a South Asian heritage now representing the US in Turkey as a Fulbright scholar and academic cultural ambassador. This is something that can happen only in the United States."

I scheduled a couple weeks of vacation to follow the work of the program, and it was wonderful to be able to stroll through the old town of Izmir with Isfana. The boys would be arriving tomorrow, along with their girlfriends, Kacie and Sausan. I had to assure their parents of this sponsorship and invitation, and in consonance with the culture and sensitivities of Sausan's parents, the Khomusis, I invited Sausan's sister, Tasneem, to join her as a companion. I had a surprise up my sleeve also. Since Isfana's fifty-second birthday would arrive while she was here, I had planned to fly her mother in from India to join us. I also thought it might be nice for her mom, the grandmother, to meet the boys' girlfriends since things clearly seemed to be getting more serious for both of them.

Isfana was delighted to see her surprise when she landed at the airport, and we spent a wonderful holiday exploring the gorgeous beaches, visiting amazing historic sites, ambling through open air markets and more. I was convinced this area had to be one of the best kept secrets in the world. Every day, we were simply blown away by the sights and history. The ancient city of Ephesus was incredible. In Istanbul, we stopped in at the world-famous Hagia Sophia, once a Greek Orthodox patriarchal basilica, later an imperial mosque, and now a stunning museum. On and on it went; I never wanted it to end.

But as everything does, my assignment and following then our family vacation ended. We said goodbye to Isfana's mother first, and then two by two, the rest of us parted ways to return to our respective parts of the US. It had been an amazing adventure all around, and I returned home rejuvenated and inspired in so many ways.

We knew they were coming after that. The calls. First came Zee. He wanted to let us know that he would ask Kacie to marry him, and she said yes! He was thrilled, and we were too. We had talked about with Zee the challenge of amalgamating culture, tradition, and religion, and they had decided to accept that challenge. The wedding planning began. We were not surprised to discover that some of our more religious relatives were upset about Zee marrying a Catholic. Likewise, some of Kacie's family, the Kellys, were uncomfortable about her marrying a Muslim. Both faiths technically require that the partner convert before marriage, so this was a tricky situation for the more traditional elements of both families. Isfana and I fielded several calls and had some long conversations with cousins, aunts, and uncles. "They are thoughtful adults," we kept telling people. "They will have to find their way."

Isfana and I were convinced that we would not try to force Kacie to convert to Islam. We knew that she would not, even if we tried. Moreover, that entailed her going through the Misaq. Misaq in the Bohra sect of Shiism that we belong to is an important oath of allegiance and commitment to the specific rules and sacrament of the faith. It cannot be taken lightly. The clergy in our sect were adamant that we get that done even if Kacie later decided not to follow through with the oath. It was considered still an important basis for the marriage ceremony. Isfana and I were not going to demean the sanctity of the oath, however. Kacie asked us what it meant to take this oath, and I explained to her what it did. We all concluded that that was not the route we wanted, and I assured her of our full support. Moreover, I was not going to diminish the importance of the Misaq and let it be a casual ceremony to suit our purpose.

I also received lectures from clergy at my mosque in Houston. They were not only concerned about Zee but also very upset that I was encouraging a blasphemous relationship by supporting my son's decision without the Bohra Islamic rites. I tried to be patient with everyone and explain our situation, but eventually I had to tune out all the negativity and focus on the joy that Zee and Kacie were experiencing and be sensitive to all family members, but mostly to Zee and Kacie. I didn't want to diminish that.

Zee and Kacie considered their options and decided to hold two separate ceremonies to celebrate each faith and culture. First came the Muslim ceremony, a modified form of the *nikah*. We invited a more moderate clergyman from a neighboring community to perform the service. At the time, there was no template for this type of interfaith marriage, so we had to make it up as we went. I approached it almost like one of my teaching curriculum. My goal was to share the beauty of the Muslim traditions without making our many Catholic guests uncomfortable or perplexed. The day began with the traditional celebrations, the henna painting, the traditional music, food, and more. Then came the ceremony itself where I narrated many of the symbolic elements, such as the traditional *mehr* (the payment and contract), the blessings of the father, the prayers, and the vows and so on. This was very basic by standards adopted later. Years later, these types of weddings would become more elaborate, ostentatious, and common, and I have attended many of them since Zee and Kacie's wedding which have been beautifully done with new features and programs that provide an interesting blend of cultures. We were trailblazing in a way and the Kellys, especially Kacie herself graciously participated. I think it touched those who observed it.

That night, there was a wonderful lively dinner, much like a traditional American rehearsal dinner, complete with touching toasts and hilarious roasts, and the next day came the Catholic ceremony in the church. It was another beautiful service and a wonderful occasion all around.

Not long after that, we received the next call. Riaz would propose to Sausan. Riaz did this while Sausan's parents, the Khomusis, visited us in New Orleans. He prepared an elaborate engagement event. He was thrilled, and we were too. Months later, the whole family traveled to Ottawa for the big event. Riaz and Sausan opted for a traditional religious ceremony, much like the one that Isfana and I had. It was like traveling back in time to see Sausan sitting on her side of the curtain, to hear the traditional prayers, and to watch the ceremony unfold. It was a fun wedding and a great mix of culture and tradition in a destination wedding.

CHAPTER 29

Five Days

There was nothing to worry about, at least not for us in New Orleans. The tropical storm was churning up past the Bahamas and heading toward the East Coast of Florida. It seemed typical as it made landfall in Florida as a category 1 hurricane.

Then everything changed. Hurricane Katrina took a hard left turn to the east, raked across the everglades and shot back into open water. The Gulf of Mexico was extremely warm in August, and Katrina quickly ballooned up to a category 2 storm. Still, her trajectory had her heading into the Yucatan peninsula of Mexico. Nothing to worry about in New Orleans, right?

Wrong again. Once more, she took a hard turn, this time bending toward to the north even as she doubled in size and intensified to a category 3. If you look back at her path, it makes an incredible S shape, almost like a cosine from trigonometry. With little more than forty-eight hours' notice, the City of New Orleans suddenly found itself in the path of destruction. Katrina continued to build in those warm waters, and people all over the Gulf South began scrambling to hardware and grocery stores for plywood, generators, food, water, extra batteries, and everything that people need to protect their homes and survive storms. The city ordered mandatory evacuations, and people began to flee. Highways became choked with traffic, and people sat for hours in the blistering heat.

Day One: Sunday, August 28

By 2005, I was taking shifts at the new Lindy Boggs Medical Center in Midcity, and I had an extended shift on Sunday, August 28, since there was a shortage of help. It was a private hospital, run by a corporation called Tenet. It was also an LSU-affiliated teaching hospital for some departments. Quite a few hospital-based doctors bailed on their shifts as the storm approached, but I was not about to abandon my patients or my residents. As I locked my car up in the parking garage, I gazed down at the umbrella in the back seat. I almost grabbed it out of habit but then laughed to myself. What good was a small folding umbrella going to do me in the middle of a category 5 hurricane? That Sunday morning, the satellite imagery of the storm was astounding. It had jumped to a category 5 storm and was so huge that it appeared to cover every drop of water in the Gulf of Mexico.

Inside, the 187-bed hospital was fairly full, and everyone was preparing to ride out the storm. Supplies were being stocked. Backup generators and batteries were being tested. Tensions were high as I checked in for my shift, but everyone was professional and collected as we enacted the emergency protocols and made our regular rounds with patients and their families, many of which gathered here in the hospital for safety and to support their loved ones.

Isfana had decided to come to the hospital also and stay with me instead of evacuating, and she would be here in a few hours. That turned out to be a fateful decision, but one that we both appreciated later. It would be hard to imagine being separated during the disaster that was about to unfold.

I met with my team of residents, all young physicians in training, and we made our plan for the night. We would be working the intensive care unit. Many of us had been through big storms before, and we shared our knowledge of how to manage different situations. When Isfana arrived, she brought biryani, a delicious spicy rice dish with chicken, that she had prepared at home. The whole ICU team ate together, and there was a great sense of camaraderie and control.

The first outer bands of the hurricane began to hit that night. Heavy winds and driving rain would sweep across the city, and we could hear the racket outside. Through the thick windows, we could see trees blowing wildly in the light of streetlamps. Then a calm would come again. These ebbs and flows lasted well into the evening until, finally, the raging rains and wind became sustained. The power, which had been flickering on and off intermittently, finally failed completely, plunging us all into the darkness as the storm whipped around the building. It only took a few moments for the hospital's backup generators to kick in, however, and we were able to reassure patients, families, and our own anxious staff that everything was just fine.

Of course, it was difficult not to notice the sensation of the barometric pressure dropping as the storm drew nearer. It was a strange feeling in the chest, and the building felt it too. As the air pressure changed dramatically, ceiling tiles would flutter over our heads and occasionally plummet to the floor. Heavy stormproof windows would bend outward, and every once in a while, there would be a pop and crash as one of the windows exploded. Most of the windows were boarded up for safety, but there were a few that we could still peer out. There wasn't much to see in the blackness outside.

Day Two: Monday, August 29

By the time dawn arrived, the eye of the hurricane was approaching landfall to the east of New Orleans, and the storm persisted. Now we could see the flooding outside, and it was bad, but not terrible. Streets were rivers. Trees were islands. Cars looked like boats. There was a street sign that we could clearly spot from our third-floor window, and we used that as a gauge to watch the water level. If the sign was about eight feet high, then the water must be about three feet deep now.

The good news was that the storm had been raging for hours and would be moving on soon. Slowly, Katrina pushed inland and drove up through Mississippi.

As the storm finally began to wane, spirits were high throughout the hospital. We had made it! It was just a matter of time now before the flooding subsided and the power was restored, phone service returned, new supplies delivered, and new staff arrived for their shifts. Everyone was looking forward to some nice cool air. The backup generators ran lights and equipment, but they did not run the air-conditioning system, and the rooms were becoming very humid and warm as a sweltering August afternoon lay over the city.

We made our usual rounds, checking on patients, administering medicines, reading heart monitors, and checking oxygen levels, ventilators, and so on. Patients and their families were feeling the stress of the heat, but they seemed to have weathered the storm very well. "Anytime now," we reassured them about the electricity and communications.

Without television, phones, or radio, we had no news from outside the walls of this place, but everyone was optimistic. Maybe we would have to ride out one more night here, but there was plenty of food for that, and the generators could run for days. "Anytime now," we assured our patients and ourselves.

Day Three: Tuesday, August 30

Something was wrong. As the first light of dawn broke over the darkened city, it was clear that something in this landscape was amiss, and it took a moment to realize what I was looking at: water. Everywhere. We had all assumed the flooding would be down or gone by this morning, but it was worse. Much worse. If the streets had been rivers yesterday, now there were no more streets—just a dark lake of water that was engulfing everything around us. Trees were now truly islands. Cars floated like submarines that had returned to the surface and rested half submerged. I looked closely at the street sign that I was using yesterday to gauge to watch the water levels. If the sign was about eight feet high, then the water must be about four feet deep now. Many lifelong New Orleanais had seen some flooding in their days, but nothing quite like this. More importantly, *where was it coming from?*

Optimism is a funny thing. It persists for a while before it gives in to reality. For a few hours, people remained curious but upbeat about the situation. This was strange, but surely things were under control by now. But the water kept coming. And coming. It was huge and murky, full of debris. The current was strong, dragging trees, cars, and pieces of houses along with it. As the water levels continued to rise, I could feel people's spirits deflate in an exact opposite reaction. What was happening? *If that street sign is eight feet high, then the water must be five feet deep now.*

Very quickly, we all realized that this was a much more serious situation than we had imagined, and it was about to get even worse. Slowly, it dawned on us: we're going to flood. As the water kept coming, it began to breach the perimeter walls of the hospital itself. It was now pouring into the basement levels. Hospital staff began scrambling to move supplies before they were destroyed. Within an hour, the backup generators were swamped and then swallowed by the water, plunging the entire building into a state of silent shock. One thought ran through my head: *the patients.* We had patients on dialysis machines, patients on ventilators, and more. Doctors and nurses scrambled to bedsides to begin manually ventilating patients, literally squeezing every breath into the patient's lungs with their bare hands.

A sense of urgency swept through the building, but not panic. Everyone knew what to do. Everyone knew how to respond to emergency situations, and surely there would be some support from outside the hospital soon.

All morning, we worked aggressively to stabilize all our patients and get some understanding of our larger situation. Luckily for us, someone on our floor had a small battery-powered radio, and for the first time, I heard the news from outside. Instead of providing any relief, however, the radio offered only grim reports. Levee breaches. Massive flooding. Houses swept off their foundations. More levee breaches. People stranded on roofs. Corpses in the water. These details began to filter in, and they quickly began to paint a bigger picture: *disaster.* The sheer scale of the tragedy was unfathomable. Eighty percent of the city was underwater. *Eighty percent.* I took a moment to find Isfana and squeeze her hand. We both knew this was now a much more serious situation than we had anticipated. Then we both went to work.

If that street sign is eight feet high, then the water must be six feet deep now.

The most important thing to do was keep a sense of calm and order in the hospital although that was becoming harder to do with each passing hour. The Lindy Boggs Medical Center had literally become an island, and we were almost completely cut off from the mainland, wherever that was now. No electricity. No running water. No phones or cell phone reception. No refrigeration for medicines. People were trying to remain calm, but it was clear to see the panic beginning to bubble beneath the surface. The thought that kept everyone going was that help was on the way. Help would be here soon. Surely help was coming.

To make matters even more complicated, people began swimming to the hospital from all over the neighborhood. Houses were submerging, and people looked toward the hospital building in hopes of finding safety and resources. But we were flooding and abandoning all the lower floors of the building. As the hospital was shrinking, hundreds more people were dragging themselves and their families out of the water and up the front steps, looking for help. Unfortunately, we had very little to offer them besides shelter.

Amid the growing chaos, we did our best to remain professional. Keep everyone fed. Keep everyone organized. Each floor should carefully monitor who enters and leaves. Wherever possible, conserve batteries. It might be a few more hours before help arrives; we have no way of knowing. Periodically, someone would peek out the window to check our flood gauge.

If that street sign is eight feet high, then the water must be seven feet deep now.

All day passed, and there was no contact from the outside world, other than the occasional news helicopter that passed overhead. As night began to fall again, I felt my first real twinges of concern. The hospital was not designed to serve as an island. It was meant to be on the grid. With hundreds of people trapped here, drinking water was already dwindling, makeshift toilets were already overflowing in places, batteries were running out, and food supplies were limited. Without air-conditioning, the hospital became a sweltering hot box. The environment was slowly deteriorating. In the darkness, orders would arrive on the floor, supposedly from management, but no one was sure who had made the orders or where they had originated. People became obsessed with projects like wristbands to identify every person in the hospital as patient, family, staff, or visitor.

Meanwhile, people began exploring the roof of the building, looking for somewhere, anywhere, that they might be able to pick up a cell phone signal. The roof was a series of a dozen or more surfaces at varying elevations, and it was quite tricky to climb around out there. Some staff finally discovered a far corner of the roof where they could reach a cell phone signal to fire off texts, and that's how we got our very first messages out from the hospital into the world. Sometimes it worked, and sometimes it didn't, but at least somebody knew we were here and needed help.

Isfana and I went to the roof also to escape into some fresh air and try our luck with the cell phone reception. Between the destroyed towers and the overwhelming numbers of people trying to use their phones simultaneously, voice calls were impossible. Text messages sometimes went through, however. One of my residents, Marc Baker, was on the roof too. He had just had some luck. He finally had been able to reach his brother who worked for the Red Cross. We asked him for help, and he took us down and up and over until we reached his lucky corner of the roof. There, we finally were able to reach our sons with messages. They were relieved to hear from us but horrified to hear our situations. By now, Riaz had taken a job in Congressman Bobby Jindal's office in Washington, DC, and he vowed to do everything he could to help us.

That was a difficult night in the ICU. I and my team of residents did everything we could to make sure the continuity of care was not affected, but we had to share flashlights to make rounds; the heat was suffocating, and everyone was exhausted. We had aggressively weaned our patients off ventilator support and moved them to manual aids, but who knew how well they would do through the night. By now it had been twenty-four hours since the first lashings of the storm, and as we hovered around the small portable radio, all we heard was a stream of officials from the state and federal government standing in front of a microphone and reciting numbers. It reminded me of a kindergarten class where each student has to take turns giving a short presentation on numbers. Everyone wanted to show off their authority, but it became painfully clear that there was no actual plan to deal with this emergency. There were simply dozens of small groups and agencies responding ad hoc.

But surely, they realized this was a *hospital*. The situation was about to get very serious.

We had our first fatalities that night. Under all the duress, several of the patients went into cardiac arrest, and there was nothing the teams could do to save them. The terrifying reality settled over all of us: *people are dying here.* There wasn't even a morgue in the hospital any longer; it was underwater in the basement. The chapel on the second floor was converted into a temporary morgue.

I spent some of that night huddled with my colleagues and Isfana, and we talked quietly. We talked about patients on the floor with my team and how best to care for them under these conditions. We talked about our friends and loved ones around the city and hoped for their safety. And finally, we took a moment to daydream about what we would like to do when we got out of here. "I'd like to take a long nap in an air-conditioned room with a beautiful bed," she said.

"I'd like an airan," I replied. The heat made me crave that lovely yogurt drink I had been introduced to in Turkey.

Then we went back to work.

The administrative team tried to contact their Dallas headquarters and were told that help could only come after water subsided. The officials and the Baton Rouge leadership would huddle and then provide details about the many challenges, but no solutions. At one point, we were told to pray. Pray we did all right, but what next? The administration leadership in the hospital convened a support session and then encouraged us all to hold hands and bond. In other words, they had no idea how to get us out of this mess. Finally, some of us created our own plan and strategy.

Day Four: Wednesday, August 31

When morning finally arrived, I went to the window to look for the street sign I had been monitoring so closely.

If that street sign is eight feet high, then the water must be more than eight feet deep.

It was completely gone.

Today was Wednesday, and this is the day the panic began to set in. Over the course of the night, five of the most vulnerable patients had died. Everyone had heard the news reports by now and knew there was no clear plan to rescue us. The hospital was overcrowded with hungry scared people, and the mood was becoming tense, verging on dangerous.

My resident, Marc, along with two other residents, Justin Spiegel and Chris Daniels, decided they weren't going to wait any longer. "We're going to go see what help we can find," Justin said.

"I'm not sure this is a good idea," I said, but I wasn't going to stop them. He was right, after all. Someone had to do something. They waded off into the murky dangerous waters.

Meanwhile, up on the roof, staff and family members made large banners that read HELP and SOS and waved them toward the sky, but to no avail. I was now reminded of the chaos that used to grip Karachi during the ethnic and political riots, when fear gripped the city, road blocks sprang up in intersections, and tire fires raged in the streets, belching black smoke. From the roof, we could hear other small groups of people wailing into the emptiness from different places around the neighborhood. *Help! Help! Help!* We couldn't see them, but with so much water, sounds carried very far. A little further off, we heard another group that had organized a loud chant of some kind. They punctuated their chanting with gunshots. *Boom! Boom! Boom!* Perhaps they thought it might help them get noticed if they fired their weapons. It was a terrifying sound to the rest of us and fueled the sense of fear and anarchy.

Isfana and I went to the lucky corner, and we were able to receive a message from Riaz: *help is on the way.*

From his position in Congressman Jindal's office, he had been able to coordinate with Marc's brother in the Red Cross. He wasn't sure what kind of help was coming, but the authorities knew about us. Isfana and I were elated. We quickly spread the word. People needed to hear some positive news, and it spread down throughout the building.

From the rooftop, we could see that the water had finally stopped rising. It was dark and still, stretching through the neighborhood as far as we could see—except for one spot. Near the Midcity Post Office, there appeared to be one small patch of high flat ground. "Look there," I said. "They could land a helicopter there."

Midafternoon, a small team of rescue workers from the Shreveport Fire Department. With a handful of small boats, it was a tiny operation, but it gave everyone in the hospital a great deal of hope to finally see someone in some official capacity arrive to help. Finally. Help from the mainland. They told us that our medical center wasn't even on the official list for rescue operations. The relatively recent name change from Mercy Hospital to Lindy Boggs Medical Center had somehow caused confusion.

They also told us about the terrifying anarchy that seemed to be raging across the entire city. Looting, murders, horrors in the Super Dome, violence in the convention center. I could only imagine thousands and thousands of people smashed together and fighting over dwindling resources.

The most chilling thing they told us, however was that they were in MCI mode, *Mass Casualty Incident*. In other words, emergency medical services resources were overwhelmed by the numbers and the severity of the situation. They were performing triage. They could only be with us for one day. They needed us to organize people.

In a mass casualty incident, it is standard protocol to evacuate the able-bodied first and then progress backward to the people with the most needs. Those people require more time, space, and resources to evacuate. Therefore, if you're working with limited resources, you can save more people by taking the able-bodied first. This is what the firemen wanted. "We'll evacuate anyone who's viable," the leader said.

Viable?

They meant anyone who could walk on his or her own, didn't require oxygen or any kind of monitoring or machinery.

"What about the rest of the patients?" one of the nurses asked.

"I'm sorry," the rescuer replied. "This is like a war. Get the able-bodied out of here first. The rest will have to wait."

With those words came the most difficult part of the entire ordeal. All the physicians were gathered, and we were ordered to categorize each of the patients in our care. We collected as a group and rounded with a team to decide on an A–D scale. "A" meant the patient was ambulatory and *viable*. "B" designated patients in wheelchairs—those who could sit up but couldn't walk themselves. "C" was for critical patients, and "D" stood for *do not resuscitate*. Those were patients in severe circumstances. The designations needed to happen immediately, and the rescuers would begin evacuating As right away.

In other words, we were asked to choose who was going to live and who was going to die, and everyone in the whole hospital knew it. If we designated a patient A or B, he or she was likely going to be evacuated. Cs and Ds were at the end of the line where things looked grim. To this day, I get the chills when I remember this process. I'm thankful that we had the group wisdom to help guide those extremely difficult moments and the ability to coordinate as effectively as we did. It was a multidisciplinary group decision we made incorporating the clergy, nurses, administration, and all MDs present at that time.

We have to move now.

In the meantime, my residents returned to the hospital with a boat that they had found somewhere. A doctor from another department also managed to retrieve a couple boats from nearby, so we were slowly growing our own private flotilla in addition to the rescuers. This was encouraging, but there was still so much work to do transferring these hundreds of people across miles of dangerous water strewn with obstacles.

Inside the hospital, the work was heart-wrenching. Patients and families literally begged me for higher designations as I marked the ones with Bs, Cs, and Ds. I was literally writing on their skin with a black permanent marker. "I'm sorry," was all I could say. "There's nothing I can do. This is an MCI."

Several times I had to retreat to an office to be alone for a few minutes when I felt an emotional breakdown coming on. The one thing I could not do was cry in front of my patients and staff. I needed to be strong.

The firefighters and our volunteer boatmen worked very hard all afternoon and into the evening, but it was a slow process. They managed to get air support for a while also. A helicopter was indeed able to land on the patch of high ground that I had spotted the day before, and the big Coast Guard chopper made trip after trip, lifting patients and flood victims into the air and shuttling them to safety. All day, Isfana and I watched the helicopter and watched those boats cruising slowly through the water, weaving around unseen obstacles like submerged cars, downed power lines, and fallen trees. They would carefully load up and then roll back out. In the distance, periodic gunfire rang out as it had since the ordeal began. Rescuers managed to move hundreds of people that day from the hospital to a landing location somewhere in the city, but still, many remained, including the most vulnerable. As the sun began to set, the firefighters' radios crackled with orders. They were to suspend operations for the day. Rescuers had to protect themselves first and foremost to keep the mission going, and no one wanted to get lost, to get caught by looters or, worse, after nightfall. Clearly, they hated to do it, but the firefighters filled their boats one last time and bid the rest of us farewell. They had done all they could do.

"Will you be back tomorrow?" I asked.

"I don't know if it will be us," one of the firefighters replied. "But someone will be back for you."

"In the morning?"

"The choppers should be back in the morning," he said. "Good luck."

It was one of the loneliest feelings I have ever felt to watch those boats disappear through the buildings and into the shadows of dusk. The sounds of their motors carried over the water for a few minutes, and then nothing. We were alone on our island. All that remained was a handful of doctors, a clutch of nurses, and dozens of the most critical patients from throughout the entire hospital. It would be another long night. But at least we had a few of our own boats now. We knew we could act on our own no matter what happened with the rescuers.

The first thing we did was move patients down to the first floor instead of having them spread out through the hospital. If we wanted to move out the doors at first light, we needed patients to be ready on the first floor. It was a grueling physical challenge to move critically ill patients down dark stairwells, and we were exhausted when we finished. Still, we swept through the hospital again and again to make sure we hadn't forgotten anyone in a dark room in some far-flung wing of the medical center. Twice, we found people like this, patients that somehow had gone unaccounted for, sitting by themselves in the pitch darkness. Other patients, we simply had to leave behind. It was agonizing to make these decisions, but the most critically ill patients who were designated Do Not Resuscitate were left in their rooms. Their situations were too fragile for such a rough transfer, and we were too short on manpower. This was the first and only time I have ever had to make decisions like this, and they haunt me to this day. I can still see those ghostly faces with the sheen of sweat glimmering in the dull light of a flashlight. I can still hear those ragged breaths in the sweltering heat of the abandoned rooms. At the time, we hoped against hope that someone would be able to make it back in time to save these people, but of course no one did. The few patients who survived the night did not survive long enough to be saved.

With heavy hearts and frayed nerves, we swept the floors again and again with our flashlights as sweat dripped off our faces and our shoes literally made squishing sounds because our socks were soaked through with sweat.

Day Five: Thursday, September 1

At first light, we began to move. My residents and I loaded up the boats with critical care patients, a painstaking process, and headed straight to the patch of ground where the helicopters landed. Overnight, it had become a chaotic scene. Survivors from all over the neighborhood had heard about the evacuation yesterday, and they had begun wading, swimming and floating to this spot all through the night. By the time we arrived, it was already crowded, and absolutely no one was glad to see boatloads of hospital patients arrive to cut line. "These patients are critical," I tried to explain to a group of people, but the shouting and shoving had already begun. Just when I thought things might get ugly and turn violent, I caught sight of a family that I knew. I had treated them at the LSU medical center, and they were friendly with me. Somehow, this sense of friendliness and camaraderie seemed to cut some of the tension. We weren't some kinds of interlopers; we were part of the community. Grudgingly, people made room for us on the high ground, and we all waited together even as more boatloads of patients arrived from the hospital, just a few blocks away.

When the helicopters began to arrive, coming through the hazy blue sky and filling the air with the roar of their rotors, it was the sound of angels. But everyone wanted to jump on those angels, and there was much scrambling and jockeying for position. It took awhile, but Isfana and I were finally able to load several of our patients onto one of the big birds and then clamber in ourselves to look after them. The helicopter soon was crowded and lifting off from the ground. As we rose up over the house tops and treetops, I got my first bird's-eye view of the flooded city. It was like Lake New Orleans. It was stunning to see it, and I had to look away quickly. It was too painful. Everyone was quiet and shocked as we flew over the city, and then the chopper descended on a stretch of Interstate 10 which had become a makeshift emergency camp. Health-care personnel were waiting to whisk the patients away to safety. Police and national guard troops were loading boats. Officers worked in a white tent. At last, we had reached safety. Finally, there seemed to be coordinated action of some kind. It was such a relief. Immediately we gathered with familiar faces who had flown in earlier from the hospital, and together we waited for the last arrivals. As these ragtag elements of the hospital staff gathered to commiserate, we were completely spent, both physically and emotionally. Several people doubled over and sobbed once they realized that we had reached safety, and they no longer were protecting other people's lives. It was a heart-wrenching scene all around.

Soon, we realized that we had one more problem to deal with. How on earth were we going to get out of here? There was a great deal of activity, but since we were not health-care emergencies or rescue workers, we found ourselves in a kind of survivor limbo. There was no clear path or process to transport the hundreds of flood victims who were gathered here. It took several hours, but we finally managed to charter one of the busses that rolled to a stop near us.

With cash right out of our pockets, we arranged to have our group driven to Baton Rouge where we could all be safe and connect with friends, family, or colleagues. Isfana and I collapsed into a seat and stared quietly out the window as the ruined city passed by and then fell away to views of the lake and swamps along the I-10 corridor. It was so peaceful, it lulled us to sleep. The Kellys were waiting for us in Baton Rouge and welcomed us to their home, which was to be our transition for the next month. Their support was invaluable and for which we will ever remain grateful.

We were able to move out soon and resume work through the state clinic in Mandeville and LSU Baton Rouge, find another temporary place to stay in Jackson, Louisiana, and gradually get our bearings, but the total lack of coordination we had seen in our rescue mirrored what we say happening all over throughout the post-Katrina period. The local authorities were not in synch with the state leadership and the state leadership were not in synch with the national leadership. Once again, the abundant resources notwithstanding, it seemed there was inaction and confusion that translated down to individuals and institutions exhibiting poverty of leadership and organization.

CHAPTER 30

Every House Had a Story

Driving back into the city was like entering a scene from a horror movie about a nuclear holocaust. A colleague of mine was driving, and we rolled up to a military checkpoint established on River Road. Humvees were parked at angles to create a barrier, and soldiers stepped into the road to greet us with automatic rifles strapped across their chests. Behind them, the landscape was brown, ashen, broken, and abandoned. It was hard to believe that what I was seeing was real. New Orleans was usually such a vibrant town, overflowing with green. It was practically impossible to stop the vines, the banana trees, the bamboo, ginger, oak trees, and azalea bushes from growing wild. Normally, it was a constant battle of man against nature. Traffic should have been thick, businesses bustling, and streetcars rattling down those tracks right over there where St. Charles Avenue met Carrolton. Birds should have been darting around the treetops and telephone poles.

Instead, the entire scene was eerily quiet. Streets were caked in dried brown mud. Broken trees were listless and covered in a patina of brown dust. Buildings were dark and quiet. Broken and empty windows seemed to watch us. The air itself seemed lifeless, without birds or the noise of daily life. "What's your business here?" one soldier asked as they approached our car. The city was still under mandatory evacuation and was occupied by the military now.

"Cars," my colleague replied. I had acquired a permit through LSU to enter Orleans Parish and retrieve my vehicle. As a health-care professional, my car was deemed a legitimate piece of medical infra-structure, which it was.

A knot of anticipation formed in my gut as the soldiers looked over our paperwork. Finally, they waved us through. "You need to go straight in and straight out," the soldier said.

"We will."

I retrieved my car from the parking garage, but instead of leaving right away, I had to see my home. I couldn't come this close and not see it. I turned down Claiborne Avenue and began driving the familiar route, only nothing was familiar any longer. The empty overpass loomed overhead, and a few of the darkened stoplights still dangled in the hot air as I passed beneath. The main roads had been largely cleared by military convoys, but I still had to steer around destroyed cars, fallen branches, rubble from collapsed walls, fallen utility poles, and whatever else had tumbled into the streets. The knot of anxiety in my stomach kept growing tighter and tighter as I drew closer to my own house. I could see the level of destruction all around, and it was tragic. The waterline was easily five or six feet high on houses here, and some of the homes in my neighborhood had partially collapsed or shifted right off their foundations to stand at odd angles from the road. Everything was covered in that wretched brown mud and dust.

The first thing I felt as I turned onto my street was relief. My house was still standing. I pulled up in front and gazed at it for a moment. The waterline was so distinct, as if someone had tried to cut the structure in half, and the front door was spray-painted with a bright-orange X, indicating that rescue workers had been by to determine if there were any survivors—or victims—inside. Every home in the flooded areas bore this same X, and the eye quickly became trained to scan the numbers, looking for the signs of survivors, pets, or fatalities. Every house had a story, and these spray-painted Xs were like a shorthand, offering these cryptic descriptions.

I walked up to the window and peered into my house. Somehow, water was still standing in the floors, inches deep inside the living room. The furniture had floated all over the place and then landed in odd locations. Dining chairs tangled by the front door. The sofa tilted against the stairs. The waterline was distinct on the inside of the home too, and even the paintings on the wall were bisected by that dreadful mark.

It was growing dark, and my sense of unease began to swell. This was my home, but now it was a place that I did not want to be after nightfall. I climbed into my car and drove back out of the city.

It took just over a month to lift the mandatory evacuation order and allow people to return to their homes, their businesses, and their city. Isfana and I had prepared a small army to help us go back in. I knew the horror that awaited us, but no one else had seen it yet. Riaz flew down from DC. My cousin arrived with his friend from Oklahoma City, armed with tools. Other family and friends arrived from all over the place to help us. It was uplifting to have the support, but gut-wrenching to pull up to our house. I noticed new features of the neighborhood this time, like the ruined car that had somehow floated right through someone's front window and now rested halfway into the living room. We were slightly surprised to realize that we were very nearly alone in our neighborhood. We had imagined that many people were waiting like us to get back to their homes, but our street felt like it was from a ghost town. Almost no signs of life. We had scheduled this day to come to open the house with the FEMA agent.

We all stood in the street and prepared ourselves for what was to come next. By now, we had all heard the horror stories of what happened inside a flooded home that was abandoned in the heat for over a month. Refrigerators were full of rot and maggots. Upholstery and carpets were fetid. Mold, mildew, and slime grew thick on walls. Floorboards rotted and buckled. Our small army of friends and family pulled on rubber gloves, slipped paper masks over our mouths and noses, laced up our heavy-soled boots, took deep breaths, and then went to work.

We pried the door open with a crowbar and entered. That's when we all felt shattered and broken. Isfana had kept it together up until now, but now that she was standing in her own living room, she couldn't fight the wave of emotion that went through her. I couldn't either. It took a few minutes for everyone to regain their composure, but we did. There was much to do after all. We hauled out furniture, pulled down drapes, and shoveled dried mud out of the living room. We taped the refrigerator shut and dragged it to the curb to join the ruined television, the dead plants, and the wretched remains of carpets. Everything from the first floor of the house had to go, along with many things that had been rain soaked on the second floor after the hurricane ripped part of the roof off. The mountain of trash at our curb grew throughout the day. It was clear to everyone that this was going to be a huge, huge job to repair and restore our home, and we were just one of thousands. No, worse than that, one of hundreds of thousands. In all, Hurricane Katrina damaged over eighty thousand homes. The scale was epic, but we tackled it the best we could—one room at a time.

Meanwhile, the local hospital systems were in a state of controlled chaos and confusion. No one knew when or how flooded medical centers might reopen or what to do with the thousands of displaced staff. Patients had been evacuated by the thousands, and there were incomplete records, at best, of where they had gone. They had to be tracked down, one by one. Electronic patient records had been obliterated, and physical files destroyed in floodwaters. Hundreds of my friends and colleagues found themselves waiting, waiting, and waiting for some news, some progress, and some assignment.

It only took a week or so before I decided that I had had enough of waiting, so I did what any enterprising physician would do. I committed a burglary. I went downtown and broke into the shuttered LSU medical center and prowled the halls with a flashlight, climbing through the dark stairwell to the Medical Education Building office where I could sneak into my office. I needed my credential files and copies of my diplomas, certificates, and licenses. Once I had retrieved these, I drove to Kenner Regional Hospital in the suburbs of New Orleans and waited to speak with a director. "I'm here to work," I said when I finally got an audience.

"We don't have an open position right now," the CEO told me.

"I'm not asking for a full-time position. Or an office. Or even a salary. I just need to work."

Within days, I was seeing patients synchronizing the start of the hospitalist service and starting the outpatient clinic. Sometimes, you just can't wait for things to fall through or come through. You just go do it. One cannot wait indefinitely for the wheels of formal structure to move amid the abundance of need.

I spent weeks with this empty, broken shell of a house in this empty, broken shell of a neighborhood. I hunted contractors every day, but it was nearly impossible to even get a call back, let alone a meeting. Every day, after work, I drove all the way to the house to clean or work on small projects for a few hours before driving back out to the suburbs where Isfana and I had rented a small condo to stay in. The house became lonelier and lonelier. The boys began advising us to sell the property. "What's the point?" they asked. "You can get a fresh start somewhere new."

It was good advice. From a financial standpoint, it made very little sense to sink more of our money back into this decrepit property, but from an emotional standpoint, I felt determined to rebuild. This was the home where we built our American Dream, where we watched it come to fruition. It was not about the house; it was about the home, and home is not just the four walls of a structure. I couldn't just walk away from it in this condition.

The thing that amazed me, however, was how few people seemed to share my sentiment. By now, it had been months since we could return, and still the neighborhood was like the setting of a zombie movie—eerie and empty. Yes, contractors were nearly impossible to find, but many houses had not even been opened or cleaned out. Only a handful of people came regularly as I did. Among us, there was a camaraderie, and often we would lean on car hoods and talk in the street, sharing Katrina stories and tips for cleaning and rebuilding. It was such a small fraternity of people though. Where was everyone else? I wondered. It was hard not to compare this event to disasters, both natural and man-made, I had witnessed in other nations like Pakistan or India. In those places, people swooped into the aftermath and began work with immediacy and energy. Here, it seemed everyone was waiting for something. Waiting for a program. Waiting for approval. Waiting for a check. Businesses were waiting to restart until they got the insurance settlement, and houses were not repaired because people were waiting for the insurance monies to rebuild with an upgrade. Doors and organizations remained unopened and unused lest the insurance claim be compromised. Restoration might happen sometime, but not in a hurry, and the whole system was in a state of suspended animation. There seemed to be a poverty of initiative amid this region of abundant resources.

One evening, as I swept the street in front of the house, I spotted something bright on the ground. It stood out immediately because it was clean. I often swept the street because I was tired of driving over roofing nails which were like a plague all over the city, but now I paused to pick up this small white card. It was a business card for a contractor named Rolando. I looked up and down the street. I hadn't seen anyone on this block for days now. Where did the card come from?

Who cares? I thought. I pulled my phone from my pocket and dialed the number. He answered on the second ring. "Hello?"

"I'm calling for Rolando."

"This is Rolando."

"I need help with my house," I said.

"I'm in the car now," he replied. "I can be there tomorrow."

He was literally driving down the interstate, on his way to New Orleans from Orlando, Florida, where he lived. He was on his way to work, to make some money, and to help rebuild New Orleans. We spoke for a short while, and he sounded both knowledgeable and was polite.

The next day, he pulled up in front of my house, and I gave him the grand tour. "What can you do?" I asked.

"I can do everything," he replied. He waved his hand around the house. "All this."

"How about we start with the roof," I said. "If that goes well, we'll talk about these other projects."

"Very good," he said. "Very good. I have to get my team together. I'll be back on Thursday to start."

I wasn't completely sure I would every see him again after he drove away. He would have unlimited work to choose from in this city for years, so would he really come back to complete this one conditional job?

Two days later, he rolled up with his crew, right on time. They were a team of Spanish-speaking immigrants, and Rolando was the only one among them who spoke English. He fired off a round of instructions, and the guys went straight to work, throwing up ladders, hauling supplies onto the roof, and making themselves busy. The sounds of voices and hammers ringing out through the empty neighborhood was music to my ears. Not only was my roof being repaired but I was not alone here for the first time in many weeks.

It didn't take long for work to pick up. In addition to working at Kenner Regional, I pitched in at a couple other LSU-affiliated hospitals, including Earl K. Long Hospital in Baton Rouge and the local community clinic where volunteers were trying to restore an old building and get a clinic running. Operating health-care facilities were few and far between. I was one of the few doctors willing and able to split shifts and work in multiple cities. In fact, I was one of only a few LSU physicians who were available at all right now. Many had evacuated with their families and had not yet returned. They were a diaspora, scattered across the nation. As such, I soon found myself in demand even as LSU administrators began the painful debates over which medical centers to rebuild, which to close permanently, and which staff would have to be cut as a result.

In addition to my hospital work, I had always been part of the state TB clinic, and now we also began to pick up the pieces. All our records had been lost in the floodwaters, and we began the arduous task of trying to track down tuberculosis patients who had fled all over the country. It was important to stay connected with them, if possible, and to help them maintain care and treatment wherever they were now. Otherwise, they could be health risks, not just to themselves, but to those around them. One by one, we reconnected with patients who had made it to Atlanta, Houston, Birmingham, Memphis, and more. We never found all of them, but we did our best. For patients who were still in our region, we had to improvise treatment and care. The TB clinic building had been destroyed, so the state TB office was able to get a trailer donated from Chicago.

As I entered that unit and we set up a desk and an X-ray view box, it reminded me of my clinics in Kenya. Those were a notch above though. "We are back to bush medicine, literally and metaphorically, and a pun intended," I said as we unpacked whatever little stationery we had. But at least we could visit patients and get the clinic going. Such makeshift clinics sprouted up everywhere possible, and those of us who did not want to wait to get some semblance of normalcy back actively engaged in them.

My routine started before dawn with work all day in the few hospitals which were functioning and occasionally with a mobile TB clinic, sometimes traveling over one hundred miles in a day. In between shifts, I would head to the house to see the progress and encourage my contractor and team. In many ways, I was reminded of my father and the way he eagerly oversaw his own teams of workers as he built his dream bungalow in Karachi. Just like my father, I always stopped for food, cold drinks, and jugs of clean water for the workers. In the suburbs, more shops, bakeries restaurants were open, so I could pick up pizzas, burgers, king cakes, or other treats and deliver them to the site where the hardworking crew would gobble them down. One by one, the projects got completed. Over these hectic months, the roof was repaired and looked like new; the electrical was replaced; the floor was ripped out and redone; exterior and interior walls were rebuilt, refinished, and painted; new doorways, windows, and moldings were installed; the kitchen was torn out and redone; the back deck was rebuilt; and more. So much more. The list seemed endless, and for every task completed, two more seemed to spring up in its place. It was a challenge of mythic proportions, like fighting a many-headed hydra.

One day, I was musing over my fortune to find this great crew, and I said to Rolando, "I've been meaning to ask you something."

"Yes?"

"How did your business card end up in the street in front of my house? You weren't even in New Orleans yet?"

"I have no idea," he said. "A friend of mine did have business cards, and he was passing them out for me in shops and hardware stores. He didn't go into neighborhoods though. I don't know how it got here."

Some things are just meant to be, I thought.

Finally, it was time to move back home. The house wasn't finished, but it was getting close. As always happens, the work crew began to divide their time between my house and new projects they were taking on. As one project begins to wind down, the focus gets shifted to performing for a new client. The rule of diminishing returns takes effect, and the final projects become smaller and smaller while taking longer and longer. I told Rolando, "We have a moving date—April twelfth. Your guys have to be out of the house before then, whether you're finished or not. I will change the lock that day and you will not be able to enter anyway." He got the message and finished the job for me.

For many months, life in New Orleans was incredibly challenging—and expensive. People like us who returned and rebuilt early were subjected to all manner of trials and tribulations. Natural gas lines were infiltrated with water which would cause them to be shut down. Repeatedly, the gas lines were repaired and shut down. Eventually, our entire street had to be dug up to replace a gas main. Meanwhile, the running water was inconsistent, and the power still flickered occasionally. We might go weeks without being able to cook on our stove, run our laundry, or bathe in our own home. I wrote to city hall, attended council meetings, visited Entergy offices, and hounded my state and local representatives. And it slowly got better. For weeks, our house was the only one with lights on after dark. The only house in the neighborhood with people living in it. But then came another. And then another. Very slowly, the neighbors began to trickle back in, and Isfana and I found ourselves in another unique role we had never anticipated: Katrina consultants. We could tell people how to find contractors, how to contact city officials, what problems to expect with their houses, and more. There was a new camaraderie in the neighborhood and an incredible bonding over these life-altering experiences and the ongoing challenges.

It took about a year for life in the house to return to some basic form of normalcy, but we persevered, and finally it came to

pass. What we learned—and some not without pain and anguish—
that while we were all in some way blessed with available resources,
we were pathetically ill prepared, dependent more on reactionary
footing, lacking coordination between what was happening at the
individual, community, city, state, and national level, resulting in
a mediocre and anemic response despite having the expertise and
abundance of resources which could be tapped. Those of us who
took the initiative were a step ahead.

CHAPTER 31

Institutionalized

By 2008, things were slowly returning to a kind of normalcy. After two and a half years, rebuilding continued at what I considered to be a glacial pace, but people and businesses were trickling back in. Before Katrina struck in 2005, New Orleans was home to about half a million people, and by now, the population had bounced back to roughly half that, including doctors, nurses, health-care administrators, and clinic workers. The greater metro area encompasses a larger population of more than 1.2 million people, all of whom needed a health-care system they could depend upon. Health-care professionals, and especially the team at Charity Hospital/Medical Center of Louisiana in New Orleans (MCLNO), did an admirable job under the circumstances of providing care and opening emergency departments, clinics, and in-patient services in makeshift facilities. The health services system at all levels, including their partners at the teaching universities, demonstrated a remarkable resilience, determination, and ingenuity to continue their work and support their local communities across the region.

I was back to teaching, working with medical students, and seeing patients, much like I had been before the storm, and my life was just beginning to feel normal again. That's when my colleague Steve Nelson spotted me in the parking garage, returning from one of my off-site clinics. I had been working with Steve for years and especially closely post-Katrina as we worked together to rebuild the LSU programs and sections we worked with. As we talked, I sensed him steering the conversation in a particular direction, and finally he asked me, "Have you ever considered a more administrative role for yourself?"

"No," I replied. I enjoyed my dual role as a physician and educator very much. There were new opportunities and challenges all the time, and never a dull moment.

"Well, consider this," Steve said. "Medical director for Charity Hospital. The position is about to be vacant, and I think you'd be a good fit for it."

"Me? Medical director? At Charity?" I was having a hard time even getting my head around this concept.

"Steve," I said, "I thought you were my friend." That position at Charity was famously clear across the state for being a very difficult job with challenges at every level. It was considered as a thankless job. Why would anyone want this?

He laughed, and we kept talking for a minute longer before heading in our separate directions. "Just think about it," he said as he waved goodbye. "You've got the perfect skill set, and you've got something even more valuable than that."

"What do you mean?"

"Respect," he answered. "Everybody respects you."

I thought I would dismiss the thought right away, but for days, it percolated in the back of my mind. In idle moments, I found myself thinking of the position with both a sense of dread and something else. *What was that? Curiosity? A sense of opportunity? A chance to make an even bigger impact on my community and profession? Did I really have anything special I could bring to the table?*

I was certainly not interested in going into management just for the sake of a pay raise, a bigger office, or some padding for my CV. If I was going to do this, it would have to be on my terms, which meant that I needed to know that I had a chance to change things for the better. For years, I had observed dysfunctional aspects of the healthcare system from many different angles, and this could possibly be a position where I could make a difference.

Charity Hospital in New Orleans was one of the largest charity systems in the nation. It was a safety net hospital with dozens of services, supporting countless clinics and smaller regional hospitals. In its heyday, it housed more than 1,500 beds, but right now it was still in a temporary situation, being housed in the university hospital, previously called the Hotel-Dieu (French for "house of God"). It had been run by the Daughters of Charity and had always been a sister hospital to big Charity. Now the sisters were living under one roof, which housed about five hundred beds.

More than just the structure though, Charity Hospital/ MCLNO was a huge presence in the city and beyond. The original hospital was founded in 1736 to take people in off the streets of New Orleans where they lay dying, and it very quickly expanded in size and scope because the need was so immense. From the Yellow Fever epidemics of the eighteen hundreds to the Level 1 Trauma Center developed in the twentieth century, Charity was a bulwark. Generations of working class and poor New Orleanians were born here; it provided care for tens of thousands of people; it supported other hospitals and clinics all across the state; the emergency room was one of the busiest and bloodiest in the nation—a sad testament to the violent nature of New Orleans poverty and gang culture—and many of the world's finest ER doctors were "graduates" of this infamous department. Despite its shabby exterior, it had an iconic facade and was a center of excellence. It was often said that *if you're really sick, you'd better go to Charity*. It certainly wasn't perfect, but Charity Hospital was a local institution.

My personal attachment to the hospital was deep too. Back in the 1970s, when I started my Touro-Tulane residency, this was one of the flagship hospitals for many rotations. When I returned on the 1991 *Mayflower II* voyage, I spent invaluable shifts in Charity. Then after Katrina, the very first patient that I treated was in the Charity-affiliated university hospital.

Steve kept encouraging me, and now my colleague Warren did also. Warren was one of the people who helped me get a conditional position in my early desperate days of trying to make a go of things in America. Now here he was, encouraging me to take a position in one of the largest health-care systems in the country. There was a growing chorus of support, and I continued to do my research. I spoke with people I knew who were affiliated with Charity, either directly or indirectly, to get their perspectives. I spoke with the current medical director as well, and she confirmed that it was a thankless position, but a very important role in the system.

"It's a special kind of doctor that can make a go here."

On the other hand, many people tried to warn me off the idea altogether. "You have such a good thing going at LSU. Why on earth would you go to this position at Charity?"

By now, it was also famous for its bitter politics and intrinsic challenges. It was bound by government civil service rules, subject to the whims of state budgets, and riven with rivalries, most notably the intense competition between Tulane and LSU.

To make matters even more complicated, all across the state, a fierce debate was raging about the strategy for rebuilding the hospital post-Katrina. The federal government had agreed to provide millions of dollars to help rebuild after the devastation, and now rival factions were drawn into a bitter dispute about how to utilize the funds. On one side of the debate, people advocated for a fresh start: a brand-new state-of-the-art medical facility to take New Orleans into the twenty-first century. On the other side of the debate were the stake-holders who argued that the historic building should be upgraded, not abandoned, to blend the legacy of Charity with that vision of the future. If you want to know just how beloved this hospital was in the community, consider that there were concerts, second lines, street demonstrations, and political rallies held in front of her gates. Passions were high, and citizens were very involved.

I knew that this was not a position for the faint of heart, but I found myself drawn more and more to the institution, especially as I realized that many of the other candidates were steering clear of the hospital or turning out to be bad fits for the position. I thought about my years working Pakistan. While there, I knew that I could not change the whole system, but I had discovered that if you focus on your own small sphere of influence and peel back the layers of the whorl one at a time, like an onion, you could make some good things happen, and hopefully, not too many tears would be shed in the process!

I thought about the thousands of people who had been able to find much-needed care and comfort in my Pakistani clinics. Many of those people would not have found quality care at all if not for the tireless work of my teams there. I knew that Charity offered a similar potential. The chance to take your work directly to the people who need it the most.

Finally, I made my decision.

My initial days on the job were slightly terrifying. I was flattered to have been recruited and to have been offered this position, but the sheer scale of the responsibility was sinking in, along with a new awareness of how complex this place was. Distrust and rivalries were deep-rooted at all levels. For example, there were technically three names for the hospital at this time, and a person could be judged harshly for whichever name he or she chose to use. If you called the hospital the MCLNO (Medical Center of Louisiana at New Orleans), it affiliated you with a certain faction. Another faction called it the ILH (Interim LSU Hospital). There was the UH (university hospital) group, the ILPH (Interim LSU Public Hospital) group and more. Then of course, there were the folks who simply used the traditional moniker: Charity Hospital. *Oh, boy*, I thought. This is going to be intense.

One of the first things I requested was an updated organizational (ORG) chart. It was like something from an engineer's fever dream. It showed every department in the Charity system, including the state leadership which was concentrated at LSU's main campus in the state capital, Baton Rouge. This chart became my bible. It told me who oversaw what and who they reported to whom. It was absolutely dizzying. One thing I noticed right away was how stovepipe the institution was. Nursing, administration, physician services, clinics, ancillary, and so on. There was very little official contact between the departments, except for the very heads of those divisions who were collectively referred to as the A-Council. Any discussion on any subject, major or minor, would have to be passed all the way up the chain, discussed by the A-Council, and then passed all the way back down the chain. It was a typical feature in bureaucracies, designed to reduce chaos, but very frustrating and inefficient to deal with, especially if open ideas and thoughts are to be encouraged.

Using the ORG chart as a road map, I embarked on a goodwill tour of the institution. I visited the A-Council and other department leaders, hoping to get off on the right foot. I learned a lot about the people I would be working with, along with the politics that gripped the place.

Phrases like *watch out, don't get her cross*, or *he is a mole* were spit out with alarming frequency.

"Duly noted," I would reply and leave it at that. I wasn't interested in getting involved in rumor mills or having discussions behind people's backs. My *modus operandi* was to keep my ears open and my mouth shut. I let people know I had no personal agenda at stake. I just wanted to help run a good hospital.

Some people were almost shocked to see me show up in their offices, like the head of facilities or the executive secretaries. They had never seen the medical director sit down across from their desks for a meeting about the important roles they played and any concerns they might have. Many people seemed to appreciate the open style that I brought to my new role, but not everybody.

CHAPTER 32

The Seven-Ring Circus

Charity Hospital (along with its alphabet soup of affiliated programs) had grown exponentially over the years, but not always in the most sensible fashion. Instead of being guided by a careful masterplan, the institution had simply sprouted new programs whenever there was a new need—or crisis—to be met. Post-Katrina recovery was a perfect example of this. By the time I arrived, it was iconic in its scope and inspiration and yet an unwieldy institution, almost like a seven-ring circus, with each of the rings competing for attention—and funding. The emergency department, the trauma program, the OT and MICU, the nursing department, and the clinics, to name a few. In each department, there might be someone being a true hero or someone acting like a clown and making a mockery of a well-set process. There might be a tightrope walker dexterously navigating the space between the bureaucracy and patient care or some trapeze artist doing daredevil measures outside the norms. Some unethical carney might be rigging the children's games for profit, but then there would be a lion tamer who was doing a remarkable job of organizing xxx to make sure the hospital could fulfill its mission. Everyone was performer, whether they belonged to the administration, the general staff, LSU, or Tulane. Each performer had their baggage and biases on one side and egos and tantrums on the other. It was at times comical as one watched this circus at work.

The organization might have been unwieldy, but each of these rings served a specific community of people in need, and that was the most important thing to me right now. With this constant motion, each day brought new adventures and new calamities. I quickly realized that I needed to be part ringmaster to succeed as medical director of this major US institution. One of my first realizations was that no one person simply couldn't watch all the rings at once. There were too many programs stretched across too many departments. This meant that any given moment, someone somewhere was doing something that was going to hijack my day. Or my week. Or my month. At times, on the other hand, it felt I may well be a fly on the wall, watch everything unfold, and be a silent spectator.

One Wednesday evening, the entire hospital almost went into lockdown protocol when a suspicious package was discovered by one of the service doors of the lab. Security police raced to the scene. The local team carefully removed the package. My phone rang off the hook all evening as I coordinated the response and directed the affected departments on how to keep their services running.

It turned out to be routine lab chemicals. A lazy deliveryman had left it by the door instead of delivering it to the lab.

On another occasion, a beautiful spring Friday late afternoon, I received a call about some lab results. "We found something bad," the lab supervisor told me. "A nasty strain of MRSA showed up in a blood sample."

"Have you enacted the safety protocols?" I asked.

"Yes."

"Excellent. So why are you calling me?"

"We can't find the actual patient that the blood came from."

"What?" I asked, suddenly alarmed. How could we have lost a patient with MRSA? "What name is on the file?"

"Monkey One."

"Have you checked with the emergency department?" I replied. "It has to be from them."

There was a protocol in the emergency room that if a patient arrived with no ID and unable to speak (such as a trauma patient), then a predetermined list would generate an odd name to temporarily designate that person until he or she could be formally identified. It was usually the name of an animal followed by a number.

The animal indicated which day the patient arrived, and the number indicated what order the patients arrived in. Owl Three. Dog Four. Tiger Eight, and so on.

"Monkey One," I repeated into the phone receiver, but no one had entered a patient by that code. "We don't even use *monkey*," the administrator told me.

"So who on earth is Monkey One?"

"I have no idea."

The lab couldn't track the patient down. Intake couldn't track the patient down, and now neither could I. We went back to the blood sample itself. Collectively, we began retracing each step that the small vial had taken before arriving at the lab. We called lab techs and hunted through delivery logs. We called the courier service and tracked down the manager there. Finally, we were able to identify the source of the blood. It had been delivered from an animal primate research center a few blocks from the medical school. Monkey One was literally the patient's name.

"You have got to be kidding me," I muttered.

Besides the frustration, this was a serious breach of protocol to send blood full of pathogens via courier with no clear warnings and a lack of documentation or follow-up. This was a public health risk. I made the trip to the research center myself to speak directly with one of the directors over there, but I was informed that they were all gone for the day.

"Can we get in touch with them? I asked.

One of the directors was at a music festival, and one was out of town and unavailable. It was the weekend.

"Would you like to leave a message?"

"No, I want to speak with someone in authority and solve this problem before everyone is really unavailable over the weekend."

We did solve the issue that day but then evaluated the process the next week, took corrective actions, and then hoped it would not happen again. There was no guarantee in this seven-ring circus, I knew well.

A few days later, the elevator in the university medical office building broke down. Again. And then again. It broke so often and was so disruptive that we had a hospital-wide emergency response code for the situation. Most codes are standard across the country. Code Blue generally means a cardiac arrest, Code Gray is a natural disaster or hurricane warning, Code Red indicates a fire, Code Orange is a response to a hazardous spill, and Code Silver warns everyone of a weapon or hostage situation. Here in our building, we now had a Code Brown, related to the recurring elevator malfunction. This was the type of problem I had been used to dealing with back in Karachi, not in the United States. More than just an inconvenience, this was a patient care and patient safety issue, and it really bothered me to see the distress we were causing patients.

It took months and months, but we were finally able to secure state funding to conduct a major overhaul on the elevators. This building had already been rehabilitated after Katrina, so the state hated sinking more money into repairs on this temporary home for the hospital, but they finally agreed that this was a significant problem. It took about two weeks for the crew to pull the old elevators and motors apart, restore them, and put them back together. I was thrilled on the day of the unveiling. Our elevators were back. No more Code Browns. No more patients lined up in the elevator waiting areas.

The euphoria lasted a few days. Then unbelievably, I heard over the overhead paging system: "Code Brown. I repeat, Code Brown."

In some regions and cultures, there is still a practice of sacrificing a black goat to chase away bad luck. It may originally stem from the ancient story of Abraham who was about to sacrifice his own son to please God when an angel intervened. Abraham sacrificed a ram instead. For many centuries afterward, animal sacrifices were a way to appeal directly to higher beings. It was not unusual in Karachi to see a family bring in a black goat around the hospital bed of a very sick patient and then later sacrifice it and feed the meat to the needy. I couldn't help thinking of this as I stood in the hallway, gazing upon the dormant elevators. The repairmen were already working on them, and I made a joke that if they couldn't get the job done, I would have to sacrifice a goat.

"You wouldn't want to have the blood of a goat on your hands now, would you?" I said to the repairmen.

In the moment, my story of the goat struck people as funny, so I went back to my office and printed a picture of a goat from my computer. I took it to the hallway and hung it over the elevator doors.

We never had elevator trouble again. *Geaux, goat, geaux.*

Many of the "fires" I had to put out were frustrating, or even semi-humorous, in retrospect, and many of them dealt with internal politics. These were issues I tackled with goodwill, hoping a "little mouse" from Karachi Grammar School Karachi could make a difference in this crazy circus. The problems that truly broke my heart, however, were the ones that affected patients in more profound ways. These were the problems that revealed the true limitations of healthcare delivery in the United States where there is a major disconnect between the demand for services and the capacity to deliver care, specially in the poorly funded systems.

It was a Monday afternoon when my phone rang, and I answered to discover one of department supervisors was on the other end of the line. "Is there something I can help with?" I asked.

"Doc," she replied, "you have to come see this."

"What is it?"

"It's...well..." she seemed at a loss for words. "Come see this."

By the time I arrived, my curiosity was stirred up with a sense of dread. What was behind this door that he couldn't tell me over the phone?

"We have a problem," the supervisor said as she opened the door to a small office. I half expected a live tiger to come roaring out into the hallway. Instead, I saw papers. Piles of papers. Boxes of papers. Shelves covered in stacks of papers.

"A filing problem?" I asked.

"I wish this was a filing problem," she replied. "This is a patient problem. These are all referrals."

"Referrals?" I peered around at the thousands of pages. With horror, I realized that each page represented a patient in need.

"Referrals," she repeated. "All of them. From all over the state. They've been backing up in here for months."

"What?" I found myself raising my voice.

It turns out the staff and the clinic team had literally been pulling referrals off the fax machine and depositing them straight into these piles without ever acting on them. We had referrals for cancer patients and referrals for colonoscopies from across the region and the community clinics.

This seemed so wrong, and it had been going on for months.

I moved a small army of people into the office, and the first thing we did was organize the referrals by date and severity. We immediately began matching more seriously ill patients to specialists within our system staffed by LSU and Tulane MDs and medical schools. For the less-severe patients, we called the original health-care providers back and informed them of the backlog. They would need to find another place to refer to if possible. It took weeks to get through all the pages. For the emergent ones, we had to use all resources we had and then some. The solution, albeit a stopgap arrangement, required an out-of-the-box approach. I approached a community clinic and a philanthropic grantor to fund me some monies for extra shifts to attend to the backlog of the most acute emergent cases. It was a drop in the bucket, but if some of these patients in need of an emergent procedure got checked earlier, it was an achievement.

One of the trickiest balancing acts of the entire seven-ring circus was trying to manage the partnership between the two universities (and their medical schools) affiliated with Charity: LSU and Tulane. The relationship had grown poisonous over the years—full of distrust and often tense. It was like having two divas who fought viciously for top billing on the posters. They had undercut each other so often in the past that they could barely be in the same room together at times.

The rivalry went back many generations. Tulane University has been providing care, conducting research, and training health-care professionals since the days of the Yellow Fever epidemics in New Orleans. They are a private institution, but very extensive and well-respected nationwide. LSU, on the other hand, is the public flagship university of the state, serving the needs of the state programs. The university is headquartered in Baton Rouge, but it has a large footprint in New Orleans. These two universities and their medical schools had been working with Charity Hospital for many years and were comanagers of the entire public health-care operation.

They were very segregated, however, working in their own silos. Patients were designated L or T, and each designation offered separate pathways of services. Most departments were cordial and professional despite this segregation, but others were downright hostile and malicious toward one another.

To make the situation more difficult, there was a very lopsided power dynamic. Charity's administration was now based out of LSU in Baton Rouge where they coordinated directly with officials in the state capital. As a result, LSU had the upper hand in budgets and negotiations.

One Monday morning, my day began with a rapid-fire barrage of angry phone calls from the deans and the heads of medicine from both schools. They were all furious and directed long bursts of frustration in my direction. I tried to get a word in edgewise. "May I ask what exactly the problem is?"

The remarkable thing was that they were both upset with *me* instead of with *each other*. This might have been the first time LSU and Tulane directors were perfectly aligned on an issue in years. It was an auspicious honor I felt.

It turns out all the furor was in response to a pilot program I had proposed. The program would have allowed care service to patients who were in need but were not integrated into the LSU or Tulane public health-care systems (or any other private care system, obviously). These were patients with chronic health conditions coupled with challenges of access. They might be treated when they arrive at one of the public hospitals or clinics, but their follow-up care and continuation of care was not ensured. During my forums with the many community clinics, I had leaned of this tremendous need among the indigent and uninsured patients who did not fit into the more traditional programs. For these patients, I had proposed something called C service (community service). It would run parallel and supplementary to but in coordination with the T and L services delivered by LSU and Tulane, respectively.

This proposal of care coordination was well received by nearly everyone within the hospital and the community clinics, except the schools. They were fiercely protective of their fiefdoms, and they believed that the C service could somehow undermine their authority through the teaching and academic mission of the hospital. I immediately recognized their legitimate concerns, but I knew that if we did this right, it was a win-win for all. I could not convince the heads of medicine, however. They worked tirelessly to squash my proposal, and it worked. I was asked to back down. In the process, I was assured that my concerns for more streamlined liaison between the community clinics patients and the hospitalists would be addressed. It never was, however, and the disconnect between academic and community clinics medicine remained a problem.

The infighting and distrust between the two medical schools and their leadership, coupled with the inherent administrative bickering at all levels, spilled, at times, down to departments: neurology, neurosurgery, psychiatry, and gastroenterology, to name a few. A simple setup of disinfection of gastroscopes, or lack thereof, became a source of paranoia. People began to fear more elaborate conspiracies among the departments and between the schools. It was simply out of control, and I could see only one way to try to alleviate some of the tension: bring the two parties to the table to communicate and work together. They viewed each other with such suspicion and distrust (if not outright hostility) right now that they probably wouldn't agree on the rising sun.

I was an LSU man, but I had worked very hard to be a trustworthy partner to my Tulane colleagues and to work well with them. In fact, my fairness was ridiculed by some. One of the best compliments I can think of was the head of a department in LSU saying, "Dr. Ali is *too* fair."

Every day was like this. I came to my office having no idea what new challenges would blow in on the wind. Slowly, I became the aerialist myself, working on this incredible high-wire act: balancing the steady progress of our long-term goals with the rapid response of putting out daily fires. It was exhausting, but there was a certain thrill to it if one was able to embrace the chaotic nature of the adventure.

And it was worth it. For every problem I encountered, there must have been one hundred successes, everything from delivering healthy babies to managing chronic diseases with long-term comprehensive care. Charity certainly wasn't perfect, but the hospital achieved world-class results in many of its programs and its services related to actual core patient care in the intensive care, surgery, and floors was extraordinary. Medical students from around the world came to observe our emergency department and the trauma team, including teams from the US military and other armed forces. Charity's work was world-renowned, particularly with the complex issues of gunshot wounds. When presidents or international dignitaries came to New Orleans, their advance teams prepared at Charity Hospital for the event of an emergency. When state senators or heads of medical programs experienced life-threatening conditions, they were airlifted to Charity even if they had been fierce critics of the hospital in the state legislature. I remember vividly a teenager who came to us during my time. He had been in a terrible car accident and was not only gravely injured but also badly disfigured. It took many months, but the teams at Charity did not rest until that young man was healthy and back out in the world with a reconstructed face and features. His future was bright once more. Charity was one of the very few hospitals in the entire region to house mental health patients, and our services were dynamic and comprehensive even as we were stretched to capacity. Charity clinics achieved near-magical levels of success in delivering care considering the resource they had to work with, and the research and information management was truly remarkable. We maintained a robust population disease management database as part of the LSU system, and the hospital was a best practice model in the early adoption of electronic medical records and piloting this comprehensively. In some respects, we were ahead of the curve.

We just had to keep our PC (Passion to Cynicism) ratio high, as I would sometimes say to my colleagues and team members.

CHAPTER 33

When It Rains, It Pours

Budget cuts. More budget cuts. And then more budget cuts. Charity hospital with all its *akas* had always known the ups and downs of state finances. As a public institution in Louisiana, anything from the weather to the price of oil could throw the entire state budget off or deliver a windfall. Charity's fortunes rose and fell with the state's, but something had clearly changed, and we were about to learn the scope of decisions being made one hundred miles away in the state capital. After Hurricane Katrina, a much more conservative administration was a strong proponent of tax cuts, budget cuts, and privatization. We did not yet realize the scale of this change, but soon enough, we would.

The first budget cuts, we weathered well by tightening our collective belts. The next round of budget cuts, less than one year later, cut a little closer to the bone, and we had to eliminate staff positions and cut back on services. But the cuts kept coming, which, predictably, caused a vicious cycle. As services got cut and morale plummeted around the hospital, complaints grew. Complaints led to more budget cuts. Rinse, repeat. Soon, a narrative emerged that Charity was a failing hospital, but this couldn't be further from the truth. The hospital was quite capable of generating its own revenue had it been given a structured charge and opportunity. Still, it inspired the state to send another round of budget cuts our way, along with a host of private sector consultants. These were state-sanctioned experts who were going to help us decide how to streamline operations.

Our number one priority was, of course, to keep serving our patients, so we did everything possible to absorb the financial blows on the administrative or facility side. Every time the consultants suggested eliminating a medical service, we fought them. Every time an academic graduate medical education program, which supported teaching and patient service, was targeted, we would fight not to let that happen. People depended on these services. The schools needed that. We could endure another year of crumbling walls in the basement if it meant we could run some needed specialty or community clinics. We could freeze hiring and pay raises if it meant we could continue providing neonatal care to vulnerable infants. I was calling in personal favors in many cases, asking LSU and Tulane medical professors to lend us their residents and students and allot more time slots. It was a hard sell though. The budget cuts impacted the schools also. The reimbursements that went to those institutions for services rendered were shrinking even as I was asking them for more. We were bleeding and slowly bled to death.

We struggled on like this for months. Every time we succeeded in absorbing a budget cut, the state legislature and the administration decided that we would manage with less and had become so efficient as to warrant another budget cut. It was absolutely demoralizing, and the vicious cycle began to spin out of control. The same politicians who undermined the institution then stood in from of television cameras to blame the institution for poor care and lack of services. The media latched onto the inevitable negative stories that emerged from a crumbling, demoralized, underfunded hospital. I was reminded of the famous proverb: *Success has many fathers, but failure is an orphan.* The leadership at all levels became toxic and the blame game started. Ideologies and biases dictated decisions. No one wanted ownership of this situation.

As this turmoil continued, predictably, medical services continued to suffer. Just when we had finally streamlined our referral and clinic process again, it was completely disrupted by lack of funding and staffing. Wait times were becoming ridiculous. A severely diabetic patient might wait seven months to see a specialist or get a retina exam. A patient with cancer might not be able to schedule an appointment immediately. It was terrible. I kept thinking to myself, *This is the United States! How can there be such poverty in a nation of such abundance?*

I was, in a way, a bystander and a nincompoop when compared to this whole political storm which raged around us, but I was not afraid to put up a fight. Whenever possible, I spoke in meetings of the leadership in New Orleans and Baton Rouge even though I knew that what was happening was above my pay grade. It seemed that the decision was made that if we bleed something to near death, it will eventually die, and the death could then be called a humane act of mercy.

In the meantime, I made every effort to patch up our existing services and still move us toward our vision of more effective twenty-first-century care. We streamlined the clinics, developed more community partnerships, and developed a telemedicine program. We worked closely with LSU sister hospitals around the state and engaged more medical school residents in improving quality and safety of care. We designed visionary progressive programs of health-lifestyle balance obesity programs, structured pain management clinics, robust discharge-planning pathways, remote telemedicine sessions, processes to reduce readmissions, improve coordination between hospital-based providers and primary care catchment clinics. Despite everything, there was still so much ingenuity, passion, and dedication here.

But then came more budget cuts. I closed my eyes and leaned back in my desk chair when I learned the news. The administration at a higher level was literally running us out of business, and everyone knew it. "Well, let's get to work," I said to my small team of administrators as I leaned forward again. We would have to redo all the budgets and deal with the resulting chaos, and the nasty word—*layoffs*—loomed over the horizon

The 2010–2011 cuts were the deepest yet, and painful. Worse still, they pitted the two medical universities against each other even more than before. By now, everyone could see what was happening. The plan seemed to bleed the institution dry of resources, undermine it in every way possible, and then, when it was on the brink of collapse, sell it to the highest private bidder and claim there was no choice. The universities played right into this plan too. Instead of spreading the pain evenly and fairly, cuts were disproportionate, and each department was fighting for its own hospital-based survival, leaving a trail of negative competitiveness behind. Predictably, leadership at each level at LSU and Tulane were enraged. One school representative would take their argument straight to the governor's office only for the other to counter that. Soon the messy argument spilled into public view as these two incredibly esteemed institutions were reduced to squabbling at the feet of the governor. This made the administration's next moves easy.

First, the senior LSU leadership was asked to step down. They were essentially fired from the job. Second, the governor announced he was officially looking into privatization.

With the LSU senior management gone and a new leadership structure developed, I was asked to step up into the role of interim CEO for the transition. Obviously, this would be a challenging position, but I agreed. Once more, I was honored to be considered for a leadership role in this institution, and I hoped that I could affect the process in some small way. I fantasized that maybe, just maybe, I could help save it from this death spiral it was in.

By now, we had long abandoned our annual budget and each department made makeshift budgets or worksheets based upon whatever the new numbers were. As I looked around, Charity was becoming a shell of its former self right before my eyes. In the past months, we had gradually gone down from 225 beds to 90. We once had more than 30 service programs delivering health care to the community, and we now had fewer than 20. We had to cut all the community clinics by now. Pain management: gone. Weight control: gone. Psychiatric and mental health services: gone. Entire operating rooms: reduced. On and on it went.

Then one morning, I received an e-mail that almost made my heart stop. During all our turmoil, the joint commission had scheduled a complete inspection and review of the hospital. As interim CEO, I was now responsible for this. I knew that recent layoffs, budget cuts, and low morale had taken a toll on the physical structure of the hospital, and we had work to do to prepare.

I did my best to motivate my departments as I directed the great spring cleaning of 2010. We repaired walls and electrical equipment, audited hospital records, reviewed intake procedures, and fine-tuned referral processes. Still, we were so limited in resources by this time that there was only so much we could do. Our priority was still delivering patient care, after all.

Inspectors with the joint commission arrived, and they combed through the hospital. They examined the building, the personnel procedures, and much more. This is an incredibly thorough inspection aimed at making sure every aspect of a hospital meets safety standards and complies with thousands of government regulations. I was nervous as the inspectors spent an entire day combing through the organization. Finally, they came to me with the report, and it was every bit as bad as I feared. We had thirty-two citations. *Thirty-two!* That was an incredible number of problems for a single institution, and it was a dark day for me as I looked over the report. When I accepted this interim CEO position, I knew I would inherit many challenges, but this was both depressing and humiliating. It was a sad day for me personally and professionally. Although not my fault, I was responsible. We now had ninety days to correct each of these problems. The joint commission would return, and if the problems persisted, the hospital could be shut down entirely.

It was just a short while later that the other news arrived. The final decision had been made in Baton Rouge. Charity Hospital/ MCLNO/ILH was going to be turned over to a private sector company with ensured state support and handing over the management of the hospital in the new premises of the university hospital. The building of the new hospital with its core planning from the ground level to the final stage of the state of the art facility had been the efforts of the LSU leadership. It had truly been a tremendous effort across the board from leadership, navigating funding, facility planning construction, and down to selecting the art pieces to make this look like the Taj Mahal as I would refer to the structure. We were now handing this over to the new management. I certainly wasn't surprised by the news, but I couldn't help feeling deep disappointment. I felt it all the way down into stomach. This fabled public institution was ending as we knew it. The question of what form it would take under the new private management remained to be seen and how would the state support that enterprise remained an open question. We were assured that the uninsured and the underinsured would be accommodated under the new management albeit with state support. It was ironical that the state was ready to support and finance the private management to run the hospital after withdrawing all its support under the previous governance of LSU.

At my end, in my own way, I turned my full attention to my hospital staff who were stunned as they absorbed the enormity of what had just happened. For starters, nearly everyone was about to be formally laid off. They would be offered an option to reapply for their own positions and possibly become employees of the private management system. That also affected their hard-earned state pensions in some cases.

For days, I had conferences with people as I waited for someone from the state government or from LSU leadership to address the staff of Charity. Surely, someone was going to address this major situation that affected the lives and livelihoods of the staff and their families. Most of the staff had been associated with the hospital for years.

But no. No one ever arrived or even returned my phone calls on the issue. I was sincerely shocked to realize that no one from the state had the guts or grace to address the hardworking employees of Charity who were all being cut loose. The politicians/bureaucrats and the top administration had made their decision, and now everyone was on their own to figure out how to respond.

So I formed a committee with the help of a few remaining A-Council members and my inner professional circle at the hospital, and we stepped in. We began a hospital-wide program to educate people on the transition and help prepare them for what came next. We held regular town hall and small group meetings where I could share information and take questions. Staffers lacked some of the most basic information at this point. When were they being laid off?

How would they manage their retirement savings after losing their jobs as civil servants? Would they have the option or opportunity to gain their jobs back in the new organization? Was there a process established for them to apply for their jobs again? Who were they competing against?

There were so many questions, and there was so much anxiety. Here was an incredibly dedicated group of people who had been with the hospital and survived Hurricane Katrina, who had persevered as an integral part of the Charity institution as it had evolved and now had been painfully dismembered, and now they were being summarily dismissed by the state and left to fend for themselves through the corporate structure of a private enterprise. These were the unrecognized stalwarts. I remember distributing service certificates with pins of recognition to employees and sending out an open acknowledgement to the "unknown unsung employee."

I did everything I could. We brought in presenters with specific skills, such as resume building and interviewing. We met with small groups of people to have more tailored discussions about their specific positions or concerns. I spoke with everyone from the nurses to the maintenance staff, and I had the same message for everyone: *Don't sell yourself short. Your experience here has been and is invaluable. Know your worth, and demand it from your new employers.*

I reminded them that while we were moving to a new fancy hospital built across the street and it looked as beautiful as ever, the Taj Mahal, it was not the building that made the institution. It was the personnel. "Unless we behave like maharajas, we don't deserve the Taj Mahal."

I reached out to the new private sector leadership also and asked for a meeting. I made it clear that I would do anything I could to help my people have a smooth transition into their new system. Many of the new managers seemed to appreciate the gesture, but there was no mistaking the open disdain that some of them had for the parent organization. The private sector administrators had negotiated a great deal for themselves, which ensured their financial growth. The new team probably never once had had to deal with a state-mandated budget cut, let alone a dozen of them in one year, so it was easy for them to pass judgement on the condition of the facility, the state of the record keeping, or the backlog of program needs. I took all that in stride. My goal was not to impress them, but to help my own staff.

As I spent time with these new managers and discussed the various aspects of Charity, I was reminded of new house buyers who arrive to survey a property they have acquired. They may sneer at a painting on the wall or at an addition built on the back of the house that they do not like. It turns out that the painting is covering a homemade repair job in the wall, and the addition was built for a sick aunt with specific needs. The previous family was working on a shoestring budget, and slowly it occurs to the new owners that there was a surprising level of ingenuity at work in this house if you pause to examine it.

As I explained the many programs we operated, showed them the array of populations we worked with, and demonstrated the incredible demand for these services, it slowly began to sink in just how much we were accomplishing with so little resources. Suddenly, the managers were more interested in talking. *How many underserved, underinsured, uninsured patients came in for each of these programs? How were you able to see that many patients on that budget? How did you manage the partnerships with outside organizations?*

In the meantime, I still had thirty-two citations from the joint commission to resolve in ninety days! I turned this mission impossible into a group effort, corralling a team of managers from all over the hospital and delegating individual problems to different departments and groups. The violations fell into three primary categories: safety codes, patient care issues, and government regulations and compliance. We divided the tasks accordingly. I would oversee the effort, participate where it was appropriate, and troubleshoot, of course, but this was such a widespread problem that it was going to require a large-scale team approach. Between the tight schedule of the joint commission and the tight regimen of the new management, the days seemed to fly by, and before I knew it, I was waking up on a hot June morning, looking at the ceiling over my bed and realizing this was my last day as CEO of Charity Hospital. My leadership tenure was all but over. It was a bittersweet feeling.

On the one hand, I wouldn't have to deal with the stress and politics any longer. On the other hand, I was losing my leadership role in an organization that I cared deeply for. Of course, that organization had already been taken over and was being merged into something that was barely recognizable. In the new medical center, it wouldn't even be called Charity any longer. Three hundred fifty years of tradition would be scraped off on the doormat of the new facility, and the hospital would be absorbed into the University Medical Center-New Orleans. At least I didn't have to deal with the joint commission any longer. I had done everything I could, and now that would fall to my successors to escort those inspectors around the building whenever they arrived for their unannounced visit. They gave us ninety days to make corrections and repairs, but they still liked to operate with an element of surprise.

I sipped my morning chai in my kitchen and prepared for my last day of office under the previous system. I imagined it would be emotional in some ways, filled with goodbyes and visits with many friends in the building. I wouldn't be going too far away, however. For the next year, I would still be chief medical officer under the new management at their request. I remembered all those years ago when I first assumed the role of CMO and I thought the pace was insane and hectic. Now that pace seemed downright relaxing to me, and I was looking forward it.

I was just climbing into my car to drive to work when my phone rang. I checked the number and realized it was the hospital calling. What could be so pressing they had to call before I even arrived? For the last time, I imagined myself as the ringmaster of that crazy circus and knew that somewhere someone was doing something that was going to mess up my day.

"Dr. Ali," said the voice. I recognized it immediately as one of the administrative assistants on my floor.

"Yes?"

"They're here."

"Who's here?"

"The joint commission."

"I'll be right there. Meanwhile, you know what to do and inform others," I told her. We hung up, and I sat in my driveway for just a moment longer, gazing through the windshield. So much for my relaxing last day as CEO.

The inspector was waiting in the conference room when I arrived, and we went straight to work. It would take hours to reevaluate all thirty-two violations and make sure that each one had been taken care of. I greeted him and walked him through a couple of the corrected violations, but the real challenge was going to be tracking down each person or team that oversaw all the other fixes. The inspector would need to be transitioned from one team to the next to access the processes in every department, to review the updated safety protocols, and so on. I spent all day bouncing back and forth between the inspector and my office, which had quickly become a war room where staffers and I worked e-mail and phones nonstop, trying to reach doctors, managers, and other team members to coordinate locations and times where they would be available to deliver results, answer questions, or clarify any query the inspection would bring up. It was stressful, especially considering the hospital could literally be shut down based upon the conclusions of this inspection.

It went like this all day long, but somehow, miraculously, everyone showed up, sometimes in the nick of time, to guide the inspector through the process. By the end of the day, I was exhausted, but hopeful. The exit meeting occurred. The lead inspector opened his file folder and turned the pages carefully.

"Well, Dr. Ali," he said, "I must say, your team has made lots of improvement."

We had passed the inspection. Thirty-one out of thirty-two violations had been completely corrected. One violation remained, related to a physician credentialing item that still needed some minor adjustments. But overall, the hospital was back in excellent standing. What a team effort!

The day might have been crazy, and it certainly didn't turn out the way I had expected, but that turned out to be one of the best parting gifts I could have received. The credit went to the tireless efforts of the hospital team who worked hard despite being on the SS *Titanic* as many people called it.

The new private sector management moved into the facility to cement the takeover and implement their rules and operating procedures. Meanwhile, on the other side of town, the controversial new hospital building continued to rise from the ground. The project might have been tainted by the scandalous political process that brought it here, but there was no question it was going to be a medical center of grand proportions. A main hospital building was flanked by an enormous clinic building and three separate patient towers. It was hard not to be excited about being able to work with such a modern and far-reaching facility. I could just imagine strolling through a brand-new, well-funded facility that didn't have thirty-two citations from the joint commission and exist in a constant state of existential dilemma.

By now, I had informed the new managers that I was willing to accept the role of chief medical officer for one year. I had given it great thought. I always enjoyed the role, and I would be able to stay with the team and continue to aid with the overall transition in my own small way. Once again, many of my friends and family were flummoxed. "Why would you do this to yourself, Juzar? You have been through so much already!" They knew that the work was stressful, the environment was chaotic.

But those weren't my concerns. I just couldn't walk away from all these programs that were so important to the community and all this wonderful staff that had been working so hard to support those programs. If there was anything I could do to help them, then I wanted to do it.

A touching moment was recounted to me a short time later by several of my colleagues. Apparently, when the new management announced my decision to remain with the hospital as CMO during a meeting in my absence, there was a spontaneous round of applause. I was humbled to hear of this small gesture of recognition and appreciation, but I have always believed that one person really can make a difference if he or she tries hard enough, and this moment inspired me to keep up my passion. I would continue to support my staff and the organization and keep my litmus test as patient care and service as much as humanly possible. Most importantly, I would, at least for now, continue to support the mission of Charity albeit in a new environment under different corporate rules and a for profit business paradigm, which ironically the new arrangement under the state brought into play.

CHAPTER 34

A New Door Opens, but
My Eyes Open More

Through my tenure at ILH, I had been engaged in my own small way in the planning of the new university medical center that would replace the old edifice of the Charity Hospital. I had toured the construction area many times but now walking into the brand-new, state of the art, architecturally stunning University Medical Center. New Orleans was a strange experience after my years in the makeshift headquarters of Charity / UMCNO / ILH with its patched walls and mishmash of names. I had been inside many modern facilities before, of course, but this one struck me differently after my recent experiences.

I strolled through the beautiful glass atriums, and I was immediately struck by the chasm that lay between health care facilities and the people it was meant to serve. This new "Taj Mahal" was stunning indeed, but was there going to be a price to enter? Gatekeepers and barriers could stand at every access point. Insurance companies and government programs and regulations with their red tape had their own barriers, and the state support to the new management behind it all was going to be crucial. This support was missing under the previous governance of ILH. A more rigorous entry point financial registration system reflected the change. One could thus not help still think of the stunning wealth of resources in the health-care industry and a persistent poverty of access just outside those glass walls.

This was a nationwide problem, I knew, but my experiences in New Orleans and elsewhere seemed a vivid illustration of the point.

I spent one more year with the hospital administration where I helped some of the remaining programs make transitions, and I guided my staff do the same. When my year was up, I exited this phase of my career with mixed emotions. On one hand, it was sad for me to see that the system was still so convoluted and driven by ideological, political, and business interests. On the other hand, I felt proud of my small contribution to the legacy of charity and my work to support the patients, the staff, and the community through that institution, especially given the paucity of resources, the challenges of the system, the demands of business, and the tsunami of politics and change.

While I moved back to my academic and clinical core in the section of pulmonary medicine and refocused on my niche subjects and interests in pulmonary medicine, I was offered the opportunity to also take on as chief medical officer for LSU Health Network Clinics. It was a familiar position, but I saw it as a new door opening for me and a chance to keep walking this path of mine. In this new phase of my career, I became even more interested in seeing what new connections I could make, what bridges I could build between communities and providers and hence close the gap between academia and community. My passion remained access to care and focused on outpatient ambulatory systems, and this position would give me that opportunity. I wanted to focus on the goal that inspired from a concept of connecting the dots in health care and implementing the "gown to town and town to gown" mantra I was so passionate about. I do not consider myself successful in having fully achieved that goal.

The Fulbright and Vietnam Educational awards I had hitherto received and the experiences it gave me across the globe, reinforced the tremendous opportunity our migration to United States gave us. For me, a Muslim born in India, who lived most of my early life in Pakistan, migrated to this country (legally I may add!) and then be given the opportunity to live and work in this country and represent USA as its educational and cultural ambassador abroad is a genuine honor. And yes, as I have said before, that cannot happen in any country of the world, but USA. Only in USA.

Meanwhile, I had also applied for another Fulbright teaching award scholarship, which conceptually dovetailed with my previous work in Turkey and Vietnam albeit with a different emphasis. This program I proposed was to try to implement my vision that despite challenges of tremendous demand and decreased capacity in health-care delivery in a resource limited environment, quality of care and patient safety programs cannot be compromised.

This was especially of personal interest too because it was to be based at the NHL Medical College and Hospital in Ahmedabad, India, where Isfana had graduated from years ago. Additionally, Ahmedabad was the city I was born in before my migration to Pakistan, and that is where Isfana's mother and family now lived. This added a personal touch to a professional endeavor. This professional opportunity would also give Isfana and I time to spend some extended quality period with her aging mother. A reward she richly deserved and a service we owed to her.

I reached Ahmedabad with a tremendous amount of trepidation and uncertainty of my professional goals. My vision of conveying my program was not in question. The reception I would receive from my would-be peers and colleagues at NHL where no one knew me and where Isfana had no connections maintained over the years was going to be lukewarm at best, their polite welcome notwithstanding. It had taken me almost a year to convince the faculty of my sincere intentions and no-agenda-unbiased approach. Being in India for an extended period and not as a tourist was déjà in one way. Wheeling through the busy streets with its mix of high-end cars and manually operated or and cattle-driven vehicles and jumping through piles of filth in some areas, was not anything new for me. I was after all a product of that environment.

What was stunning was the dichotomy of health-care delivery that continued to exist. One of the aspects of my program related to infection control. It was striking to see the public sector health care field struggle with the basics of infection control, not because there was no awareness or expertise but because there was a blasé attitude of resignation to the obvious. These very experts in a state-of-the-art hospital next door would practice top class medicine that would put USA doctors to shame.

In March 2017, WHO announced its list of the top "Dirty Dozen" difficult to treat bacteria in a health care environment. A public hospital dealt with this, as a matter-of-fact, casual curiosity as its long clinic lines dictated another priority for the patients and providers alike. The Taj Mahal next door, where the elite and the rich got their medical care, would not allow anyone to even enter the hospital area with shoes.

Poor health may be a misfortune or a result of many factors including socio-economic disparity, but limited access and difficult navigation of care could surely be improved. I remember talking about this in Pakistan. These are the mandatory Cs of care: competency, compassion, care, and continuity of care.

In underdeveloped systems with high demands and limited resources, this is understandably challenging. I ask, though, what is the excuse we have in a developed system? Surely, we can overcome this poverty in abundance here in the US by focusing on streamlining care, thus preventing redundancy and eliminating waste. This can be done without going into the politics and ideological debate of health care. This poverty of health care affects us all and not just the uninsured or those living below the poverty line. Some of us just do what we need to do with personal mechanisms and pathways to navigate the hurdles.

In countries like Pakistan and India, there is a landscape of poverty of resources and access with pockets of abundance and wealth. In the US, especially in the health care but not limited to, it is the opposite and there is a landscape of abundance one can see or perceive but with pockets of abject poverty of streamlined-coordinated care and access. The net result especially to the elderly, disadvantaged, non-resourceful or needy is the same—fragmented episodic care. Discussions about the multiple versions of payer systems that we endlessly debate about every couple of years seem so fruitless and nonproductive. The energy and resources we spend debating about the insurance system year after year, at every election cycle, can better be spent, one can argue, on streamlining the existent health-care infrastructure. This can and should be done irrespective of what payer system we adopt or maintain. Some may argue or believe that a single-payer system is the answer to all these issues, but I hasten to add that that may not be entirely correct.

Insurance coverage is not synonymous with health-care access and coordination of care and examples of Medicare and Medicaid, and the VA system show us that time and again. Obtaining a card showing a PCP assigned in a managed-care Medicaid system, does not necessarily guarantee access to structured streamlined care. Access to care is determined by payers, types of insurance coverage, and group practices rates and rules set by conglomerate partnerships of health systems and insurances. Co-payments, deductibles, and other hidden costs prevent patients from accessing care and impede doctors in implementing treatment plans.

Tier system medication pharmacy coverage and costs are, at times, prohibitive and confusing to both the patient and provider. There is no doubt that the patients I see and work with, by and large, have the best medical, technical care, and expertise once they get it. That is the best part of our system. But that is only so if they get it. The hurdles they must overcome to get this expertise of care, whether from payers, systems, or providers, and depending upon coding and stratification of their insurance plan is agonizing to hear as I see my patients on a day-to-day basis. It is tragic to see that a patient can get one appointment and not another, one medicine but not another one, one imaging test but not another one, a breathing machine but no medicines to use in that machine, oxygen tubing but no oxygen. Health-care providers and patients must use extraordinary resources and persistence in navigation of the process through the maze of pre-authorization and appeals.

Patient care and services are dictated more by the premium, co-pay, and types of coverage. The speed and level of care is dependent upon the type of plan. Health care delayed is health care denied. Health care fragmented is health care broken. The cost of health care is a separate issue by itself. That cannot be comprehensively addressed unless all the stakeholders in the cost including the patient, are not included in the decision-making. To control costs, we have moved from providing care to managing care to administrating care to budgeting care, and in some instances, to rationing care.

To determine value of care, we have established guidelines of quality of care under the umbrella of performance metrics. However, every practicing physician and knowledgeable patient knows that achieving performance metrics in not synonymous with achieving quality of care. This remains my struggle as I navigate through the maze of health-care delivery currently in the United States. It is every doctor's or health-care provider's struggle. We all remain in our silos of delivering point of care on an incident of care basis. I at times, claim that if I do a good job technically during that point of care, I am the best doctor, and nothing else counts; some of us get upset about the hurdles to deliver this care; some just accept it as part of the system and shrug our shoulders; some become temporarily agitated; and some transiently passionate to remedy this on a case-by-case basis. I, too, remain doing all of the above, depending on the day and time of the day. For the patient, it is the luck of the draw.

CHAPTER 35

Dimming the Lights: Footprints

I can say without an exaggeration that I have had an eventful non-boring life although, at times, I may have appeared boring. Well, even relaxation for me sometimes appeared boring too as some of my friends would remark!

By now, my most ambitious years are behind me, at least from a career standpoint. Maybe?

I hope the passion of my career directed toward the As and Cs of patient care with a focus of streamlined coordinated care continues in some form or the other and the challenges we face in this country that are roadblocks to such a care are overcome. The TAHA (Toward Achieving Health Care and Access) Foundation that Isfana, Murtuza, Riaz, and Sausan and I have formed, albeit in its infancy and evolution, is a small symbol of that dream that reflects my experience on how difficult it is for patients to navigate their care without using extraordinary efforts and resources in this land of abundance. Interestingly, the name of the foundation, other than its spiritual origin and its acronym, is also representative of Tahir Ali and Hasan Ali, the two people at Venus Medico in Karachi when I was growing up, who taught me by example what health-care access meant.

I have settled down and turned the light switch to a dimmer mode. Retirement is around the corner, but I enjoy working and mentoring my junior colleagues at work and gently reinforcing the legacy of care and service that we all sworn to participate in. I see myself trying to continue a structured career if health allows as long as I am vertical, as I sometimes say.

My life has, up until now, been always looking for the next mountain to climb. My story is not unique by any means, and many have helped me through those ascents. I started in a single-room apartment off Elphinstone Street in humble beginnings and ended up reasonably well at this stage of my life (AIMS).

There may be still adventures ahead. There may not be mountains to scale as age and perception of age precludes such a quest, but now I look for beaches and smooth terrain to stroll upon with Isfana. Isfana remains the strong source of unqualified love and support, and she is what she is—no facade, no show; you get what you see, you see what you get; she is what she is with no pretensions. Our life has taken on the sweetness that comes with age even as we deal with some of the bittersweet emotions and swings that come with life's many changes and continued ongoing struggles through the prism of person, family, friend, and colleagues.

Murtuza and Riaz have created their own paths with their hard work and with successes and failures through their personal and career growth. They have done this mostly on their own with some help from us as parents and unconditional love and emotional support. As the cycle of life continues and they go through their phases, we see that with immense pride and joy and sometimes with some trepidation as all parents do. Our grandchildren, Raiyan, Samad, and Amaal, through their parents, have given us renewed vigor of life. Three unique and charming personalities that are an amalgam of the past, present, and future. They are the wonderful continuation of this journey. MaashaAllah

Like in all families, some family events have been traumatic, and we just must accept these with grace and patience. Most families do that. The passion and hard work of the moment, notwithstanding the ups and downs of life, must be borne with moderation and balance dictated by the phase and cycle of life journey one is in at that time. The Monday morning quarterbacking of could have and should have must be kept to the minimum. Having said that, do I have any regrets? Many. Could I have done this or that better? You bet.

One of our other great joys we treasure is connecting with the extended family around the globe. Isfana and I try not to take anything for granted, especially relationships even with our children. We believe in maintaining these connections. Of course, today's technology makes it easy. A message here, a note there, without sending annoying forwards and holier-than-thou sermons!

Every two years, we also enjoy a family reunion in the US. We call it the Monabao connection, and although it does not have the participation of all the families and the "Bawan Pataa" (the full deck of cards), we enjoy the company, noise, food and the game of Daadu. Years ago, my father had miraculously maneuvered dozens of relatives across the forbidding border of Pakistan and India for Shirin Bahen's wedding. The symbolic Monabao connection was the train journey that carried us across the border between India and Pakistan at that time. Over the decades, several of us, including young cousins and siblings who were on that journey, migrated to the United States for school, work, and other opportunities. We all tried to stay in touch throughout the world with sporadic efforts and success.

As we spoke, we all realized that we had a common goal of making sure our children knew their extended family as well as possible. We had all been raised amid sprawling familial connections back in Pakistan and India, and we cherished that part of our culture. The digital age on one hand and the ease of travel and some physical proximity on the other enables us to celebrate togetherness. These reunions have thrived although I am curious to see if we and the next generation picks up the gauntlet and continues the tradition, not formalities, culture, not rituals, language, not dialect, values, not preachy opinionated sermons all under the umbrella of faith, not a particular religion or any cult, and with tolerance and not biases.

In the meantime, I continue to cherish the closeness, love, and support of my sisters, Shirin Bahen, Cheeko, Mukha, and their families. With Isfana, I feel the closeness with Iloo, Asmi, Anjum and family. Her friends are my friends and mine hers, and it is now a neat little garment of fun and joy that we wear. It is a treasure. It is a blessing. Unbiased, non-judgmental continual connections with families and friends add value to the relationships at all levels and we treasure that immensely. Isfana and I try to reach out as much as possible even when we do not have to. We do this for ourselves as much as we do for others.

Just like my parents, Isfana and I are trying to light a pathway for our immediate family to follow as they deem fit, now more by quiet examples and tolerance. I do hope, however, with all my faults and shortcomings, mistakes, and missteps, they sense the faith passion, patience, perseverance with which I have pursued my life, career, and relationships. I hope they know the dignity and values Isfana and I have tried to demonstrate through it all, more by example and less by preaching or dictating.

Isfana and I continue to try to adopt and adapt, tolerate and forgive, and move on with humility and dignity. A sprinkle of wit and humor here and there helps too, though we realize that at this age, all humor does not necessarily match. We hope that we will get the respect and tolerance as we become annoying to some due to our quirks and idiosyncrasies.

I know the footprints of my life will inevitably get washed away on the sands of time. I do hope, though, to leave behind some positive impression of value on those I have had the privilege to cross paths with through this journey. As we dim these lights, we hope that we have spread many nice pebbles, few unique seashells, and may be some pearls on the way.

ABOUT THE AUTHOR

Juzar Ali is a resident of New Orleans, Louisiana, where he lives with his wife, Isfana. They have two sons and three grandchildren with an extended family and friends settled in different parts of the world. Born in India, Juzar Ali grew up in Pakistan after his parents migrated after partition of the Indian subcontinent. He has traveled and lived across the globe at various times of his life. He is a physician who has practiced in both the public and private sector and is now an academic clinician, clinical educator, and researcher at the LSU Health Sciences Center, New Orleans. He has also served in a variety of roles in health-care administration through his professional and academic career.